Komi Can't Communicate

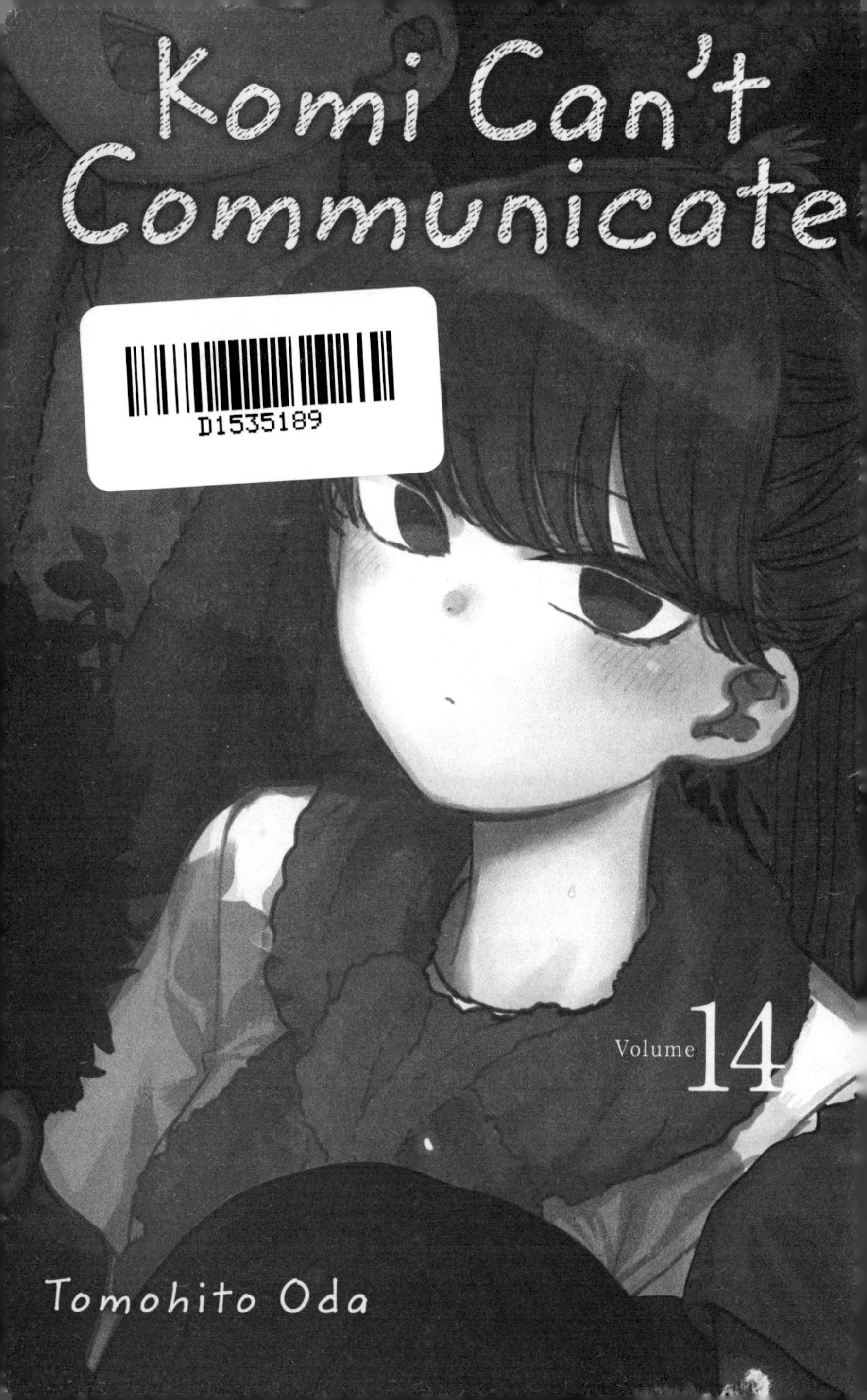

Volume 14

Tomohito Oda

Contents

Komi Can't Communicate

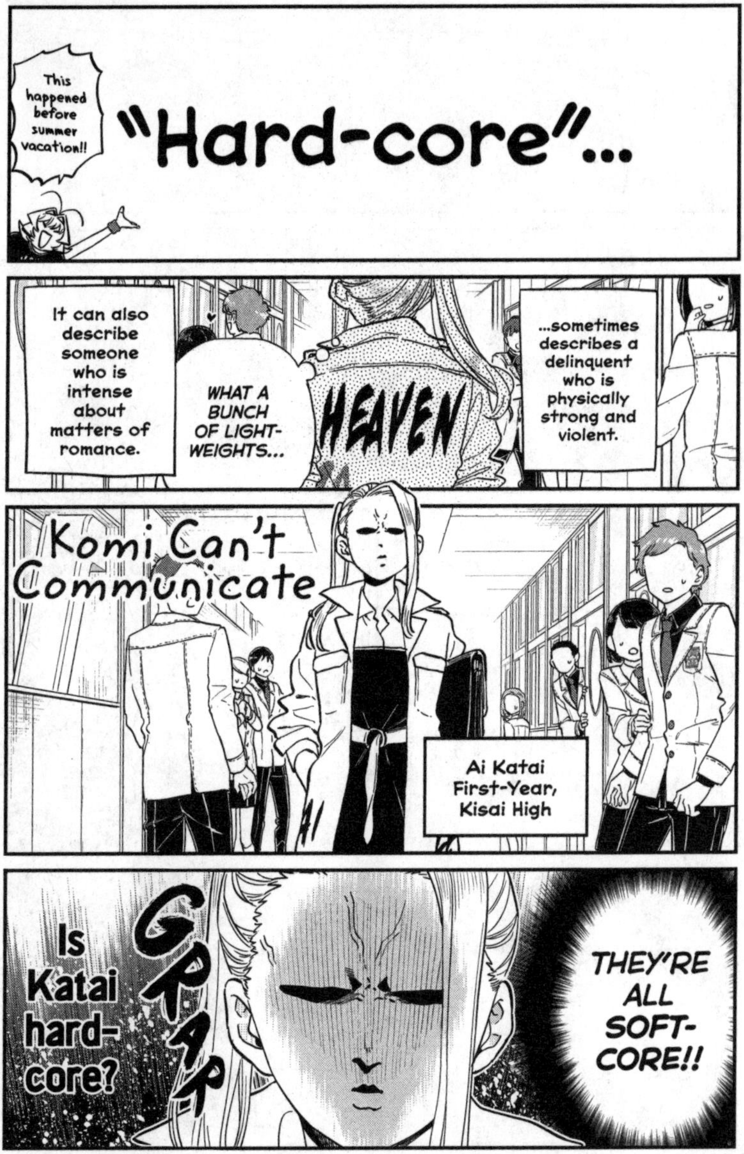
"Hard-core"...
This happened before summer vacation!!
...sometimes describes a delinquent who is physically strong and violent.
HEAVEN
WHAT A BUNCH OF LIGHT-WEIGHTS...
It can also describe someone who is intense about matters of romance.
Ai Katai First-Year, Kisai High
Komi Can't Communicate
AI
THEY'RE ALL SOFT-CORE!!
GRAR
Is Katai hard-core?

Communication 182: Hard-Core

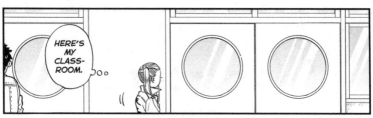

HERE'S MY CLASSROOM.
WHAT'S UP.
BAM
FLINCH
?!
WHO'S THAT?
HAS SHE BEEN SKIPPING SCHOOL UNTIL NOW?!
A DELINQUENT!!
SHE'S COMING IN!!
SHE DRESSES LIKE A GANGSTER!!
SHE MUST BE IN OUR CLASS!!
Yikes!!
I DIDN'T WANNA GO TO THE SAME SCHOOL AS MY STUPID BROTHER, SO I CAME HERE, BUT...
...THE STUDENTS ALL LOOK SO PATHETIC!
THEY'RE ALL SOFT-CORE!

TCH... I NEVER SHOULDA COME!
SPARKLE
BABWUMMMP
Ooh! What a mancake! ♥
AI KATAI ♥
SPARKLE
GASP
GAH!
WHAT JUST HAP-PENED?!
UH-OH! THAT WASN'T VERY HARD-CORE OF ME!!
HEAVEN
AND

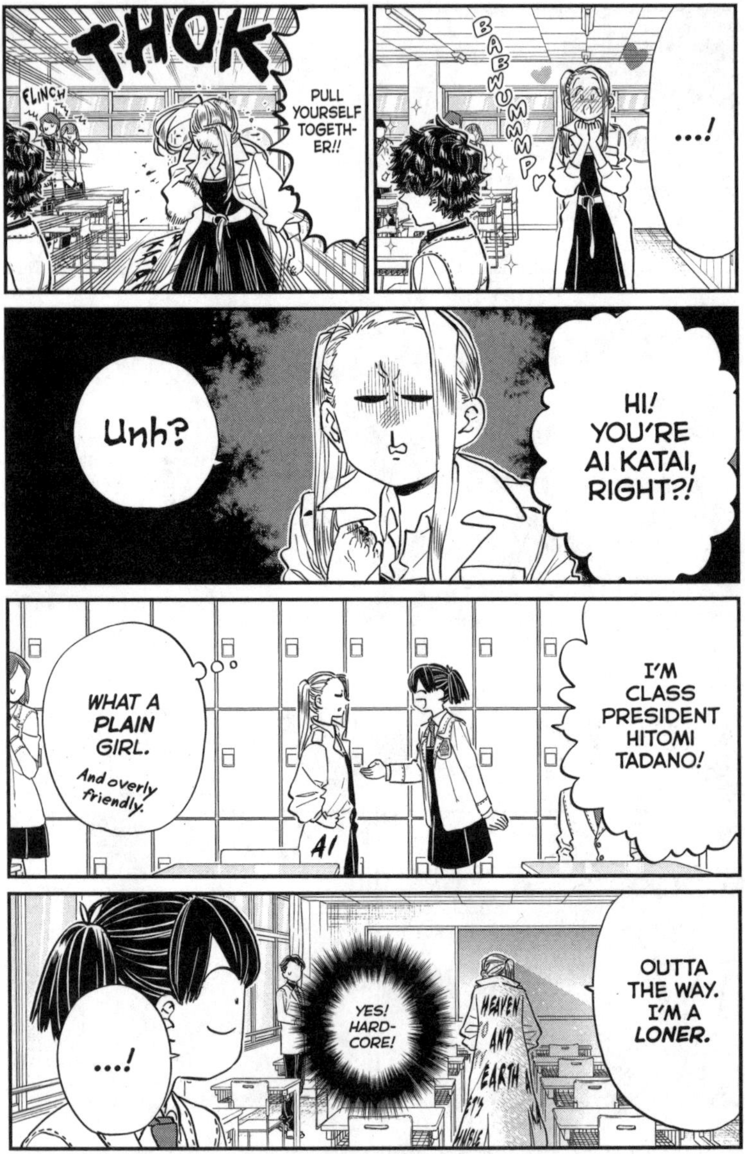
...!
BABWUMMP
THOK
PULL YOURSELF TOGETH-ER!!
FLINCH
HI! YOU'RE AI KATAI, RIGHT?!
Unh?
I'M CLASS PRESIDENT HITOMI TADANO!
AI
WHAT A PLAIN GIRL.
And overly friendly.
OUTTA THE WAY. I'M A LONER.
HEAVEN AND EARTH
YES! HARD-CORE!
...!

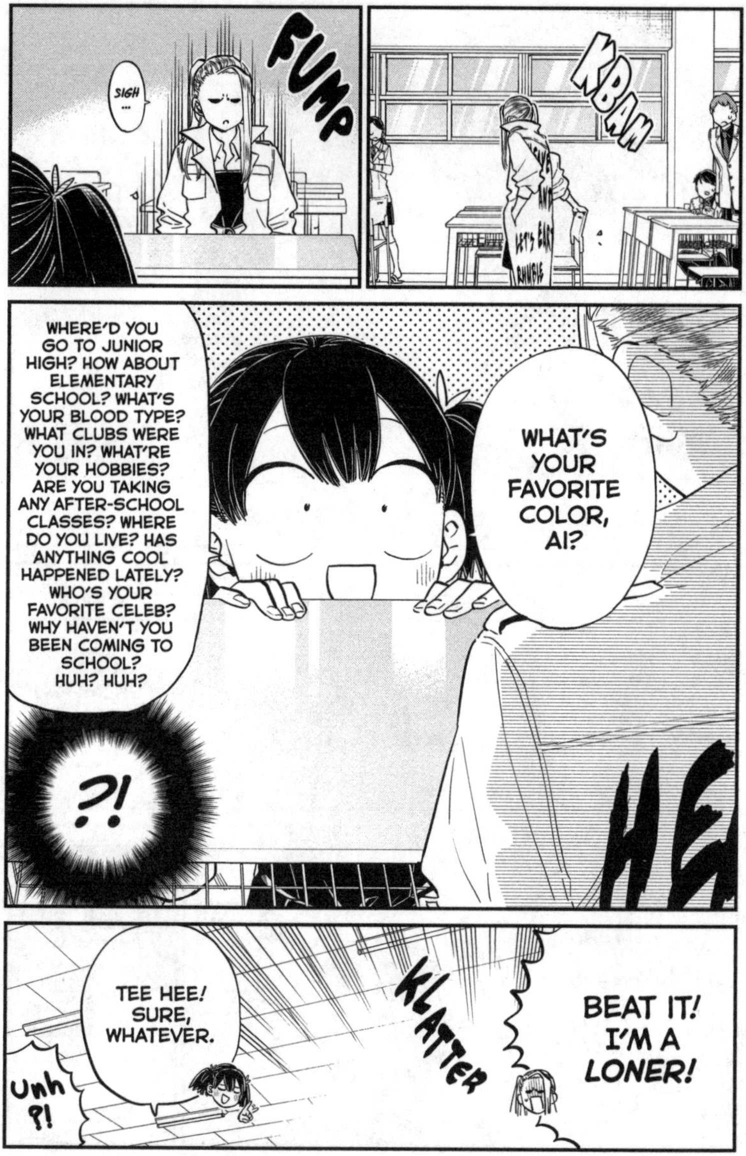
KBAM
SIGH...
FLUMP
WHAT'S YOUR FAVORITE COLOR, AI?
WHERE'D YOU GO TO JUNIOR HIGH? HOW ABOUT ELEMENTARY SCHOOL? WHAT'S YOUR BLOOD TYPE? WHAT CLUBS WERE YOU IN? WHAT'RE YOUR HOBBIES? ARE YOU TAKING ANY AFTER-SCHOOL CLASSES? WHERE DO YOU LIVE? HAS ANYTHING COOL HAPPENED LATELY? WHO'S YOUR FAVORITE CELEB? WHY HAVEN'T YOU BEEN COMING TO SCHOOL? HUH? HUH?
?!
BEAT IT! I'M A *LONER!*
KLATTER
TEE HEE! SURE, WHATEVER.
Unh ?!

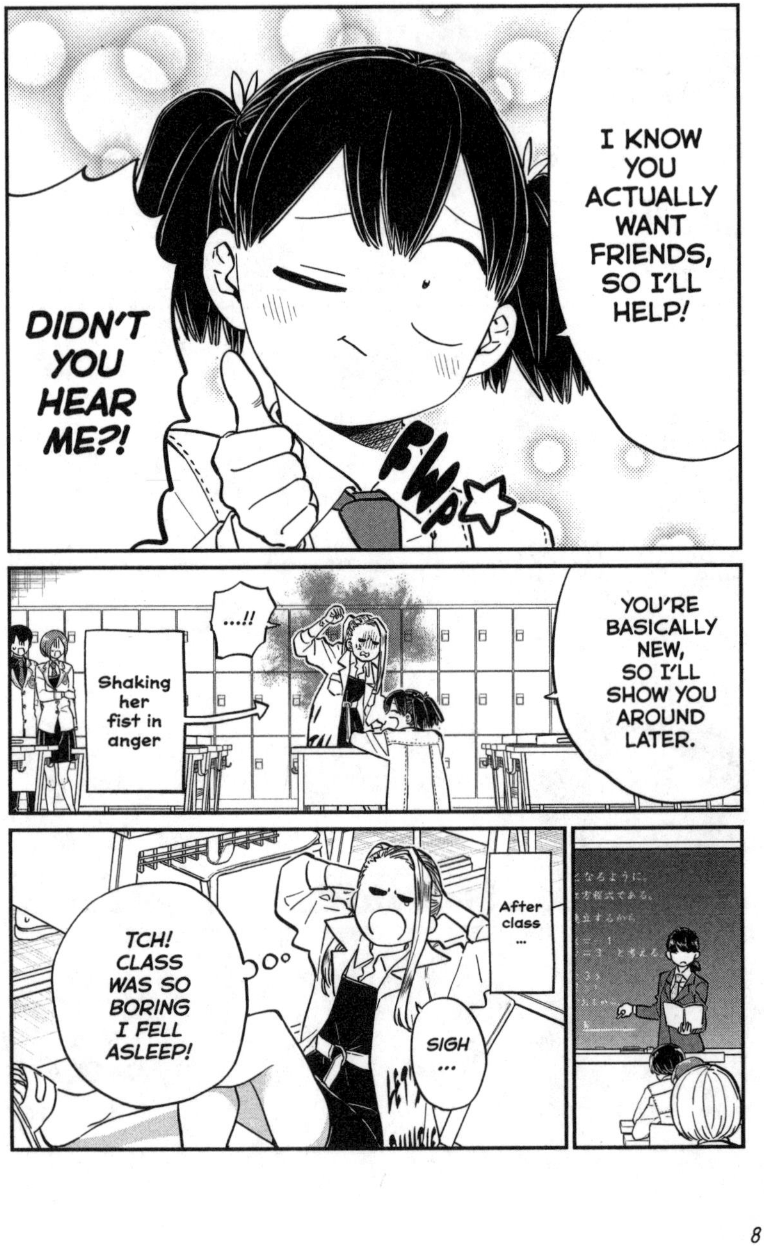
I KNOW YOU ACTUALLY WANT FRIENDS, SO I'LL HELP!
FWP
DIDN'T YOU HEAR ME?!
YOU'RE BASICALLY NEW, SO I'LL SHOW YOU AROUND LATER.
...!!
Shaking her fist in anger
After class ...
SIGH ...
TCH! CLASS WAS SO BORING I FELL ASLEEP!

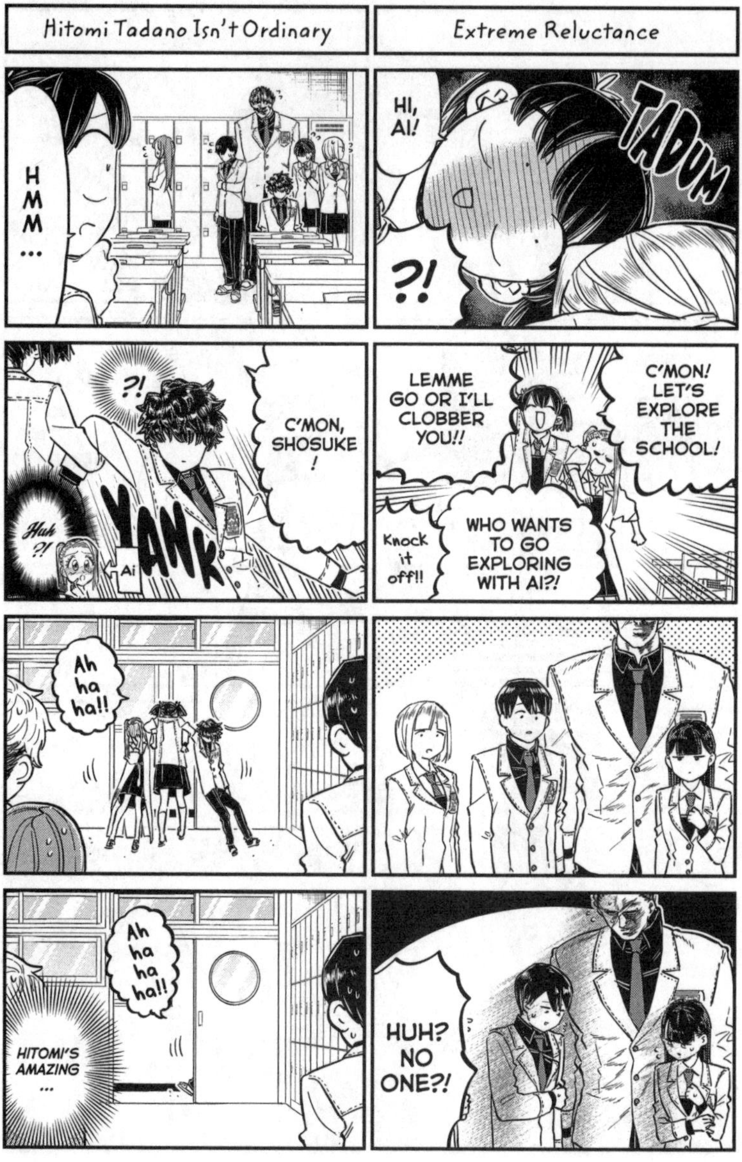
Extreme Reluctance
HI, AI!
TADUM
?!
C'MON! LET'S EXPLORE THE SCHOOL!
LEMME GO OR I'LL CLOBBER YOU!!
WHO WANTS TO GO EXPLORING WITH AI?!
Knock it off!!
HUH? NO ONE?!
Hitomi Tadano Isn't Ordinary
HMM...
C'MON, SHOSUKE!
?!
YANK
Huh ?!
Ai
Ah ha ha!!
Ah ha ha ha!!
HITOMI'S AMAZING...

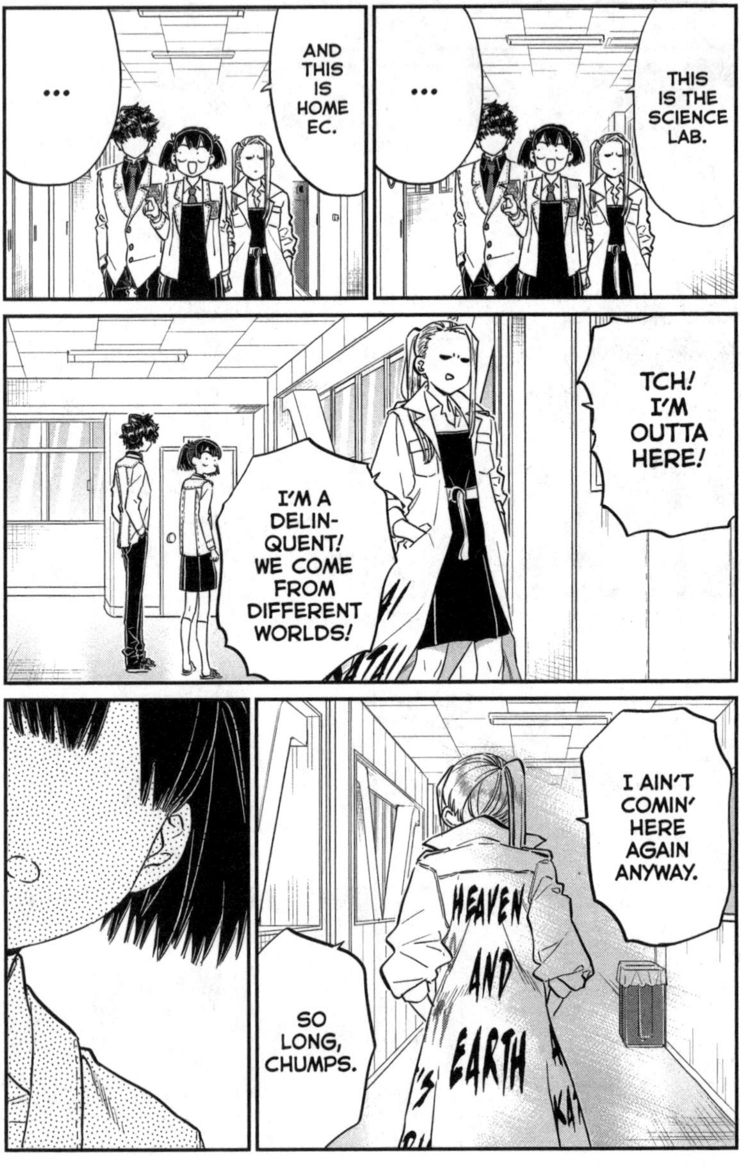
THIS IS THE SCIENCE LAB.
...
AND THIS IS HOME EC.
...
TCH! I'M OUTTA HERE!
I'M A DELIN-QUENT! WE COME FROM DIFFERENT WORLDS!
I AIN'T COMIN' HERE AGAIN ANYWAY.
HEAVEN AND EARTH
SO LONG, CHUMPS.

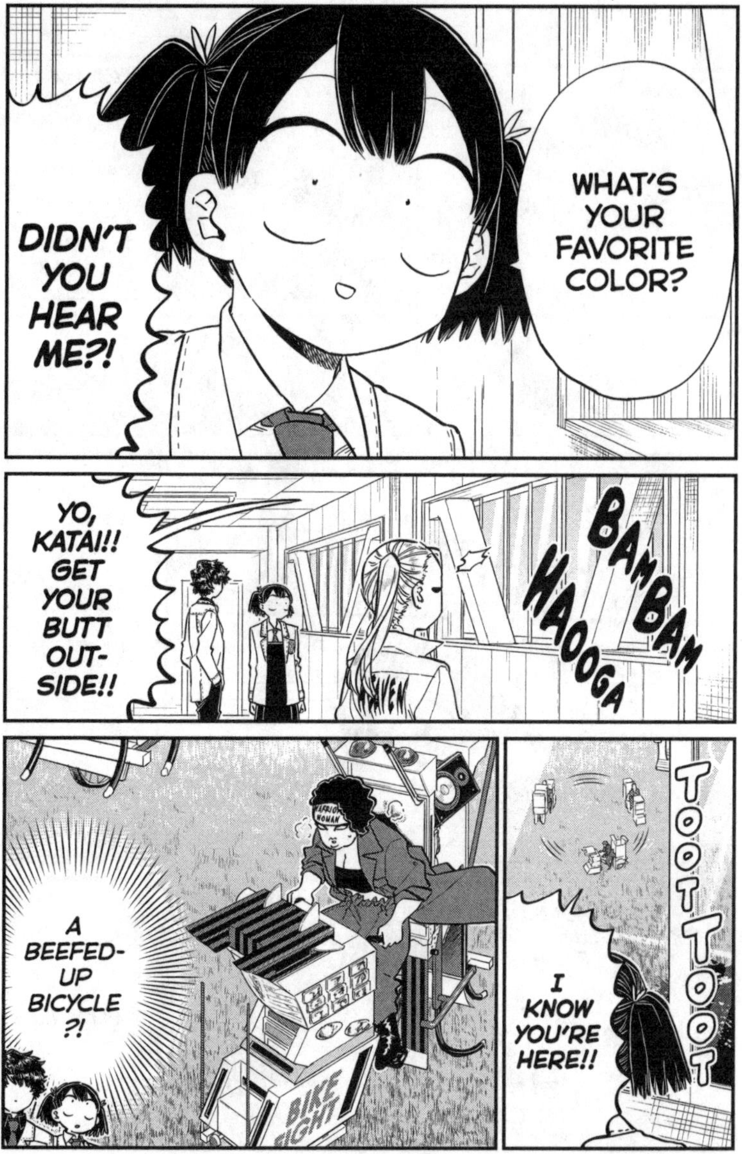
WHAT'S YOUR FAVORITE COLOR?
DIDN'T YOU HEAR ME?!
BAMBAM
HAOOGA
YO, KATAI!! GET YOUR BUTT OUT-SIDE!!
TOOT TOOT TOOT
I KNOW YOU'RE HERE!!
A BEEFED-UP BICYCLE?!
BIKE FIGHT

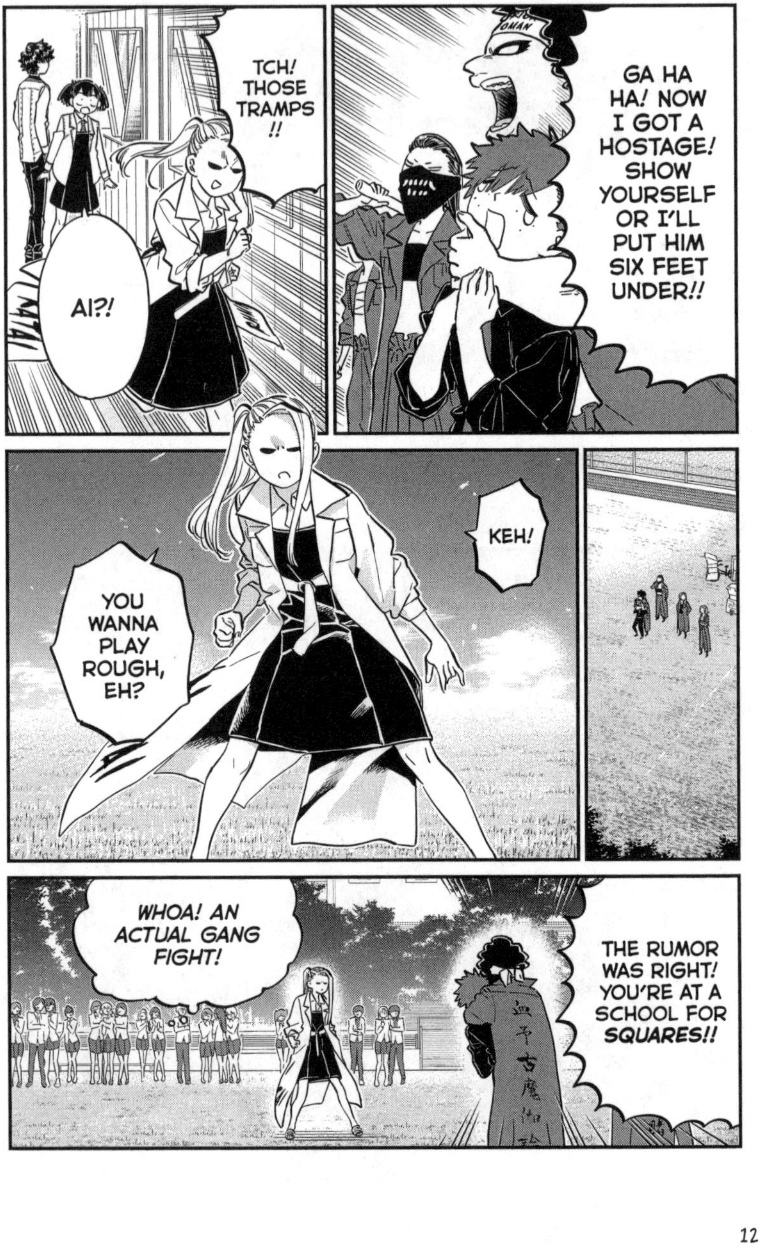
GA HA HA! NOW I GOT A HOSTAGE! SHOW YOURSELF OR I'LL PUT HIM SIX FEET UNDER!!
TCH! THOSE TRAMPS!!
AI?!
KEH!
YOU WANNA PLAY ROUGH, EH?
THE RUMOR WAS RIGHT! YOU'RE AT A SCHOOL FOR SQUARES!!
WHOA! AN ACTUAL GANG FIGHT!

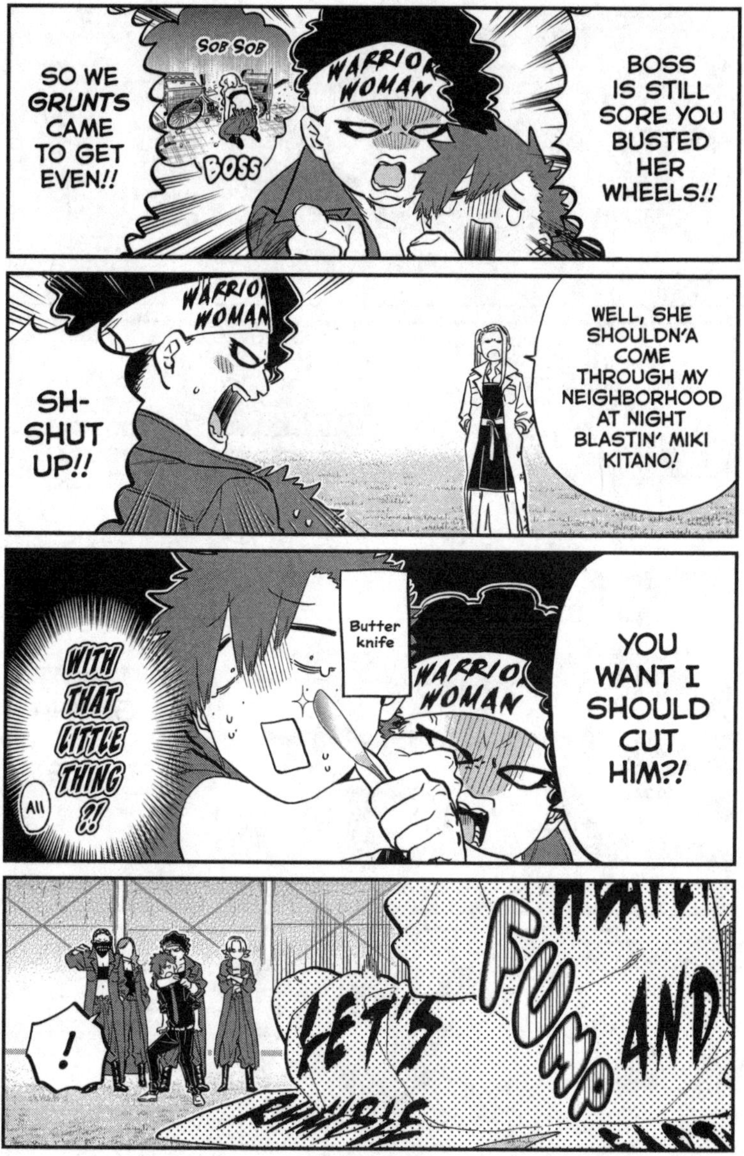
BOSS IS STILL SORE YOU BUSTED HER WHEELS!!
SOB SOB
BOSS
SO WE GRUNTS CAME TO GET EVEN!!
WELL, SHE SHOULDN'A COME THROUGH MY NEIGHBORHOOD AT NIGHT BLASTIN' MIKI KITANO!
SH-SHUT UP!!
YOU WANT I SHOULD CUT HIM?!
Butter knife
WITH THAT LITTLE THING?!
All
!

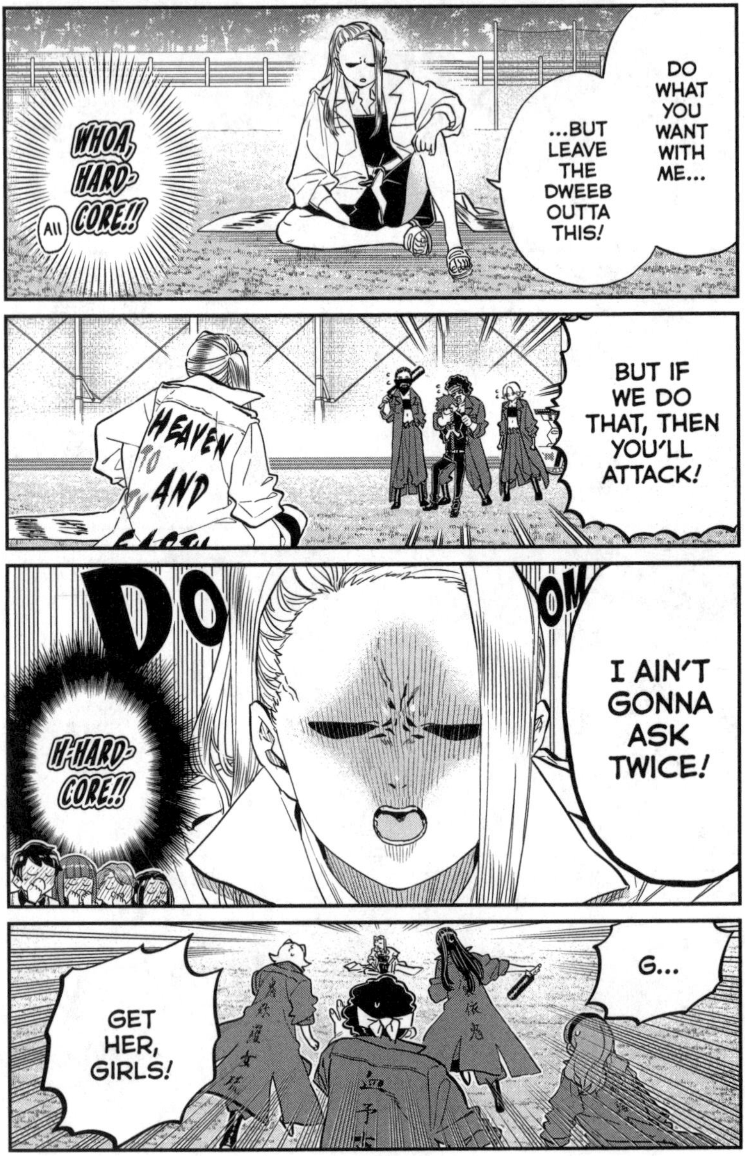
DO WHAT YOU WANT WITH ME...
...BUT LEAVE THE DWEEB OUTTA THIS!
WHOA, HARD-CORE!!
All
BUT IF WE DO THAT, THEN YOU'LL ATTACK!
HEAVEN AND
DOOM
I AIN'T GONNA ASK TWICE!
H-HARD-CORE!!
G...
GET HER, GIRLS!

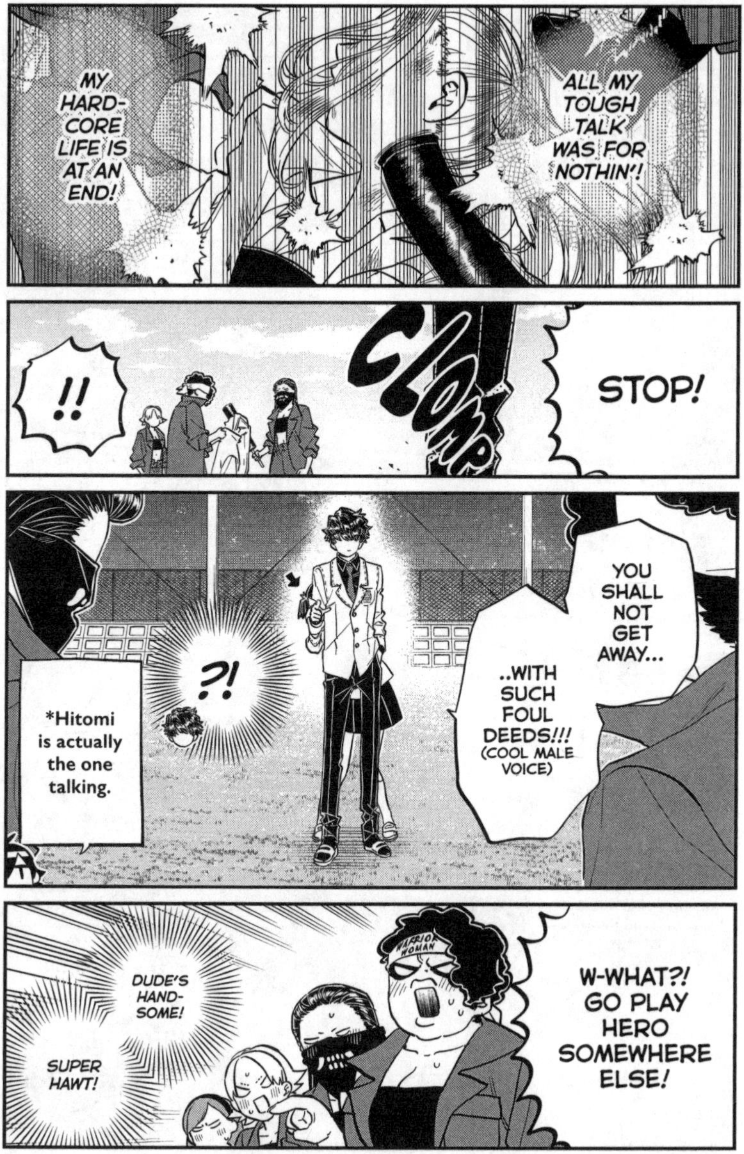
ALL MY TOUGH TALK WAS FOR NOTHIN'!
MY HARD-CORE LIFE IS AT AN END!
STOP!
CLOMP
!!
YOU SHALL NOT GET AWAY...
..WITH SUCH FOUL DEEDS!!!
(COOL MALE VOICE)
?!
*Hitomi is actually the one talking.
W-WHAT?! GO PLAY HERO SOMEWHERE ELSE!
WARRIOR WOMAN
DUDE'S HAND-SOME!
SUPER HAWT!

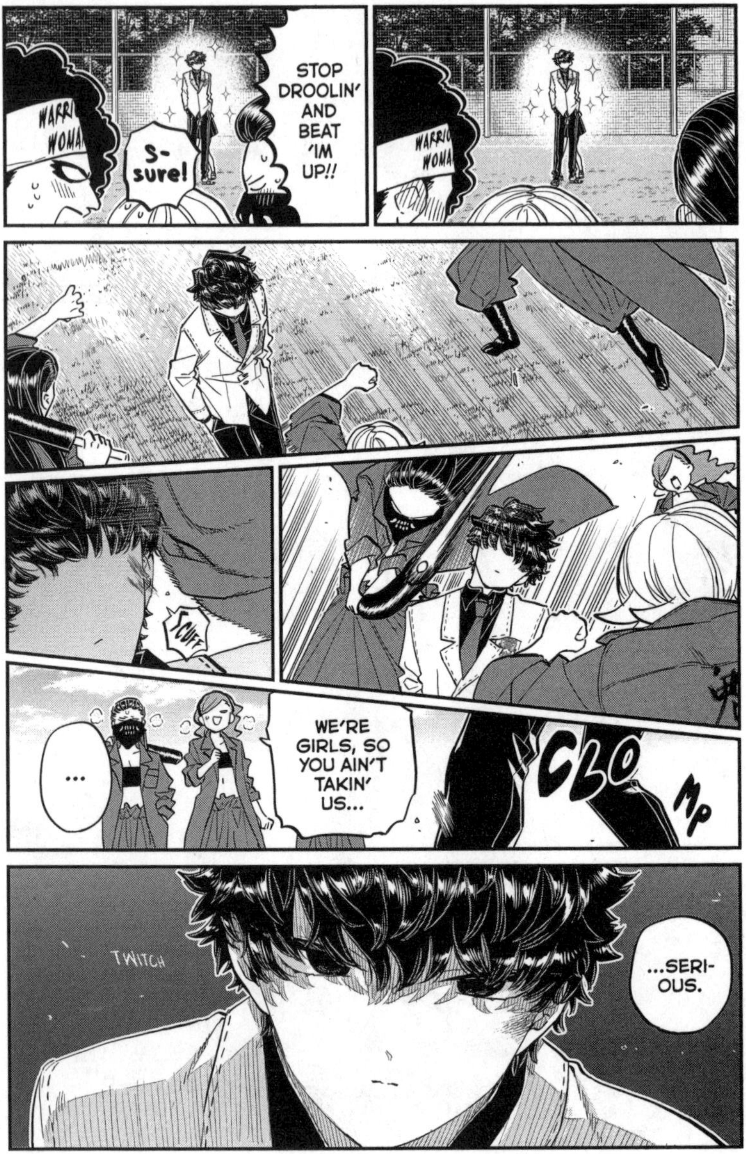
STOP DROOLIN' AND BEAT 'IM UP!!
S-sure!
SCUFF
CLOMP
WE'RE GIRLS, SO YOU AIN'T TAKIN' US...
...
...SERI-OUS.
TWITCH

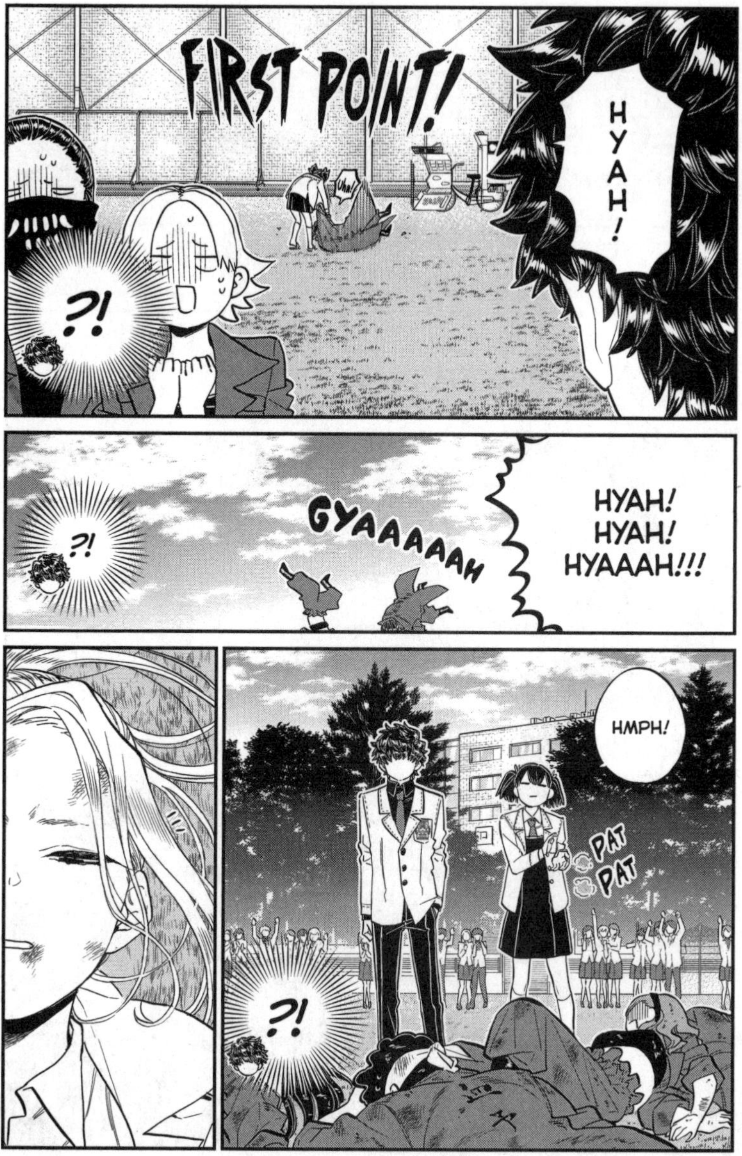
HYAH!
FIRST POINT!
?!
HYAH! HYAH! HYAAAH!!!
GYAAAAAAH
?!
HMPH!
PAT PAT
?!

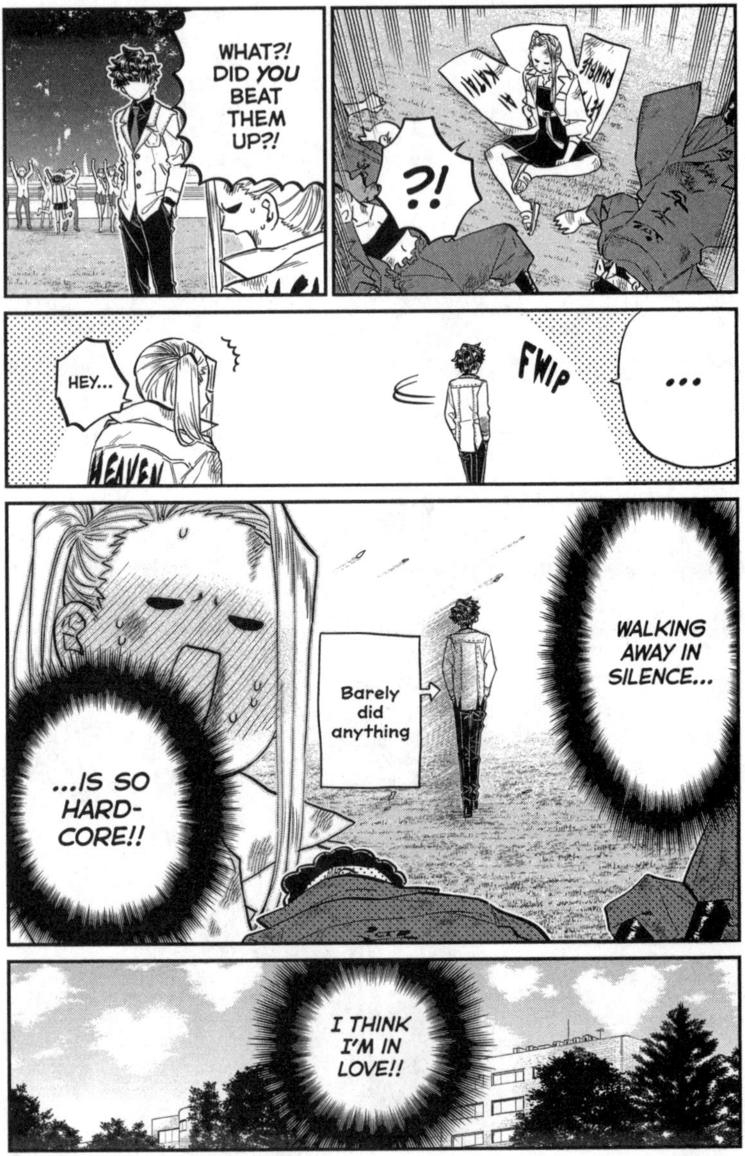
?!
WHAT?! DID YOU BEAT THEM UP?!
...
FWIP
HEY...
WALKING AWAY IN SILENCE...
Barely did anything
...IS SO HARD-CORE!!
I THINK I'M IN LOVE!!

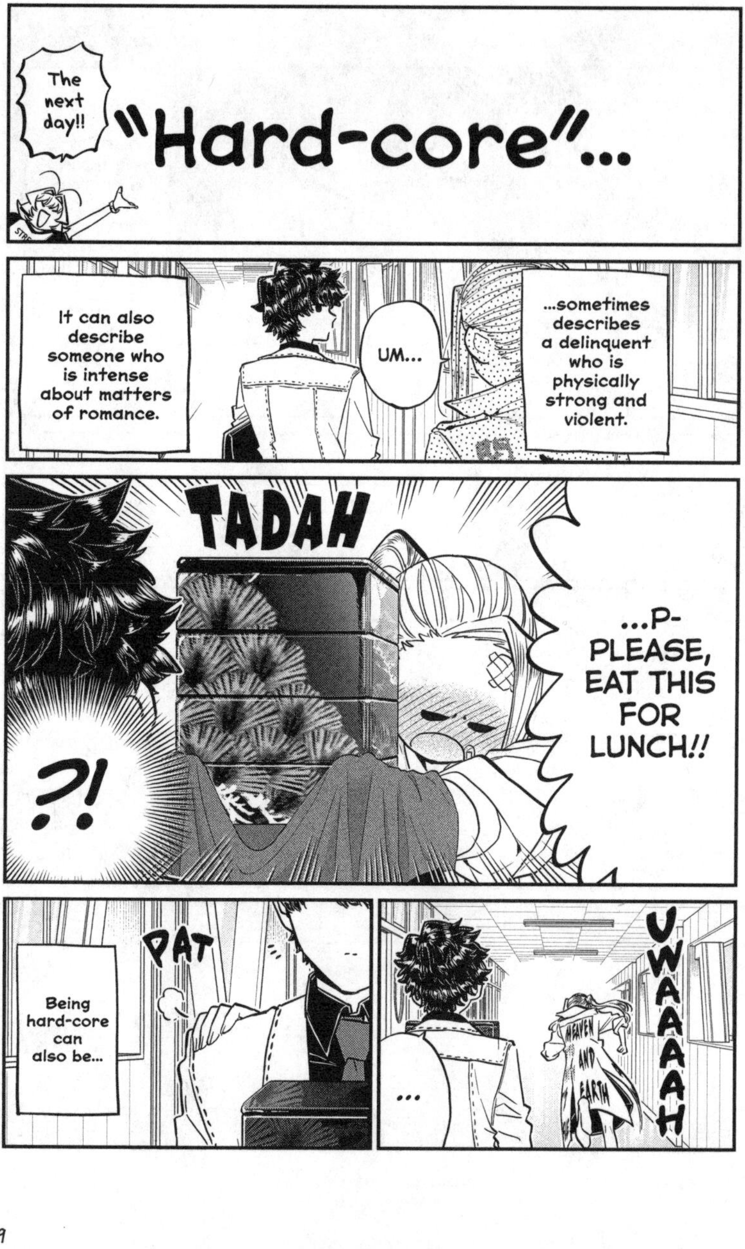
"Hard-core"...
The next day!!
...sometimes describes a delinquent who is physically strong and violent.
UM...
It can also describe someone who is intense about matters of romance.
TADAH
...P-PLEASE, EAT THIS FOR LUNCH!!
?!
UWAAAAH
HEAVEN AND EARTH
...
PAT
Being hard-core can also be...

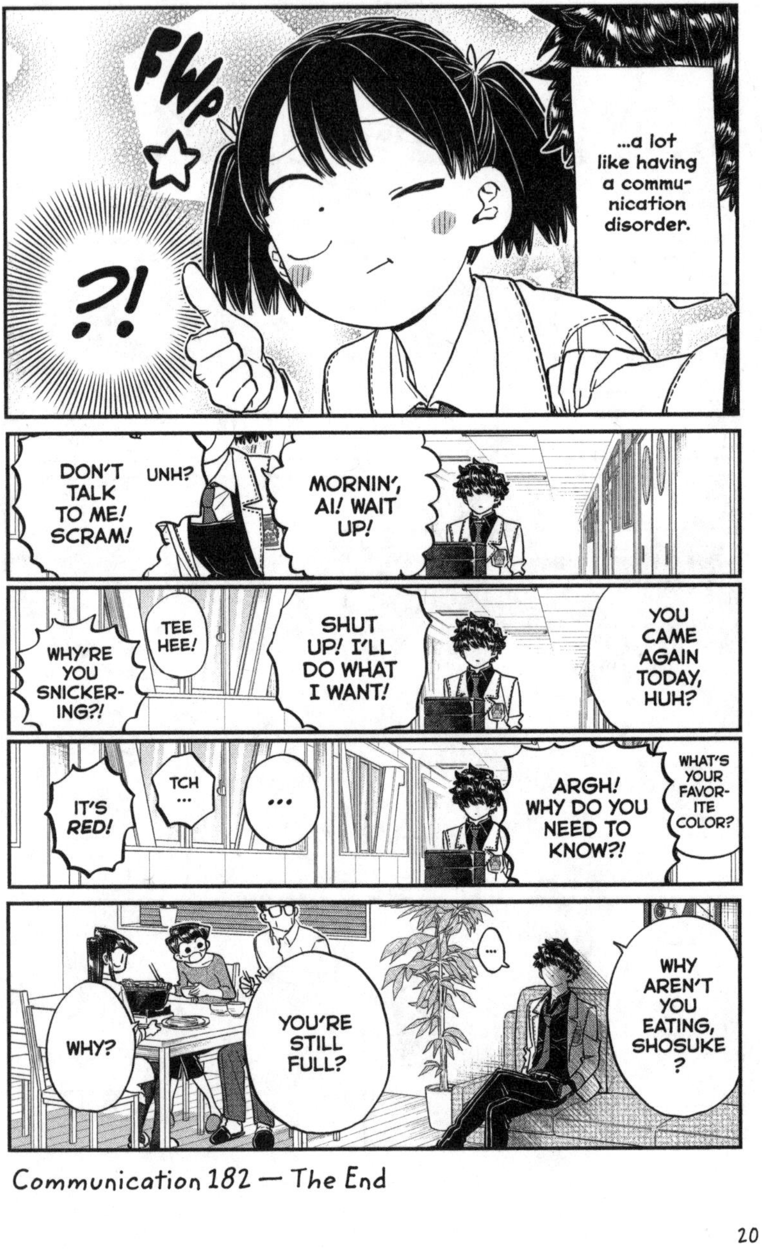
...a lot like having a communication disorder.
FWP
?!
MORNIN', AI! WAIT UP!
UNH?
DON'T TALK TO ME! SCRAM!
YOU CAME AGAIN TODAY, HUH?
SHUT UP! I'LL DO WHAT I WANT!
TEE HEE!
WHY'RE YOU SNICKERING?!
WHAT'S YOUR FAVORITE COLOR?
ARGH! WHY DO YOU NEED TO KNOW?!
...
TCH ...
IT'S RED!
WHY AREN'T YOU EATING, SHOSUKE?
...
YOU'RE STILL FULL?
WHY?

Communication 182 — The End

Komi Can't Communicate

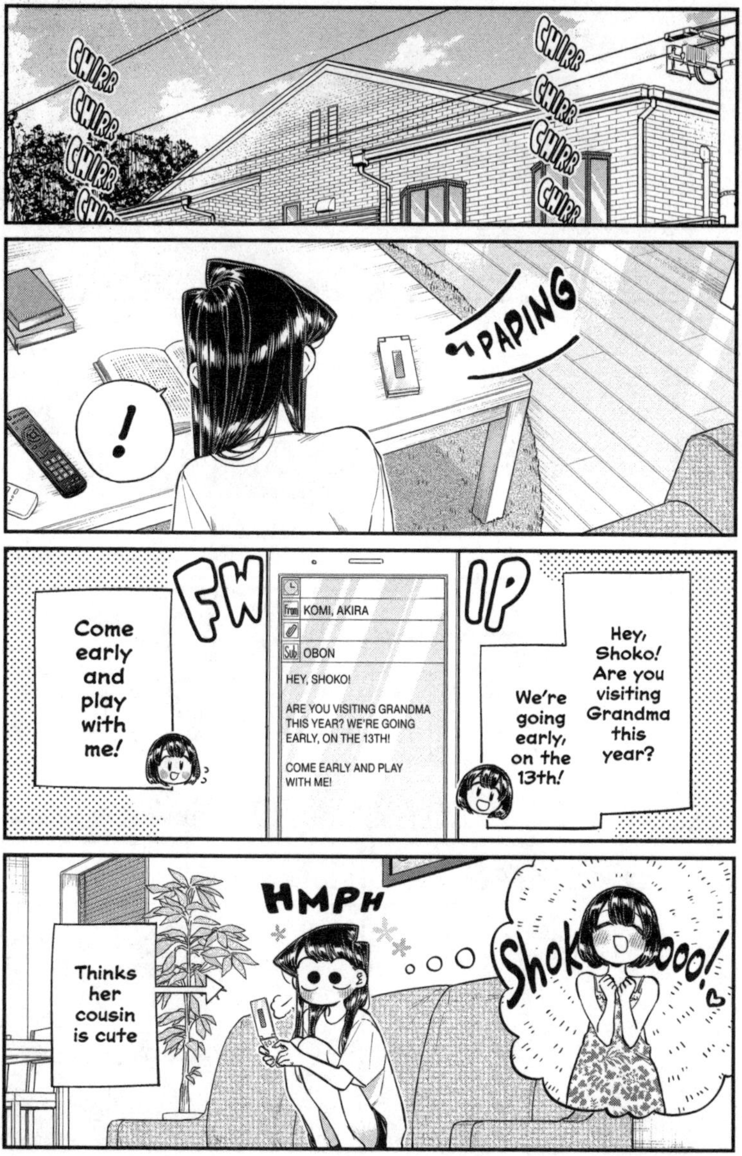
CHIRR
CHIRR
CHIRR
CHIRR
CHIRR
CHIRR
CHIRR
PAPING
!
FW
IP
Hey, Shoko! Are you visiting Grandma this year?
We're going early, on the 13th!
From KOMI, AKIRA
Sub OBON
HEY, SHOKO!
ARE YOU VISITING GRANDMA THIS YEAR? WE'RE GOING EARLY, ON THE 13TH!
COME EARLY AND PLAY WITH ME!
Come early and play with me!
Shokoooo!
HMPH
Thinks her cousin is cute

YOU WANT TO GO EARLY THIS YEAR?

...

WE PLANNED ON GOING ON THE 15TH, BUT...

!

...YOU CAN TAKE THE SHINKANSEN AHEAD OF US!

H-HMPH

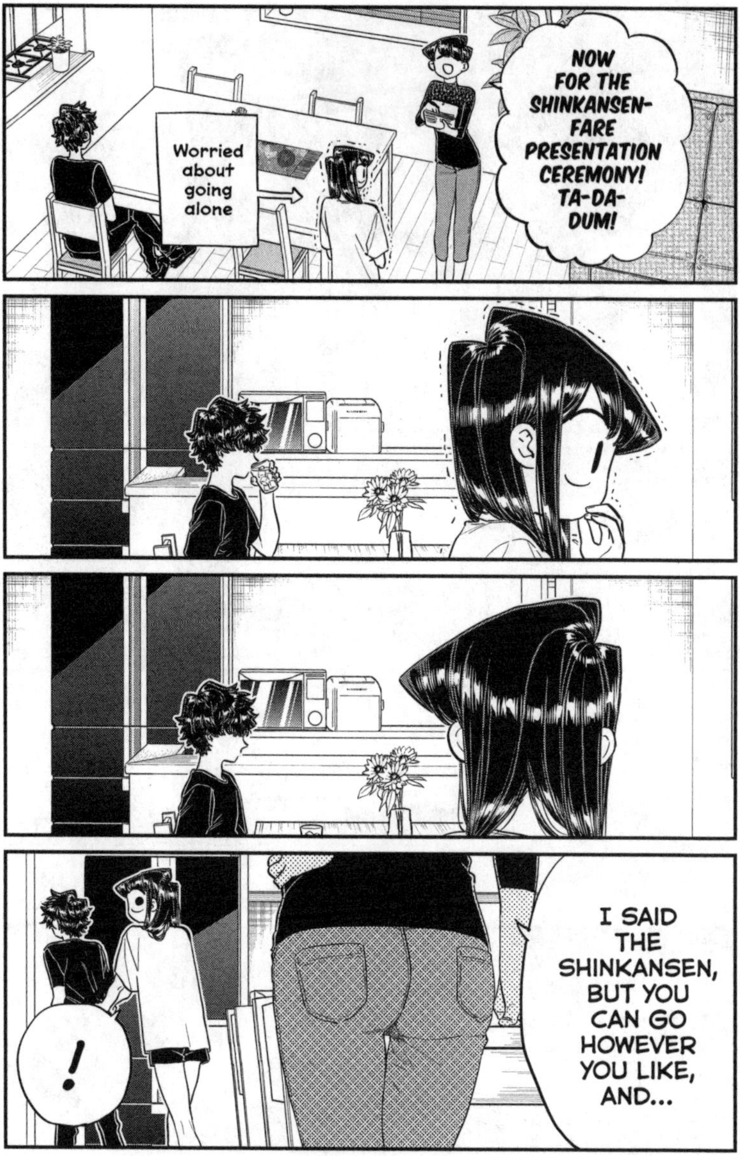
NOW FOR THE SHINKANSEN-FARE PRESENTATION CEREMONY! TA-DA-DUM!
Worried about going alone
I SAID THE SHINKANSEN, BUT YOU CAN GO HOWEVER YOU LIKE, AND...
!

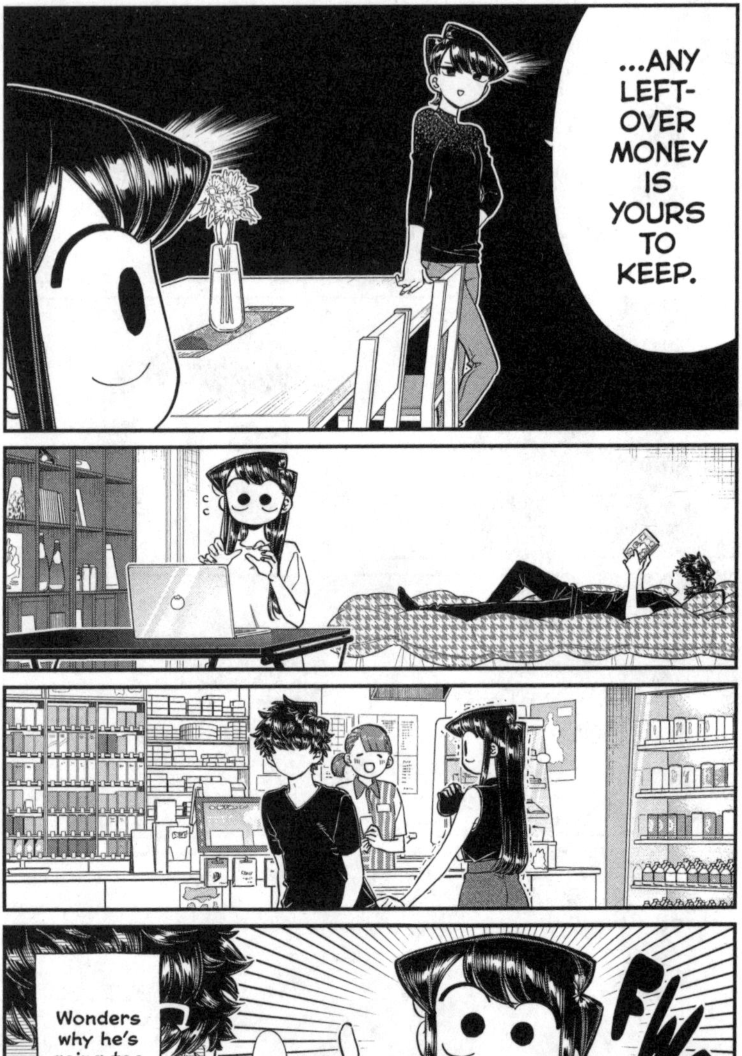
...ANY LEFT-OVER MONEY IS YOURS TO KEEP.
FWP
...
Wonders why he's going too

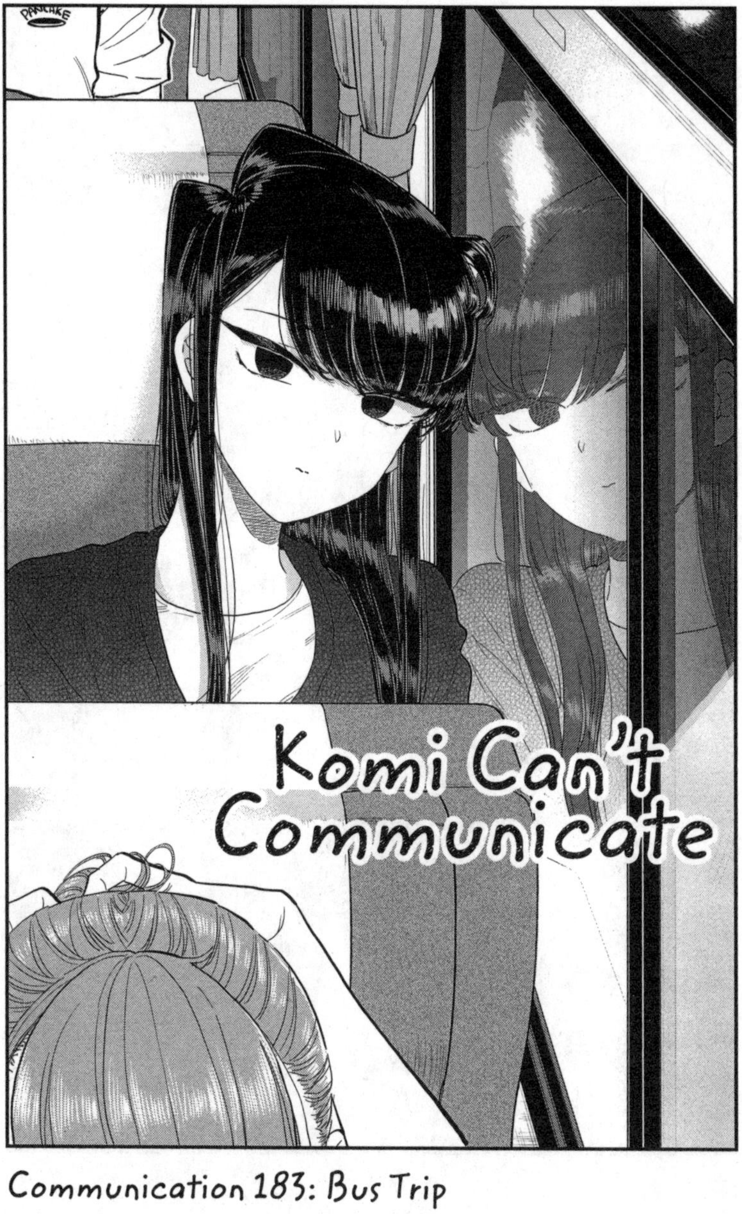
PANCAKE
Komi Can't Communicate

Communication 183: Bus Trip

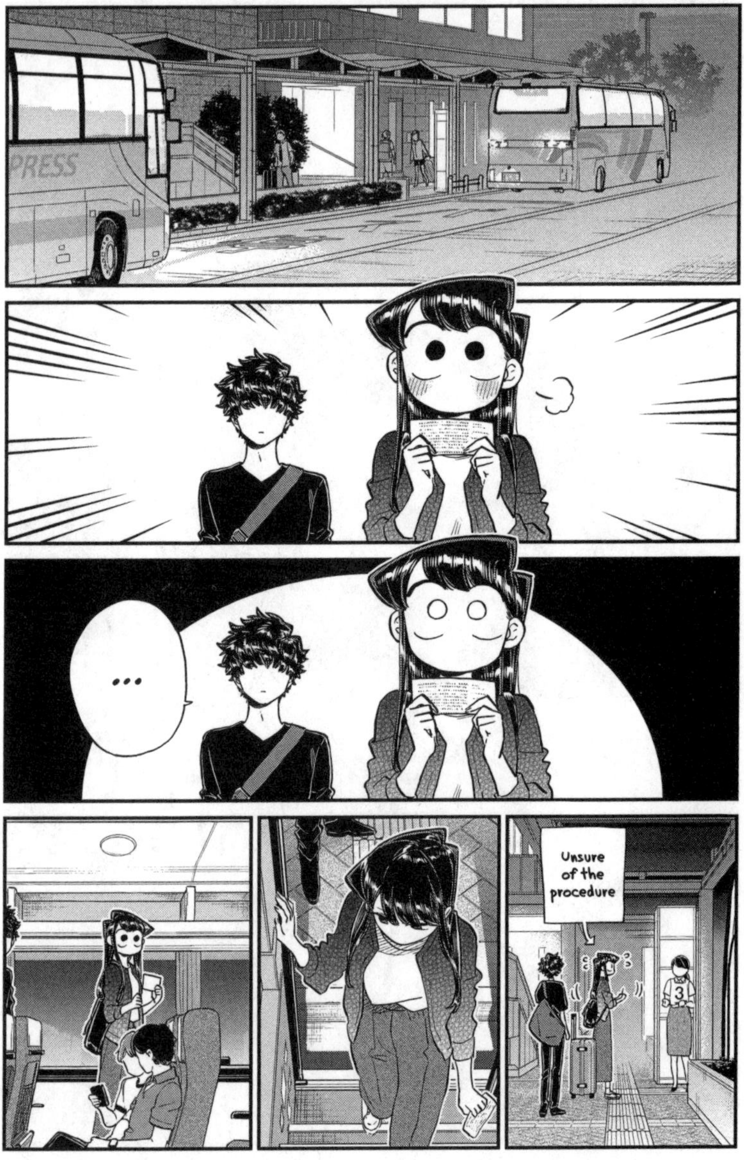
...
Unsure of the procedure

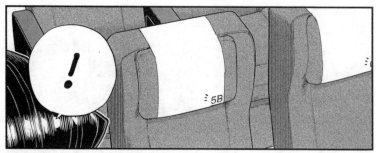

Pointing out their seats like a good big sister

Quite pleased with herself so far

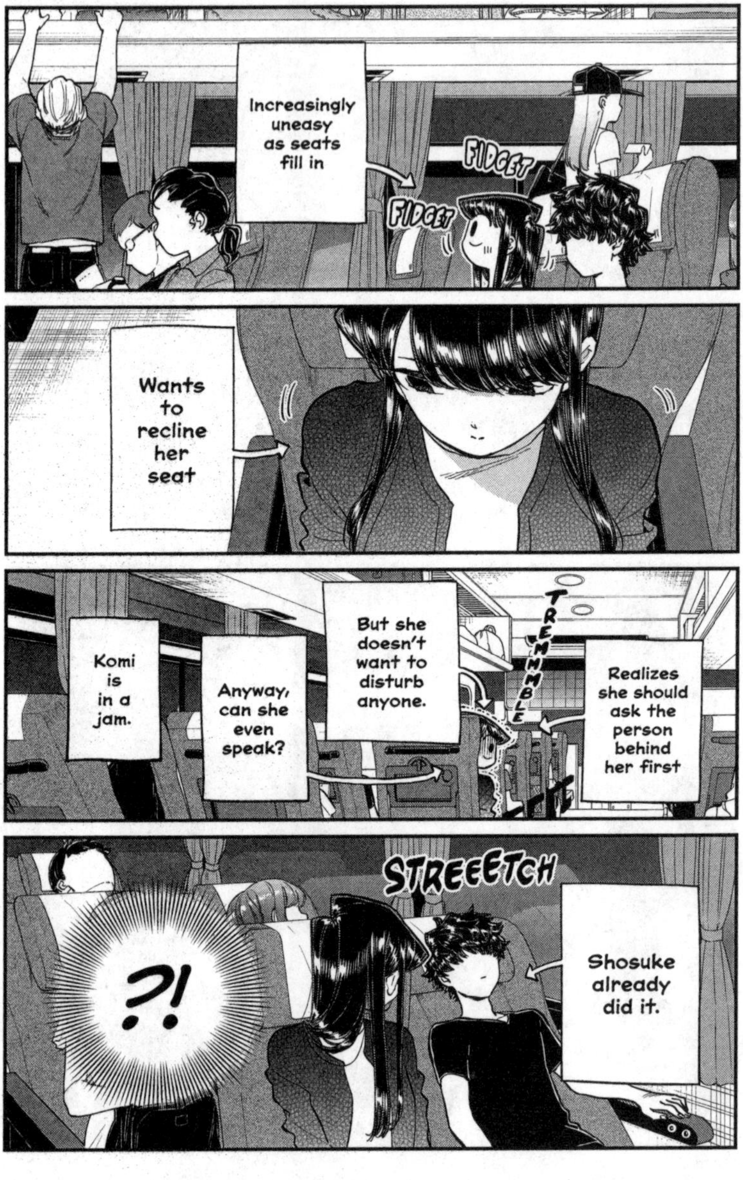
FIDGET
FIDGET
Increasingly uneasy as seats fill in
Wants to recline her seat
Realizes she should ask the person behind her first
TREMMMBLE
But she doesn't want to disturb anyone.
Anyway, can she even speak?
Komi is in a jam.
STREEETCH
Shosuke already did it.
?!

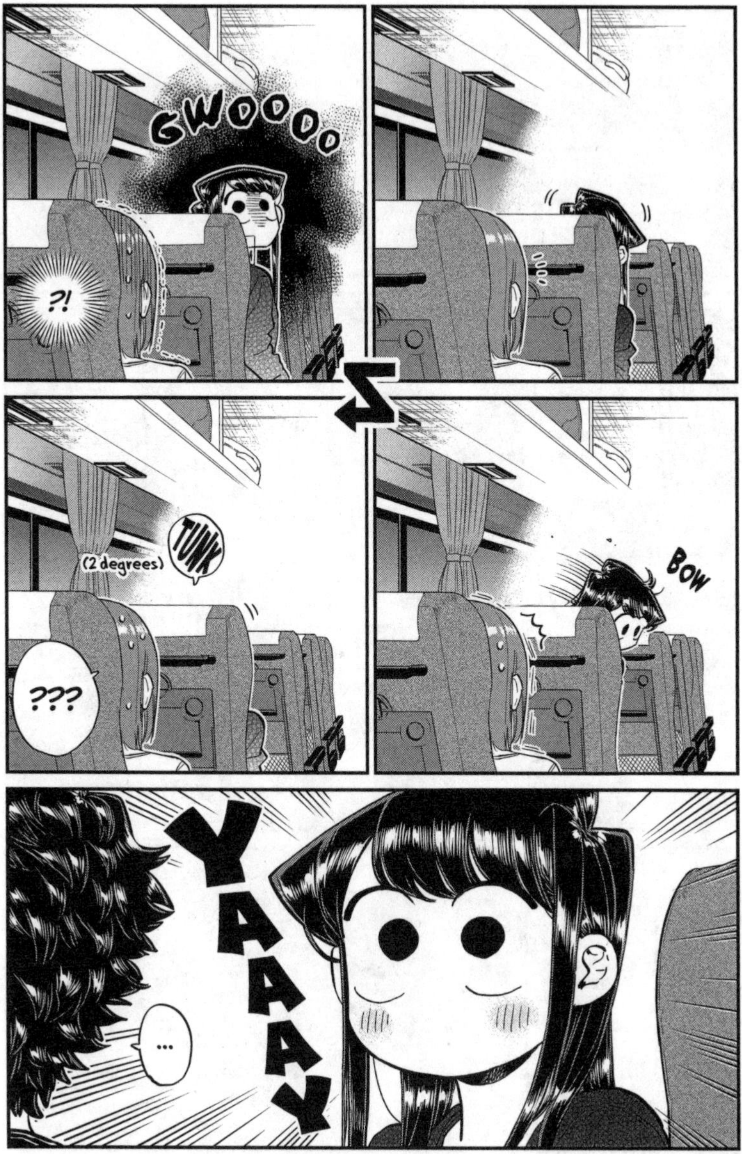
GWOOOO
?!
BOW
TUNK
(2 degrees)
???
YAAAAY
...

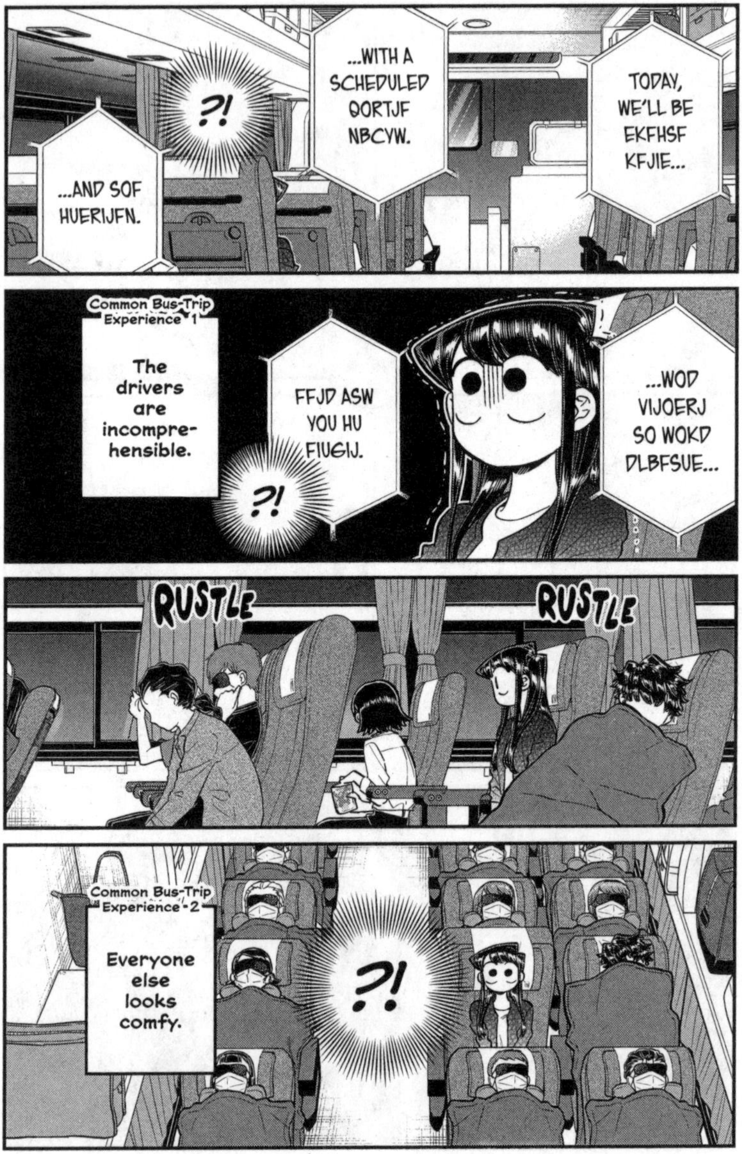
TODAY, WE'LL BE EKFHSF KFJIE...
...WITH A SCHEDULED QORTJF NBCYW.
?!
...AND SOF HUERIJFN.
...WOD VIJOERJ SO WOKD DLBFSUE...
FFJD ASW YOU HU FIUGIJ.
?!
Common Bus-Trip Experience 1
The drivers are incomprehensible.
RUSTLE
RUSTLE
?!
Common Bus-Trip Experience 2
Everyone else looks comfy.

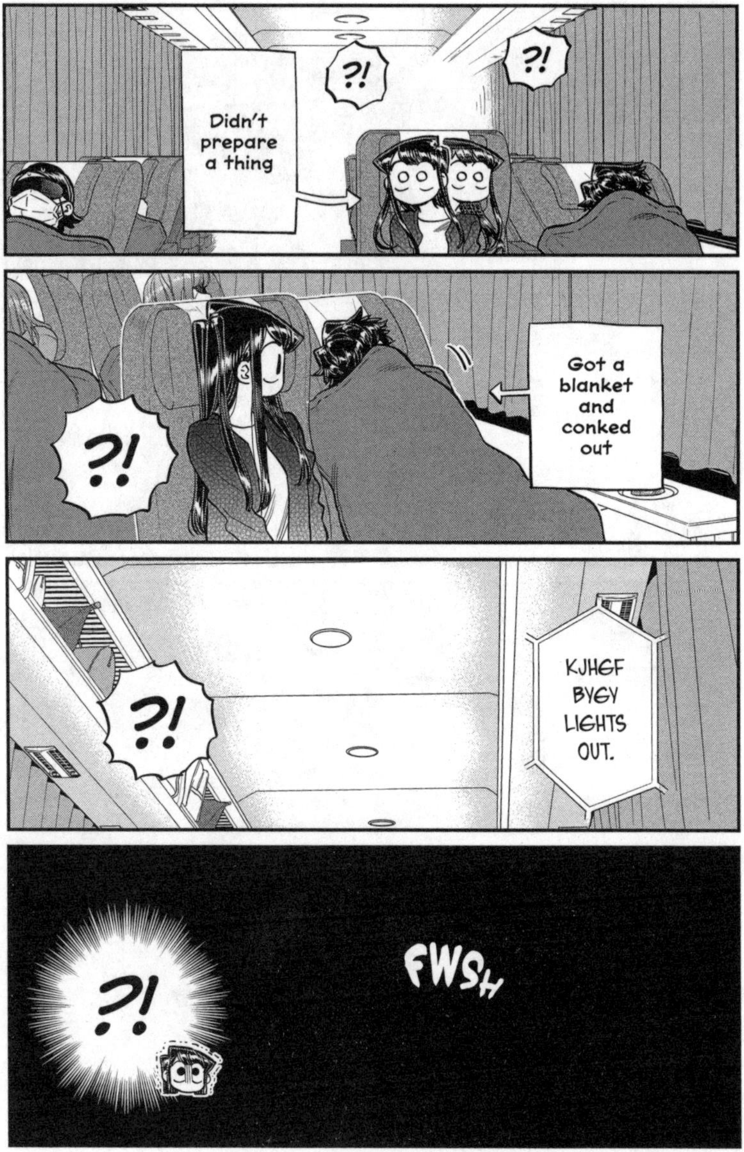
?!
?!
Didn't prepare a thing
Got a blanket and conked out
?!
KJHGF BYGY LIGHTS OUT.
?!
FWSH
?!

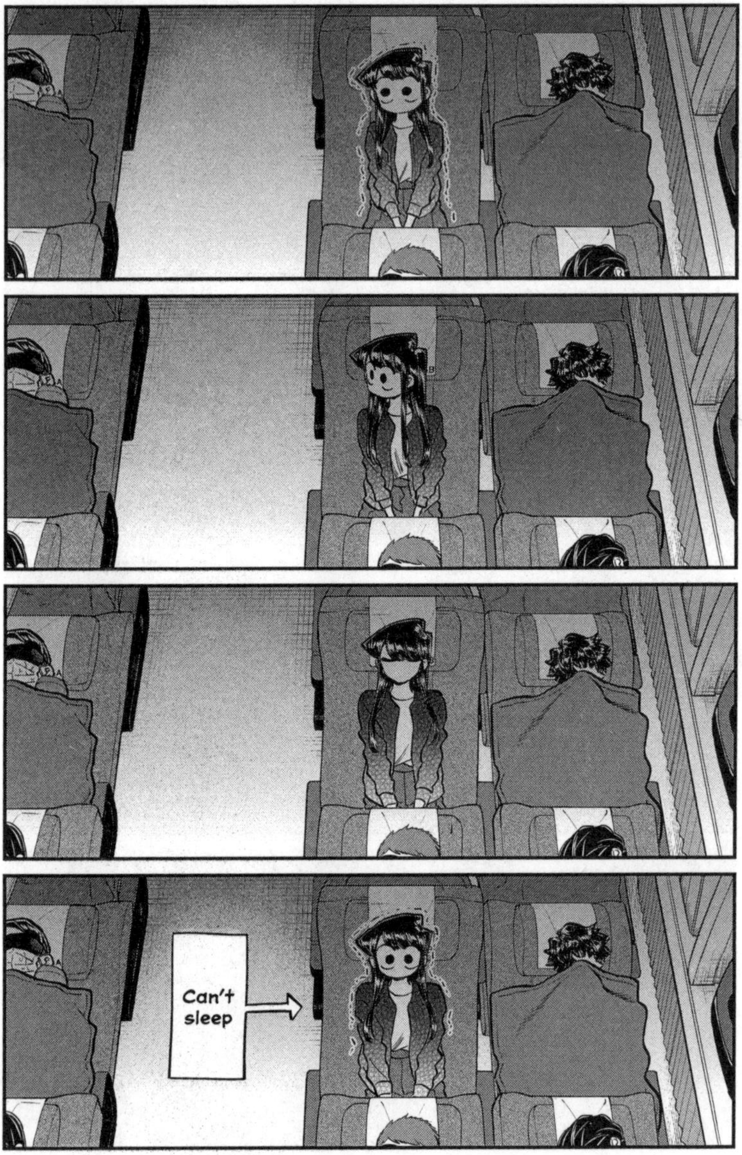
Can't
sleep

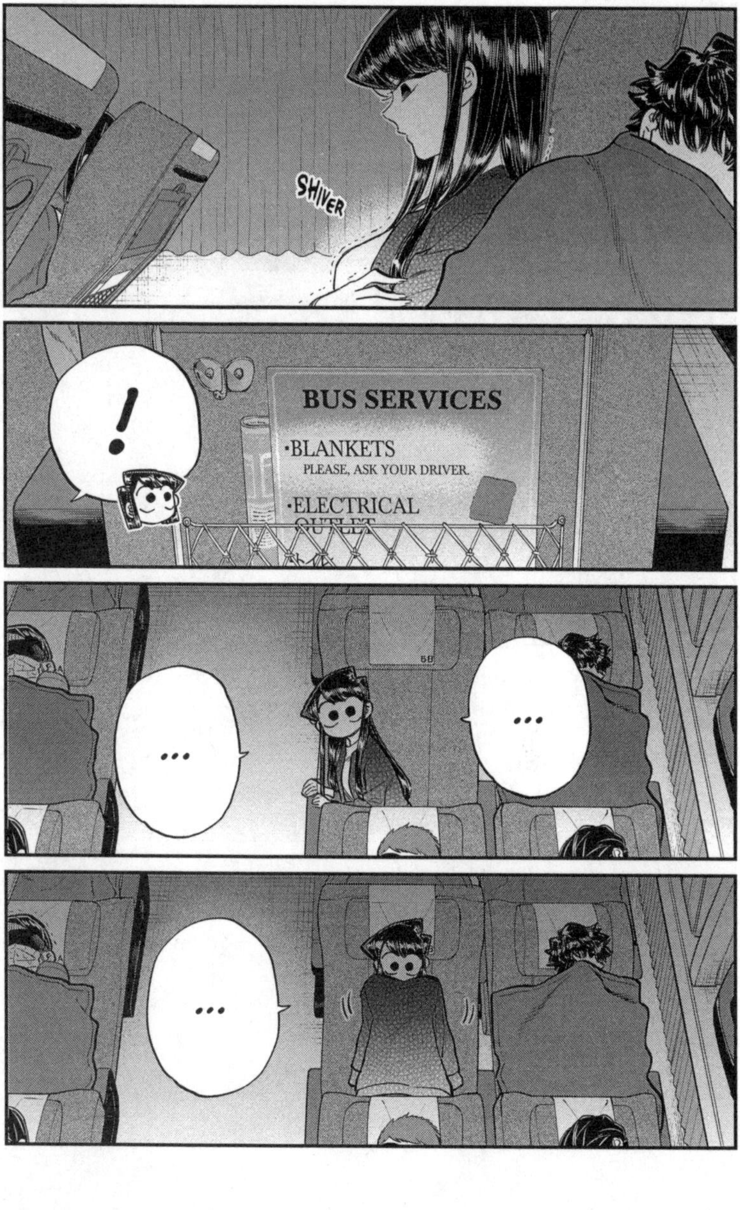
SHIVER
!
BUS SERVICES
•BLANKETS
PLEASE, ASK YOUR DRIVER.
•ELECTRICAL
...
...
...

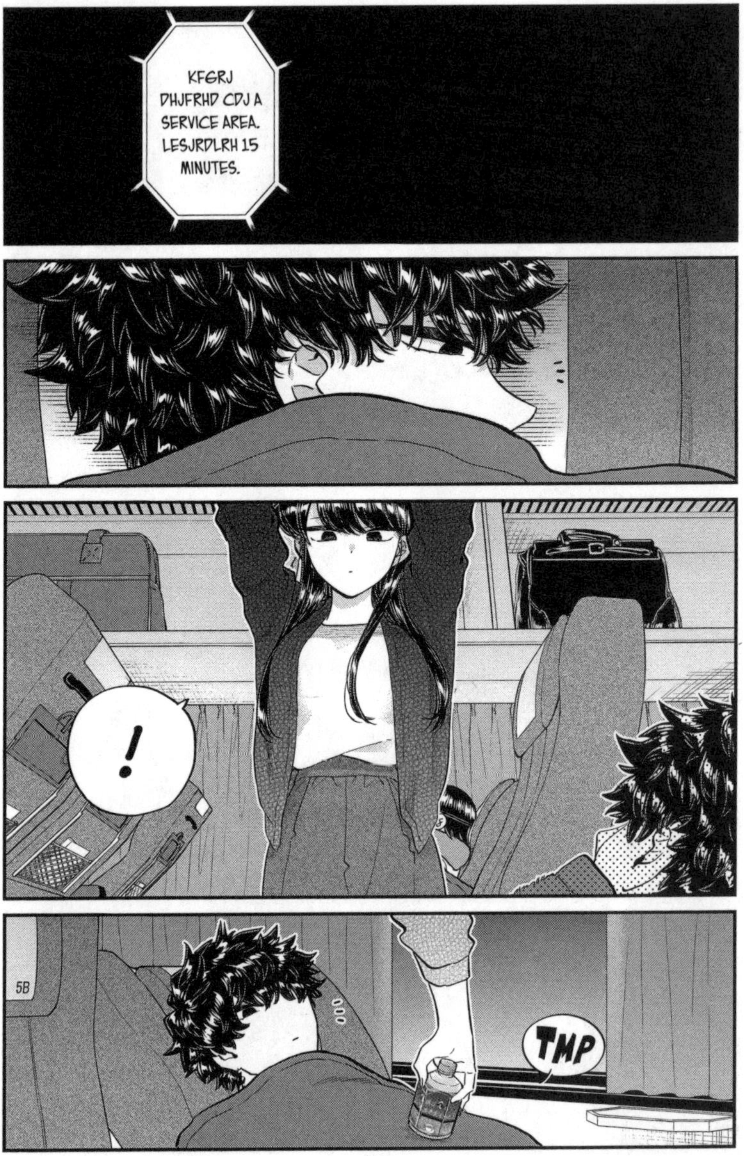
KFGRJ DHJFRHD CDJ A SERVICE AREA. LESJRDLRH 15 MINUTES.
!
5B
TMP

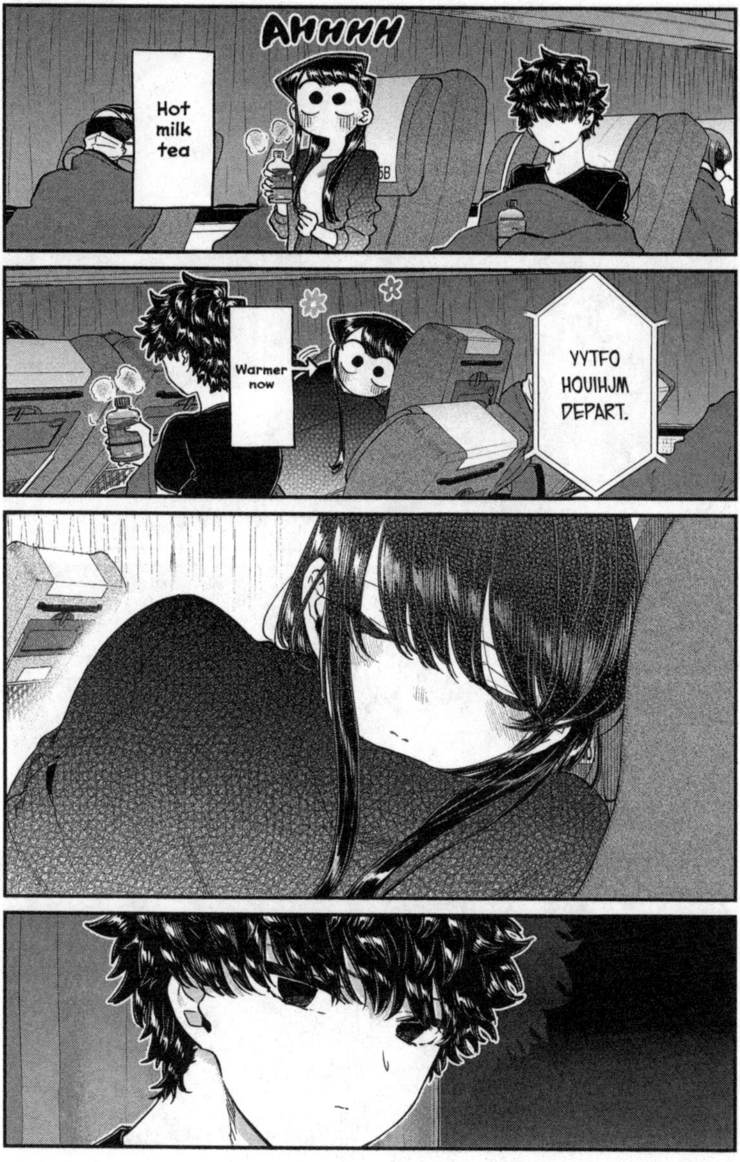
AHHHH
Hot milk tea
YYTFO HOUIHJM DEPART.
Warmer now

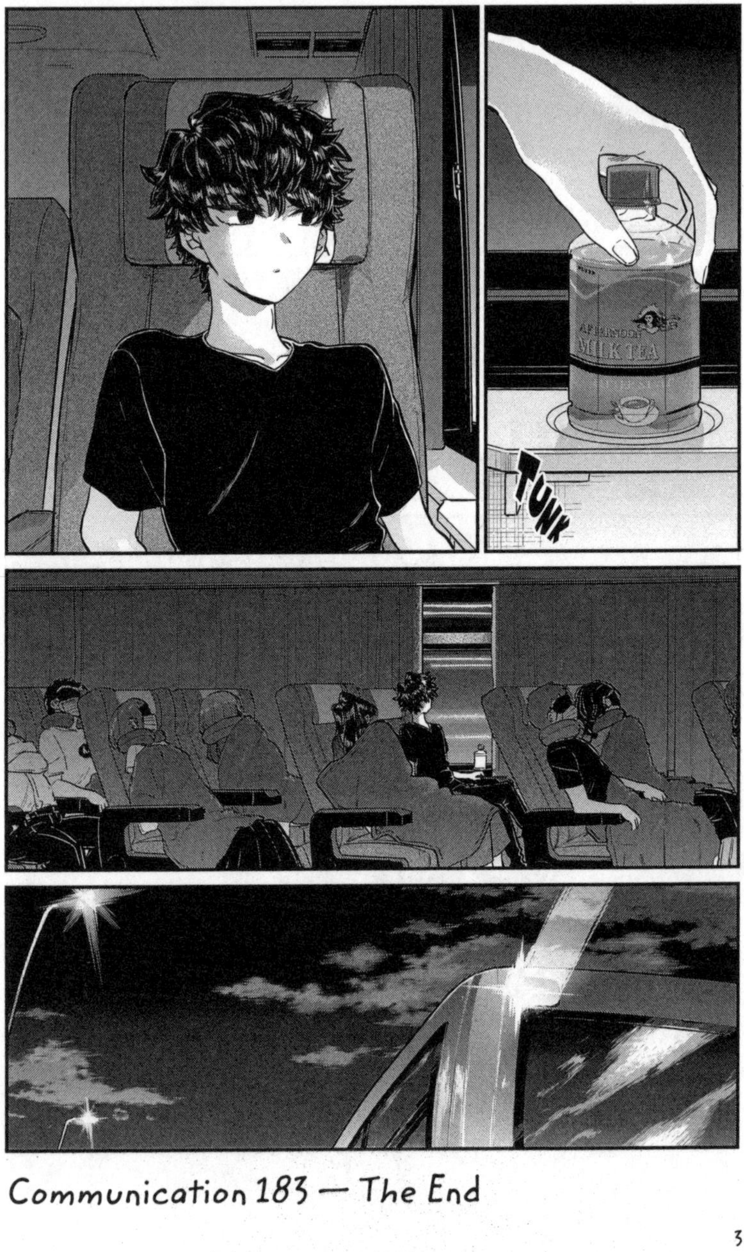
MILK TEA
TUNK

Communication 183 — The End

Bonus

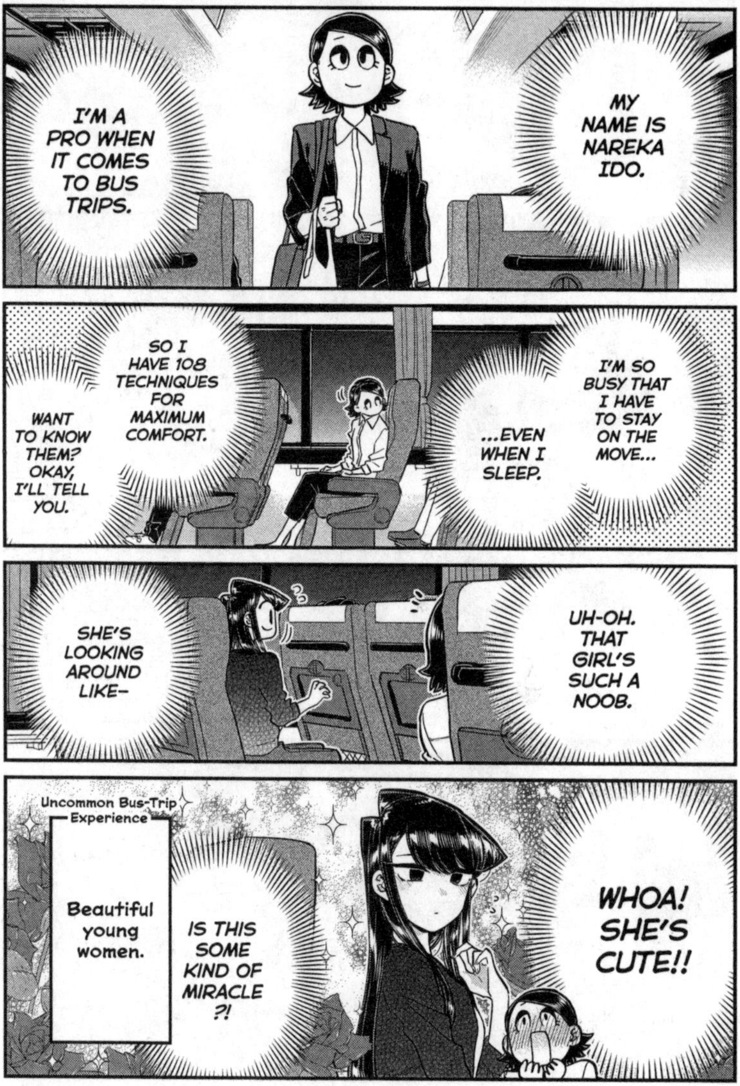
MY NAME IS NAREKA IDO.
I'M A PRO WHEN IT COMES TO BUS TRIPS.
I'M SO BUSY THAT I HAVE TO STAY ON THE MOVE...
...EVEN WHEN I SLEEP.
SO I HAVE 108 TECHNIQUES FOR MAXIMUM COMFORT.
WANT TO KNOW THEM? OKAY, I'LL TELL YOU.
UH-OH. THAT GIRL'S SUCH A NOOB.
SHE'S LOOKING AROUND LIKE–
WHOA! SHE'S CUTE!!
IS THIS SOME KIND OF MIRACLE ?!
Uncommon Bus-Trip Experience
Beautiful young women.

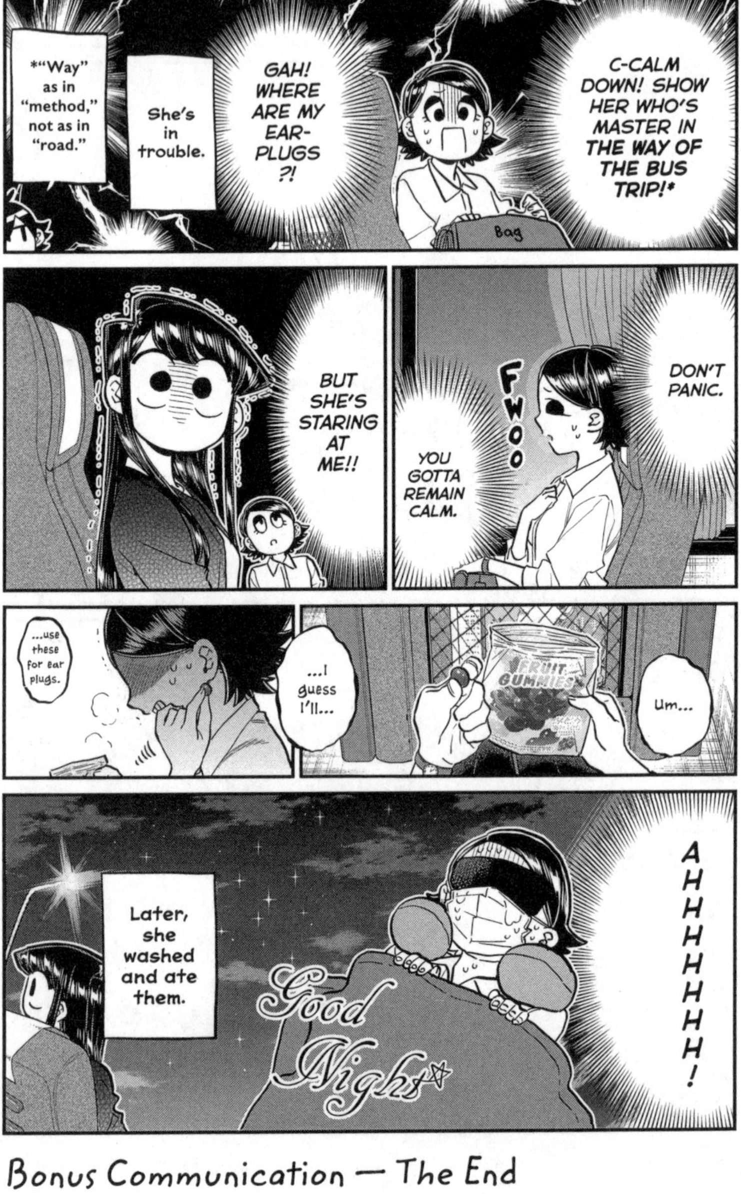

C-CALM DOWN! SHOW HER WHO'S MASTER IN THE WAY OF THE BUS TRIP!*
GAH! WHERE ARE MY EAR-PLUGS?!
She's in trouble.
*"Way" as in "method," not as in "road."
Bag
DON'T PANIC.
FWOO
YOU GOTTA REMAIN CALM.
BUT SHE'S STARING AT ME!!
Um...
FRUIT GUMMIES
...I guess I'll...
...use these for ear plugs.
AHHHHHHHH!
Good Night☆
Later, she washed and ate them.

Bonus Communication — The End

Common Bus-Trip
-Experience-3-

Your body gets stiff.

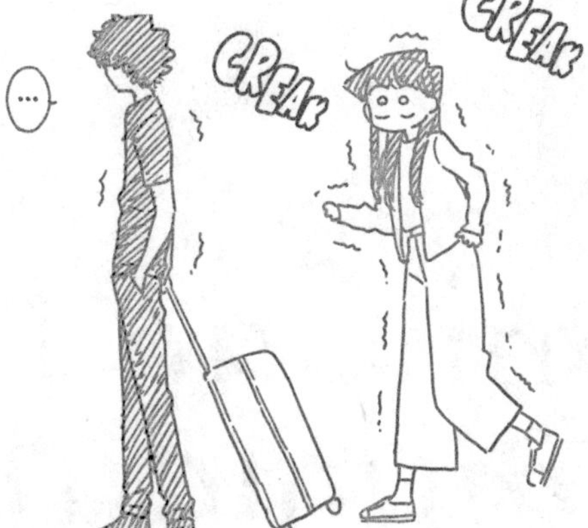
CREAK
CREAK
...

Komi Can't
Communicate

Komi Can't Communicate

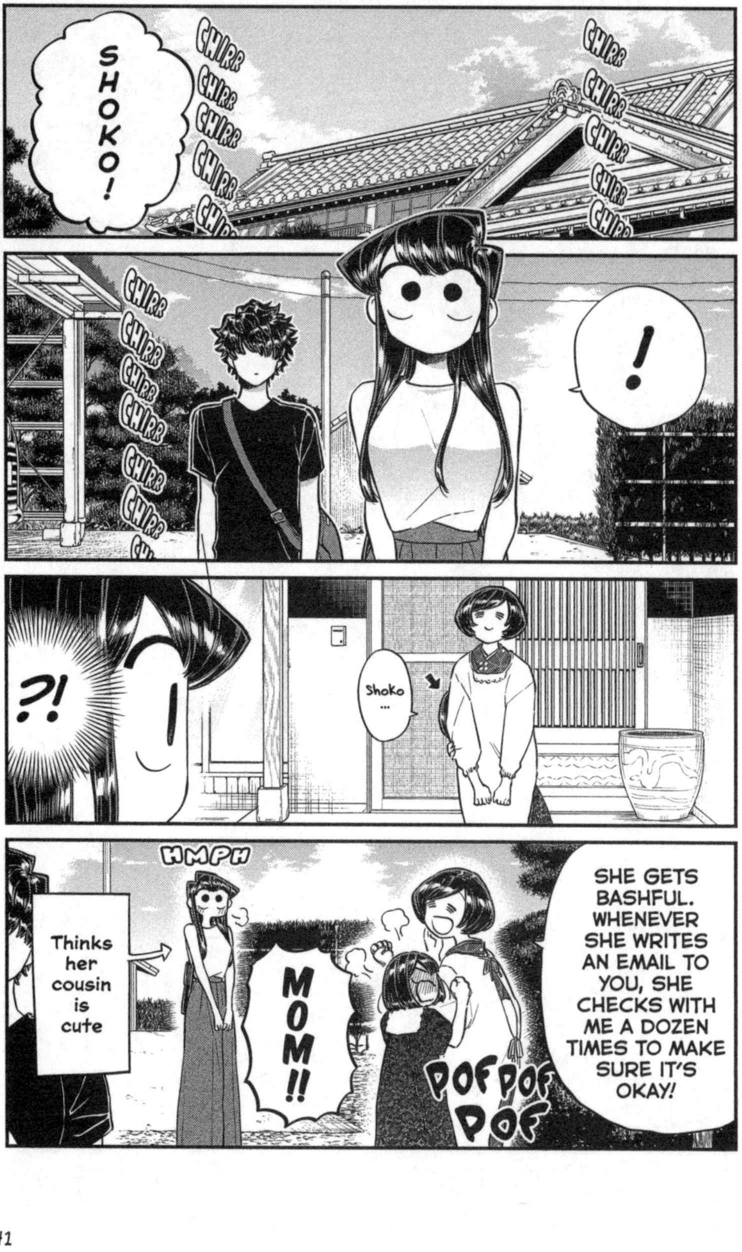
CHIRR CHIRR CHIRR CHIRR CHIRR
SHOKO!
CHIRR CHIRR CHIRR CHIRR CHIRR
!
CHIRR CHIRR CHIRR CHIRR CHIRR CHIRR
Shoko ...
?!
SHE GETS BASHFUL. WHENEVER SHE WRITES AN EMAIL TO YOU, SHE CHECKS WITH ME A DOZEN TIMES TO MAKE SURE IT'S OKAY!
POF POF POF
MOM!!
HMPH
Thinks her cousin is cute

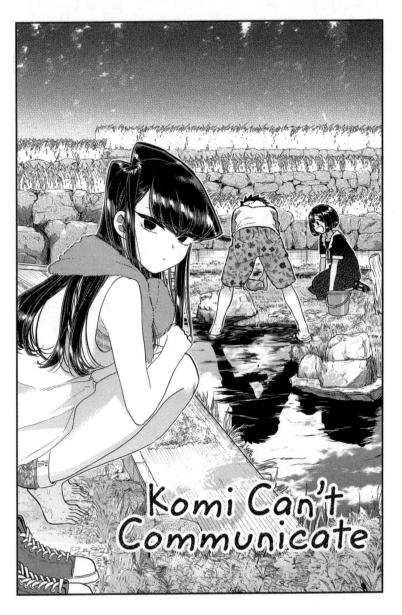

Komi Can't Communicate

Communication 184: Playing in the Country

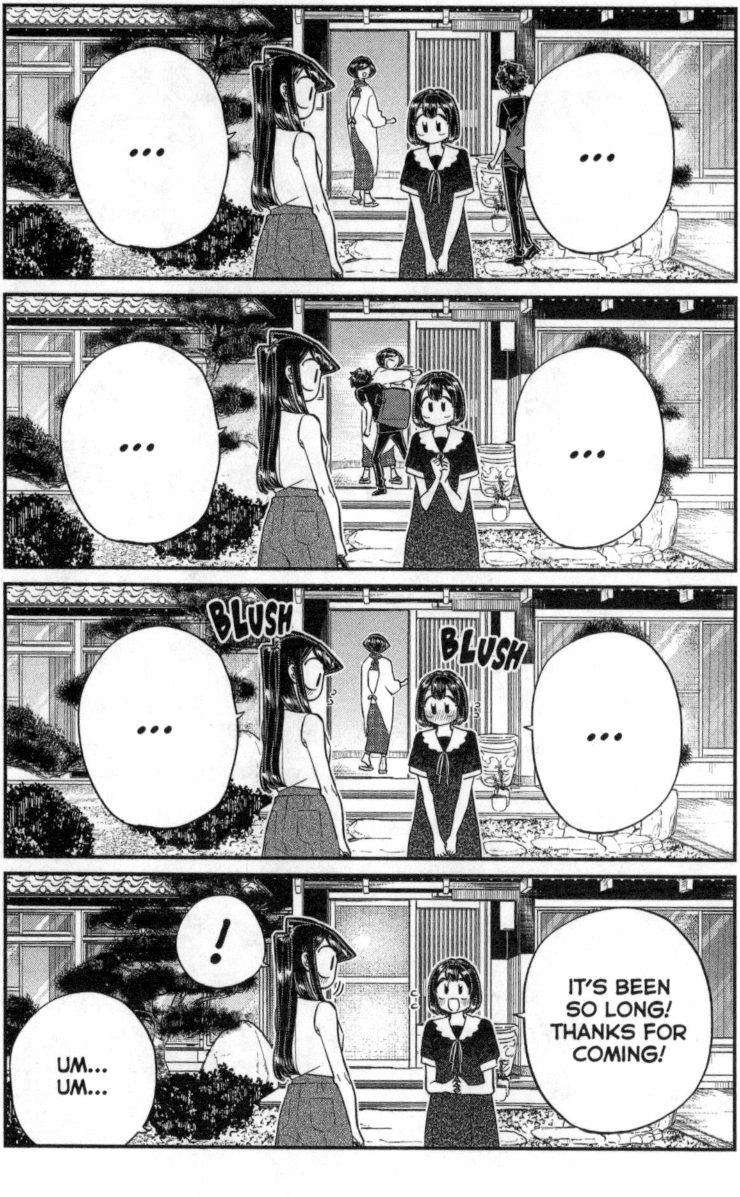
...
...
...
...
BLUSH
BLUSH
...
...
IT'S BEEN SO LONG! THANKS FOR COMING!
!
UM... UM...

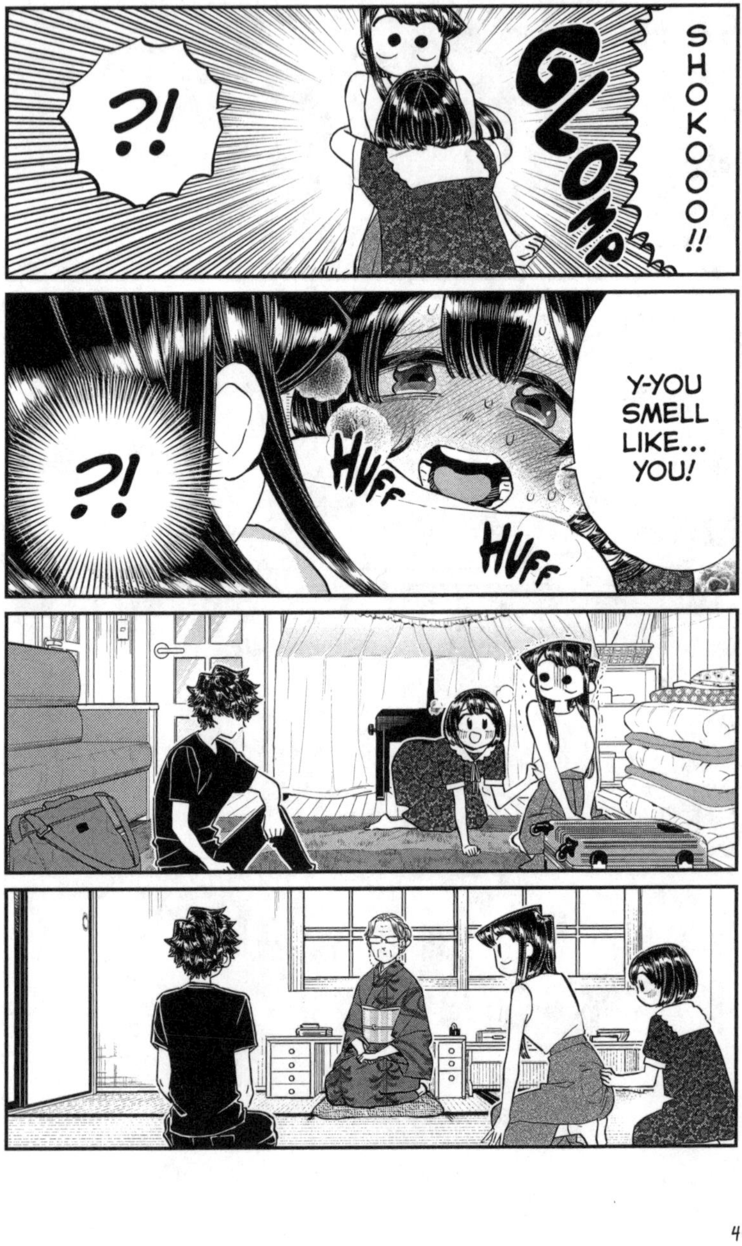
SHOKOOO!!
GLOMP
?!
Y-YOU SMELL LIKE... YOU!
HUFF
HUFF
?!

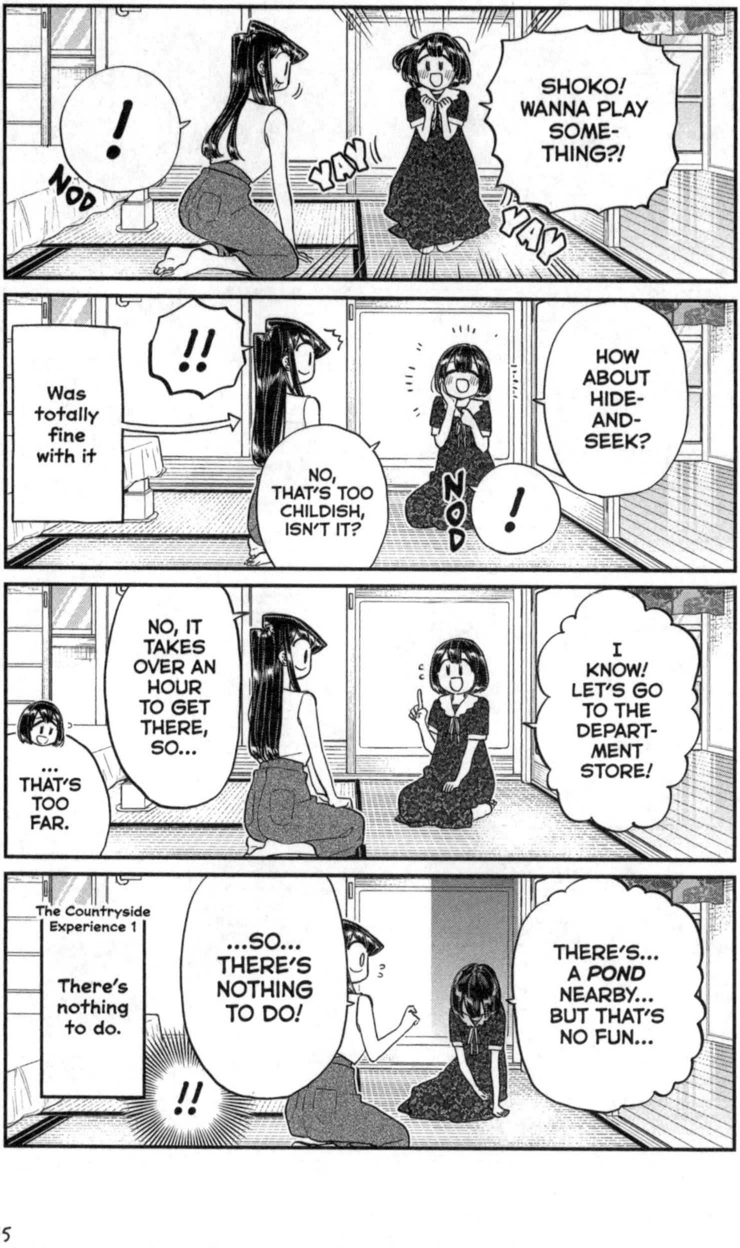
SHOKO! WANNA PLAY SOME-THING?!
YAY
YAY
!
NOD
HOW ABOUT HIDE-AND-SEEK?
!
NOD
NO, THAT'S TOO CHILDISH, ISN'T IT?
!!
Was totally fine with it
I KNOW! LET'S GO TO THE DEPART-MENT STORE!
NO, IT TAKES OVER AN HOUR TO GET THERE, SO...
... THAT'S TOO FAR.
THERE'S... A *POND* NEARBY... BUT THAT'S NO FUN...
...SO... THERE'S NOTHING TO DO!
!!
The Countryside Experience 1
There's nothing to do.

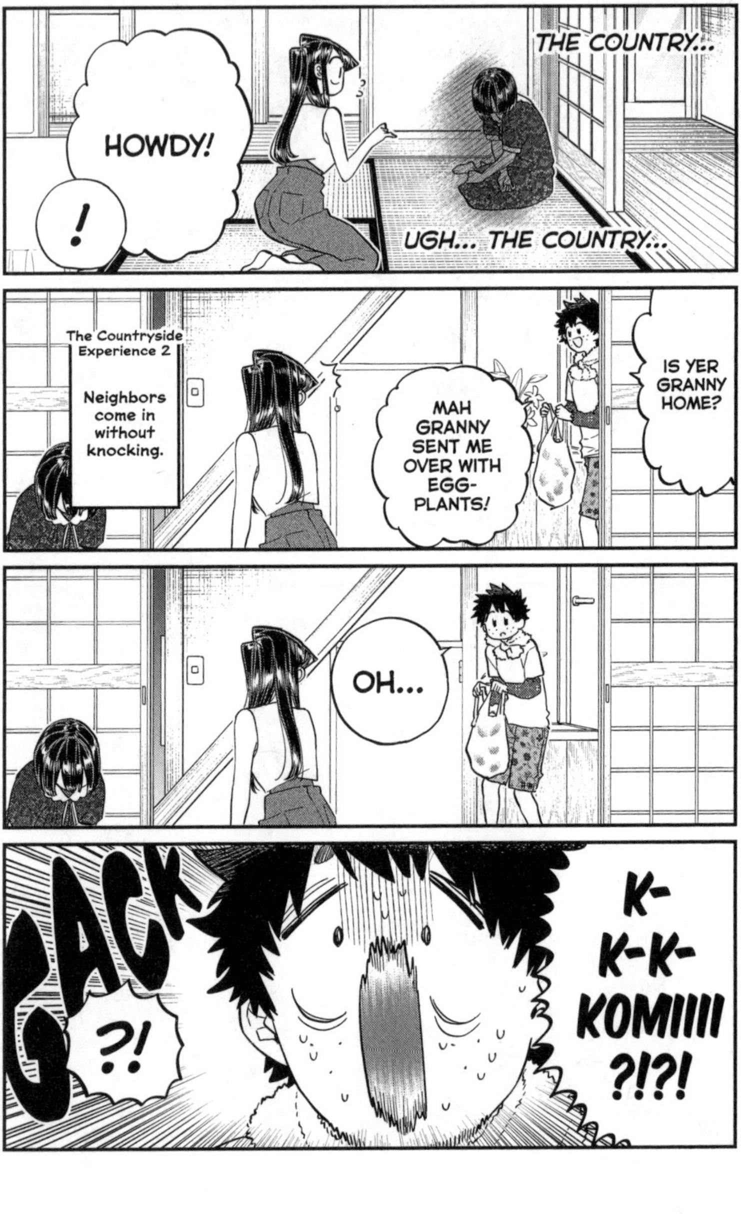
THE COUNTRY...
UGH... THE COUNTRY...
HOWDY!
!
IS YER GRANNY HOME?
MAH GRANNY SENT ME OVER WITH EGG-PLANTS!
The Countryside Experience 2
Neighbors come in without knocking.
OH...
K-K-K-KOMIIIII?!?!
?!
GACK

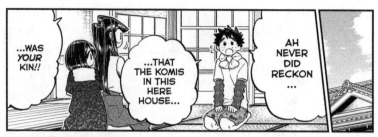

AH NEVER DID RECKON ...
...THAT THE KOMIS IN THIS HERE HOUSE...
...WAS YOUR KIN!!
DO YOU TWO KNOW EACH OTHER?
WE'RE CLASSMATES! YER GRANDDAUGHTER IS A REAL PEACH!
Surprised to see Inaka's true self
WELL, MY GRANDCHILDREN HAVE BEEN BORED.
WILL YOU KEEP THEM OCCUPIED?
UH... ME?!
I LEAVE THEM TO YOU.
THANK YOU FOR THE EGGPLANTS.
AGH!

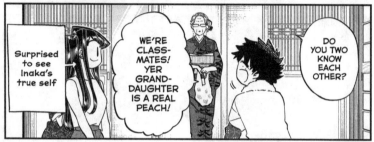

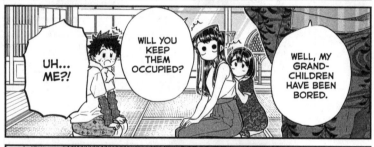

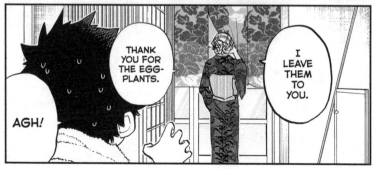

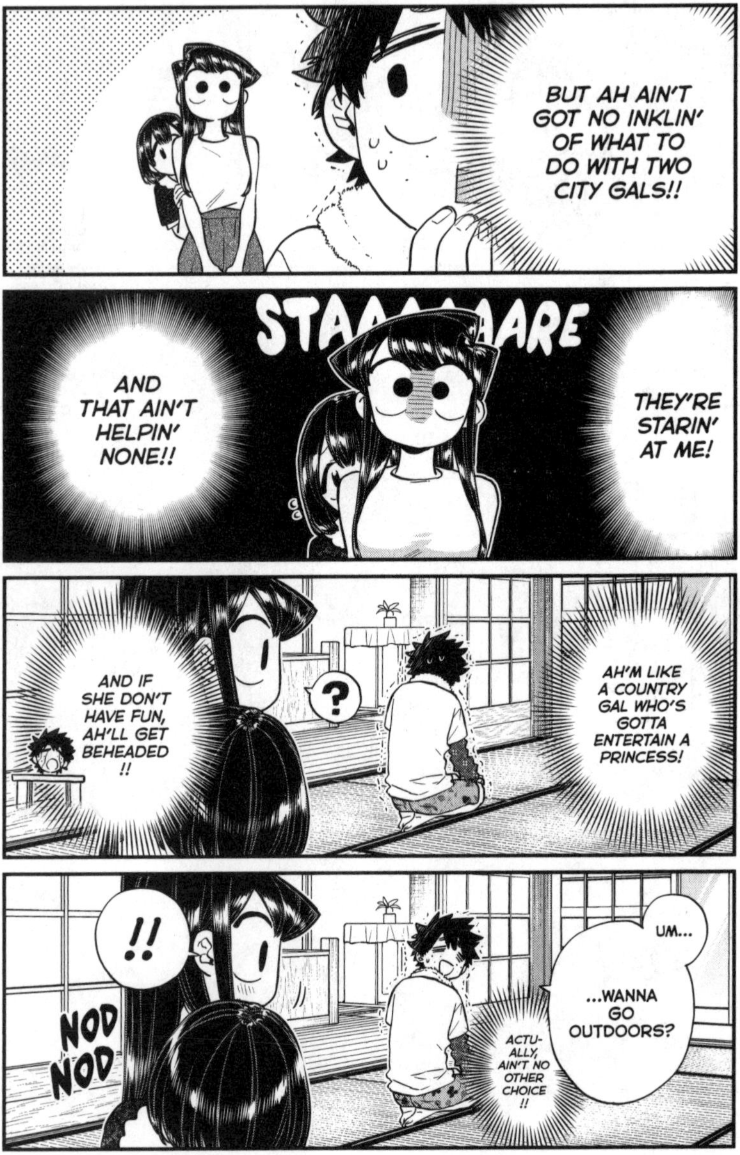
BUT AH AIN'T GOT NO INKLIN' OF WHAT TO DO WITH TWO CITY GALS!!
STAA AARE
THEY'RE STARIN' AT ME!
AND THAT AIN'T HELPIN' NONE!!
AH'M LIKE A COUNTRY GAL WHO'S GOTTA ENTERTAIN A PRINCESS!
?
AND IF SHE DON'T HAVE FUN, AH'LL GET BEHEADED!!
UM...
...WANNA GO OUTDOORS?
ACTUALLY, AIN'T NO OTHER CHOICE!!
!!
NOD NOD

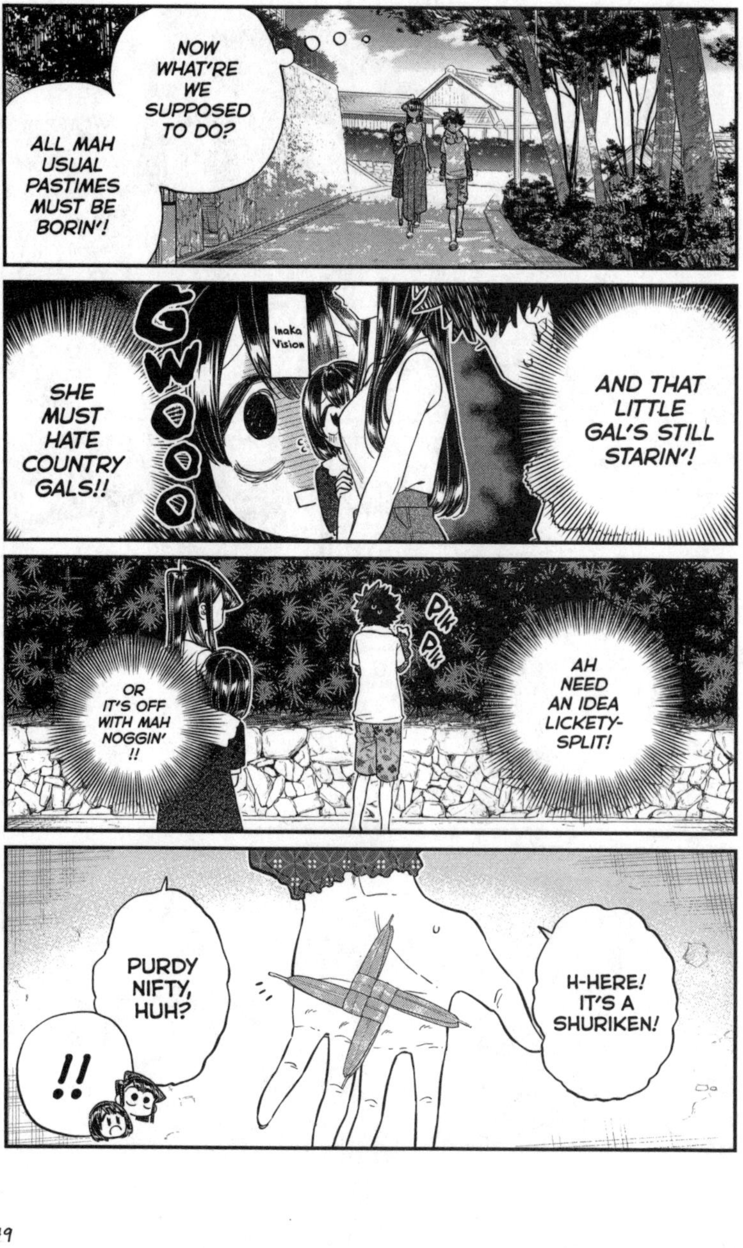
NOW WHAT'RE WE SUPPOSED TO DO?
ALL MAH USUAL PASTIMES MUST BE BORIN'!
AND THAT LITTLE GAL'S STILL STARIN'!
Inaka Vision
GWOOOO
SHE MUST HATE COUNTRY GALS!!
PIK PIK
AH NEED AN IDEA LICKETY-SPLIT!
OR IT'S OFF WITH MAH NOGGIN'!!
H-HERE! IT'S A SHURIKEN!
PURDY NIFTY, HUH?
!!

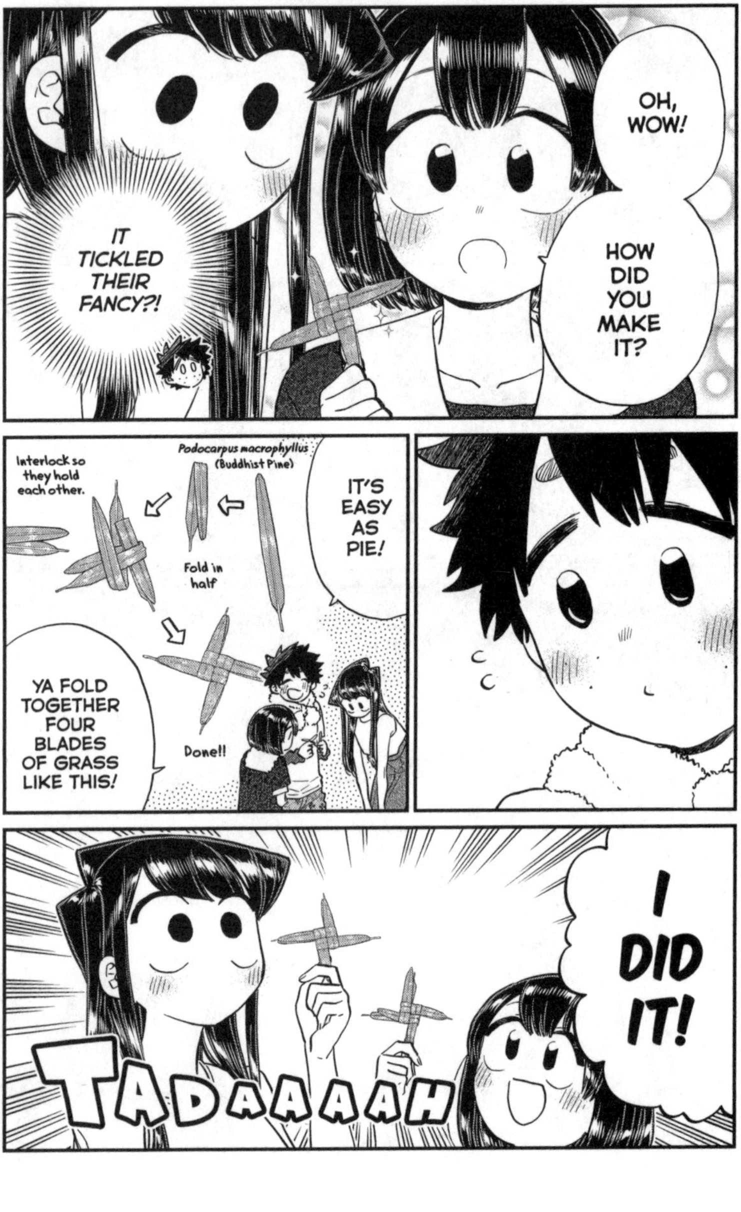
OH, WOW!
HOW DID YOU MAKE IT?
IT TICKLED THEIR FANCY?!
IT'S EASY AS PIE!
Podocarpus macrophyllus (Buddhist Pine)
Interlock so they hold each other.
Fold in half
YA FOLD TOGETHER FOUR BLADES OF GRASS LIKE THIS!
Done!!
I DID IT!
TADAAAAAH

DO YA KNOW THIS TRICK?
?
PYOOO OOOOOOOOOINK
Cat-tail
WHOA!
THIS HERE'S A *MIRABILIS* FLOWER.
IF YA PEEL OFF THE GREEN PART AND PULL THE ROUND THING, THE PISTIL COMES OUT.
Pistil.
WHIRRRRRRRR
THEN YA GOT *FLOWER PARA-CHUTES!*
THIS IS AWE-SOME!!!!
AW, IT'S NOTHIN'.

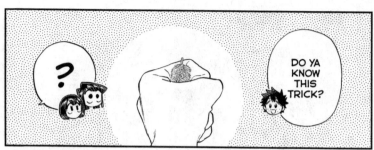

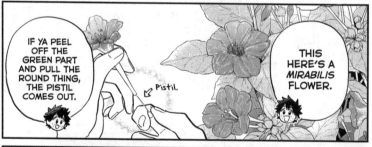

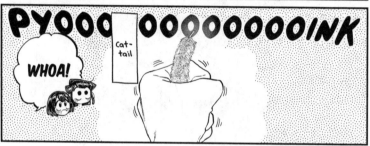

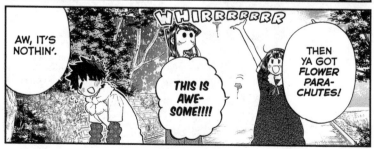

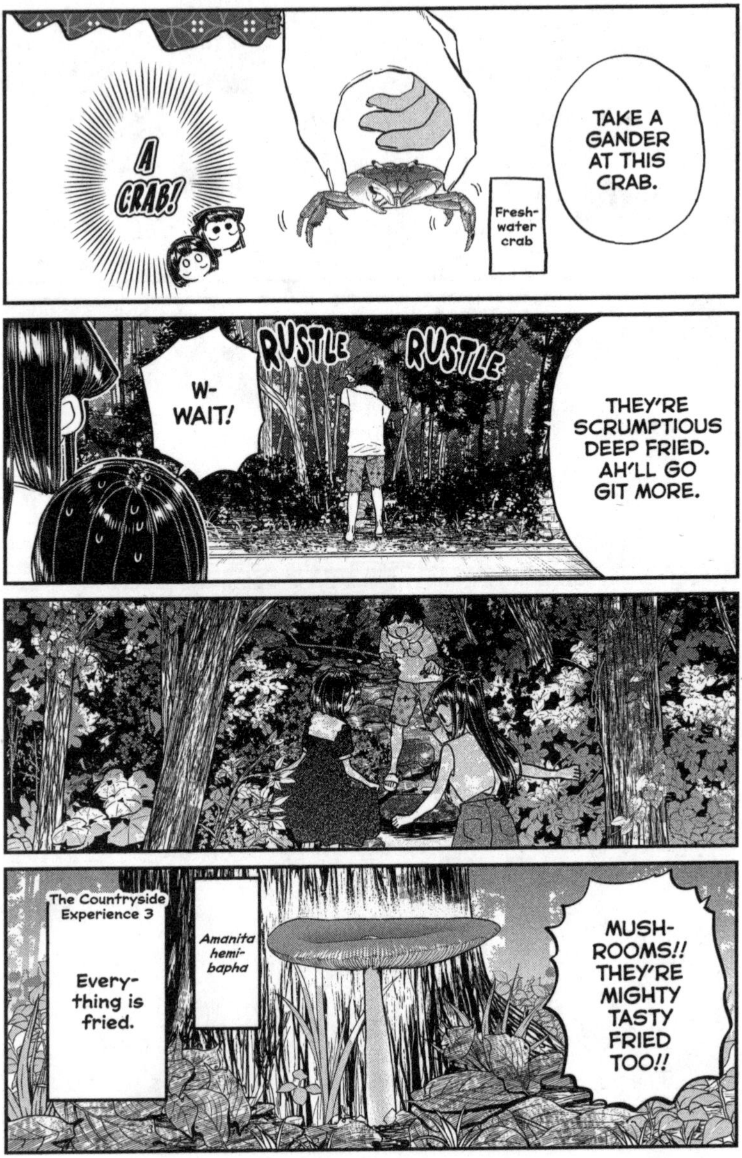
TAKE A GANDER AT THIS CRAB.
Fresh-water crab
A CRAB!
THEY'RE SCRUMPTIOUS DEEP FRIED. AH'LL GO GIT MORE.
RUSTLE
RUSTLE
W-WAIT!
MUSHROOMS!! THEY'RE MIGHTY TASTY FRIED TOO!!
Amanita hemibapha
The Countryside Experience 3
Everything is fried.

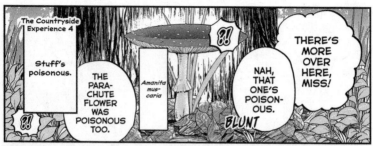

THERE'S MORE OVER HERE, MISS!
?!
NAH, THAT ONE'S POISONOUS.
BLUNT
Amanita muscaria
THE PARACHUTE FLOWER WAS POISONOUS TOO.
?!
The Countryside Experience 4
Stuff's poisonous.
HMM...
THIS IS FINE BAMBOO.
WE CAN MAKE FISHIN' POLES AND CATCH MINNOWS FOR COOKIN' LATER.
SHING
?!
The Countryside Experience 5
People just carry around saws.
Give it a pull!

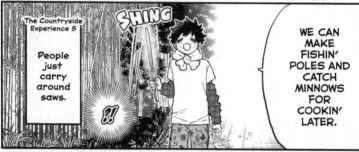

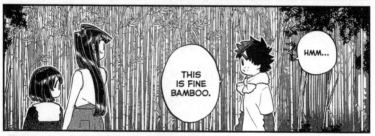

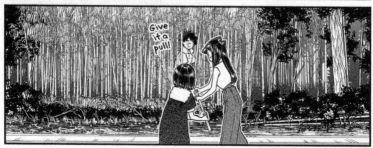

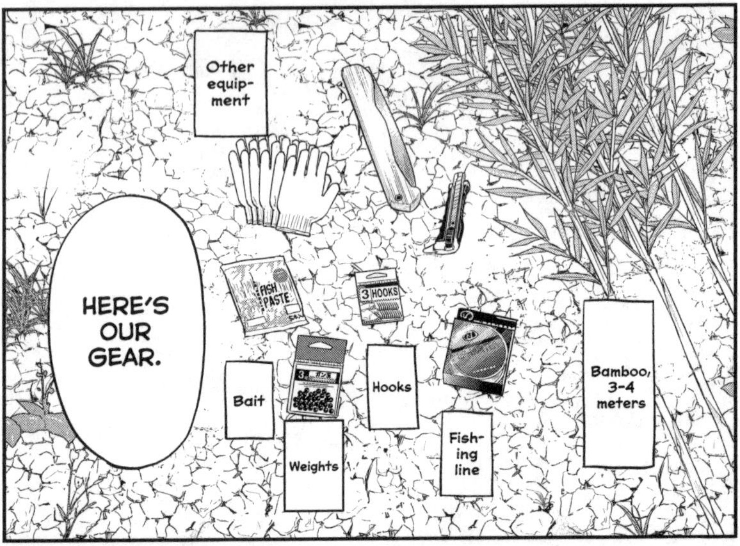
Other equipment
Bamboo, 3-4 meters
Fishing line
Hooks
HOOKS
FISH PASTE
Bait
Weights
HERE'S OUR GEAR.

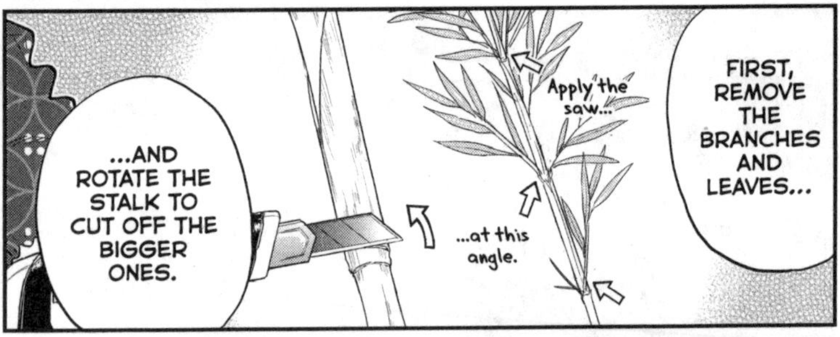
FIRST, REMOVE THE BRANCHES AND LEAVES...
Apply the saw...
...at this angle.
...AND ROTATE THE STALK TO CUT OFF THE BIGGER ONES.

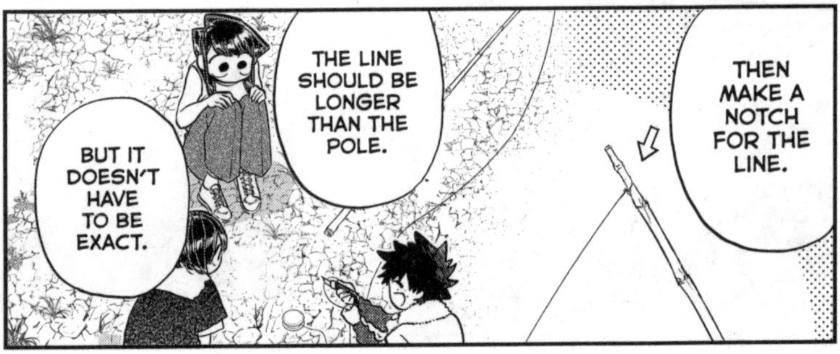
THEN MAKE A NOTCH FOR THE LINE.
THE LINE SHOULD BE LONGER THAN THE POLE.
BUT IT DOESN'T HAVE TO BE EXACT.

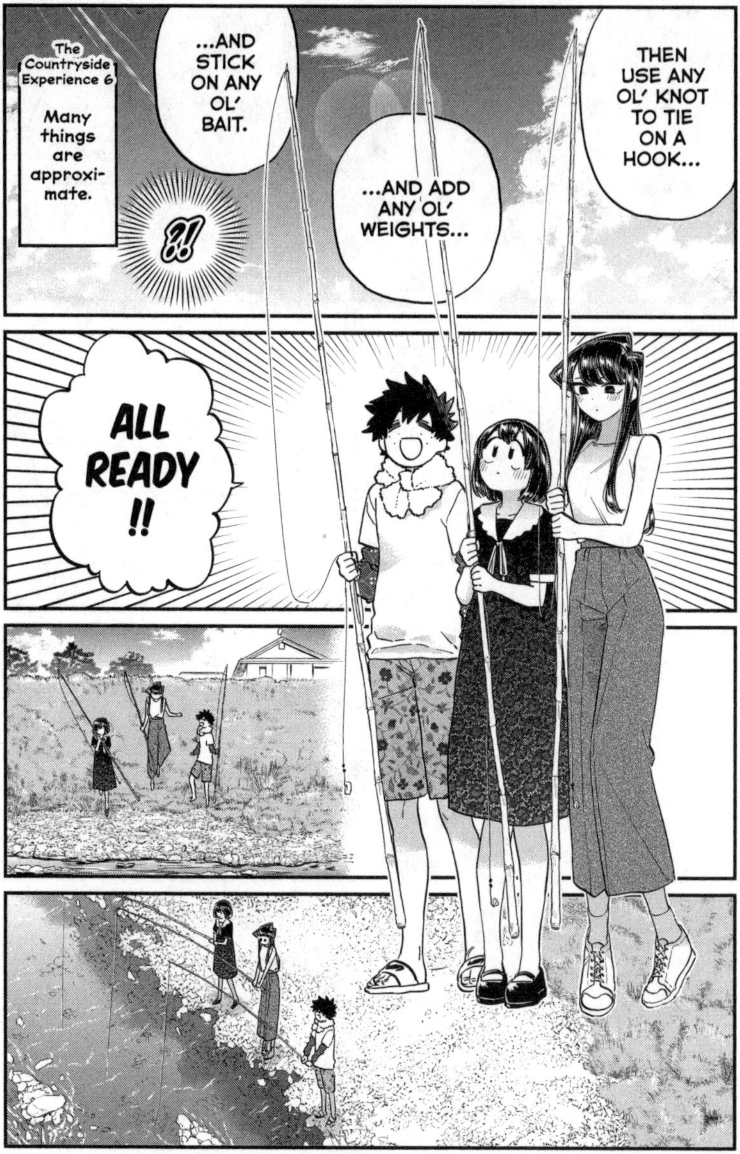
THEN USE ANY OL' KNOT TO TIE ON A HOOK...
...AND ADD ANY OL' WEIGHTS...
...AND STICK ON ANY OL' BAIT.
?!
The Countryside Experience 6
Many things are approxi-mate.
ALL READY !!

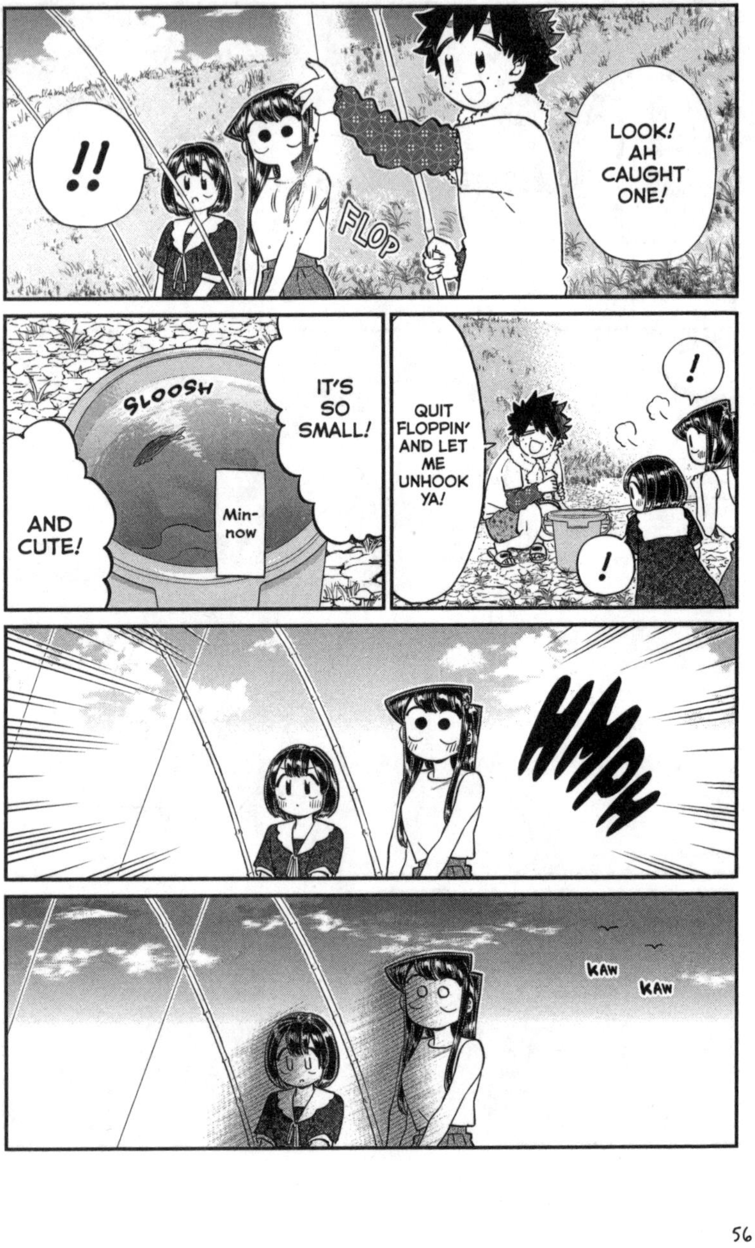
LOOK! AH CAUGHT ONE!
FLOP
!!
!
QUIT FLOPPIN' AND LET ME UNHOOK YA!
!
IT'S SO SMALL!
SLOOSH
Min-now
AND CUTE!
HMPH
KAW
KAW

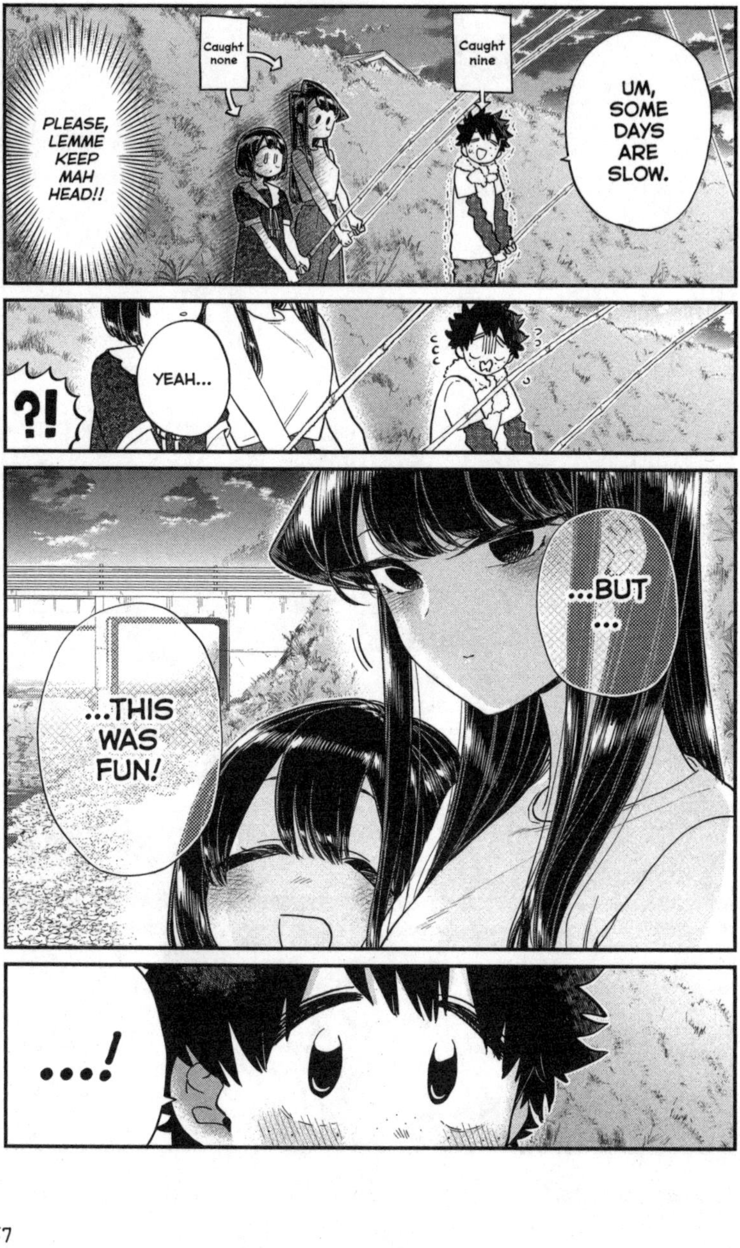
UM, SOME DAYS ARE SLOW.
Caught nine
Caught none
PLEASE, LEMME KEEP MAH HEAD!!
YEAH...
?!
...BUT ...
...THIS WAS FUN!
...!

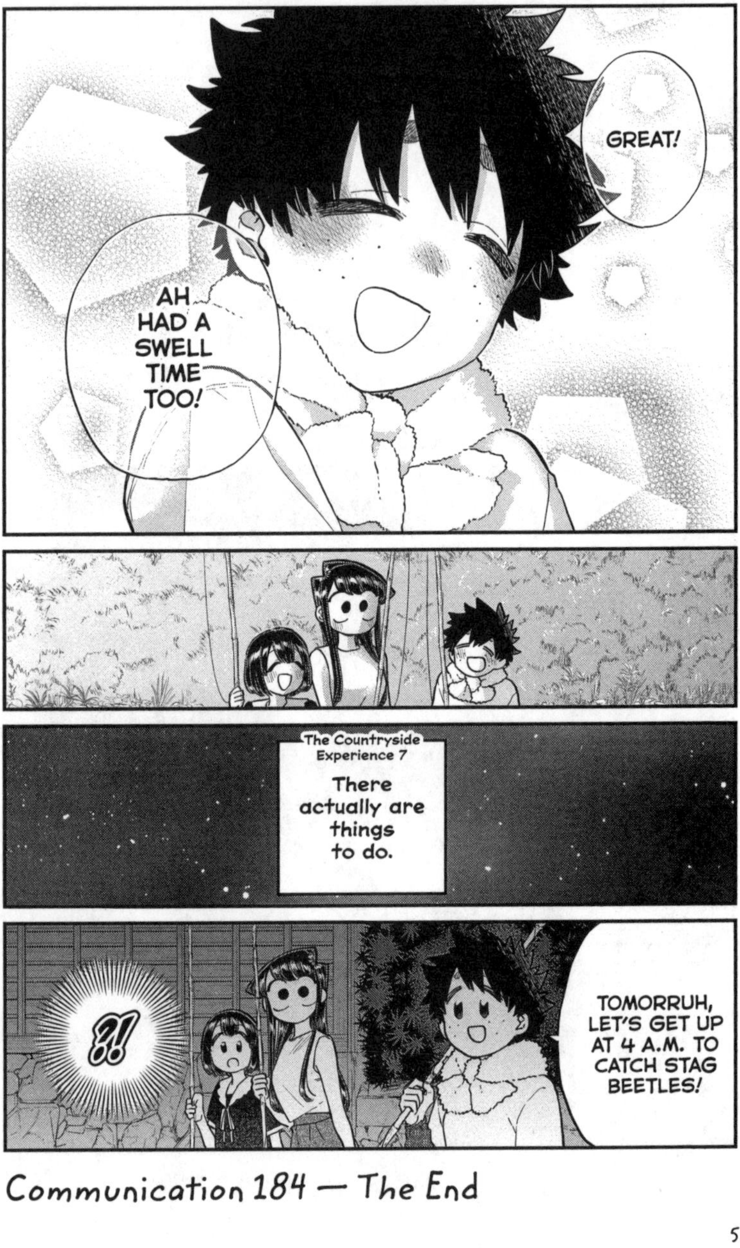
GREAT!
AH HAD A SWELL TIME TOO!
The Countryside Experience 7
There actually are things to do.
TOMORRUH, LET'S GET UP AT 4 A.M. TO CATCH STAG BEETLES!
?!

Communication 184 — The End

Komi Can't Communicate

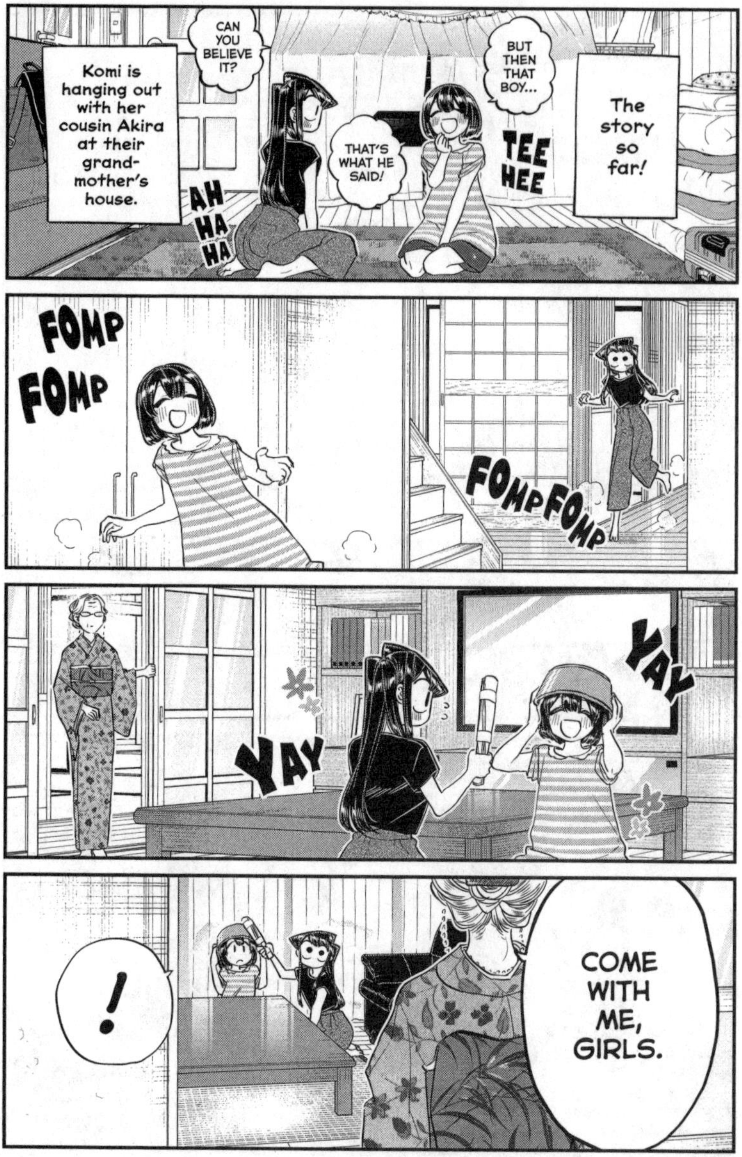
The story so far!
BUT THEN THAT BOY...
TEE HEE
THAT'S WHAT HE SAID!
CAN YOU BELIEVE IT?
Komi is hanging out with her cousin Akira at their grand-mother's house.
AH HA HA
FOMP FOMP
FOMP FOMP
FOMP FOMP
YAY
YAY
COME WITH ME, GIRLS.
!

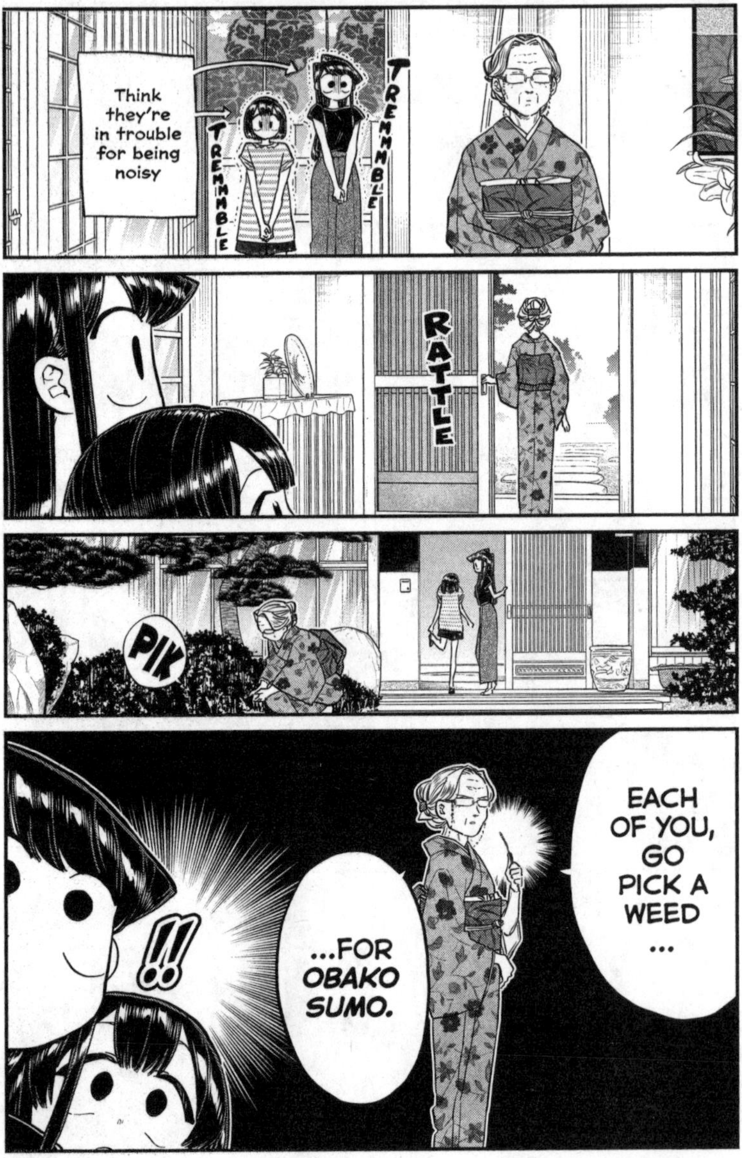
Think they're in trouble for being noisy
TREMMBLE
TREMMBLE
RATTLE
PIK
EACH OF YOU, GO PICK A WEED ...
...FOR OBAKO SUMO.
!!

Communication 185: Obako Sumo

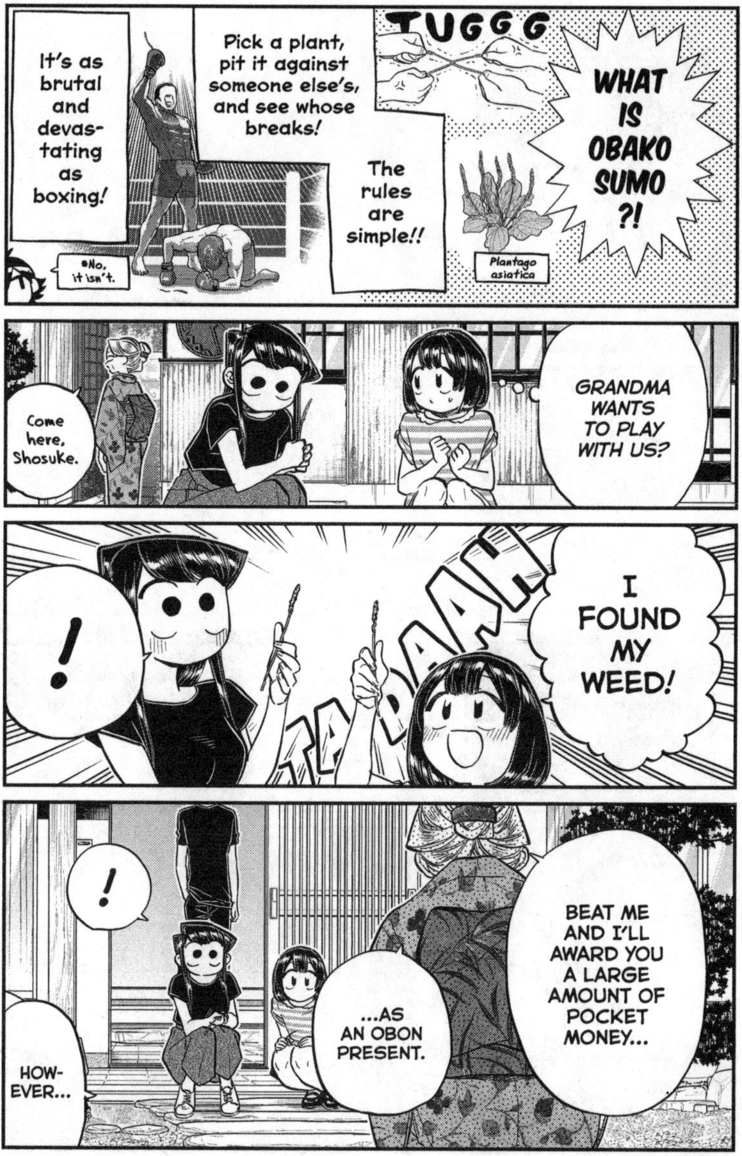
TUGGG
WHAT IS OBAKO SUMO?!
Plantago asiatica
Pick a plant, pit it against someone else's, and see whose breaks!
The rules are simple!!
It's as brutal and devas-tating as boxing!
*No, it isn't.
GRANDMA WANTS TO PLAY WITH US?
Come here, Shosuke.
I FOUND MY WEED!
TADAAH!
!
BEAT ME AND I'LL AWARD YOU A LARGE AMOUNT OF POCKET MONEY...
...AS AN OBON PRESENT.
!
HOW-EVER...

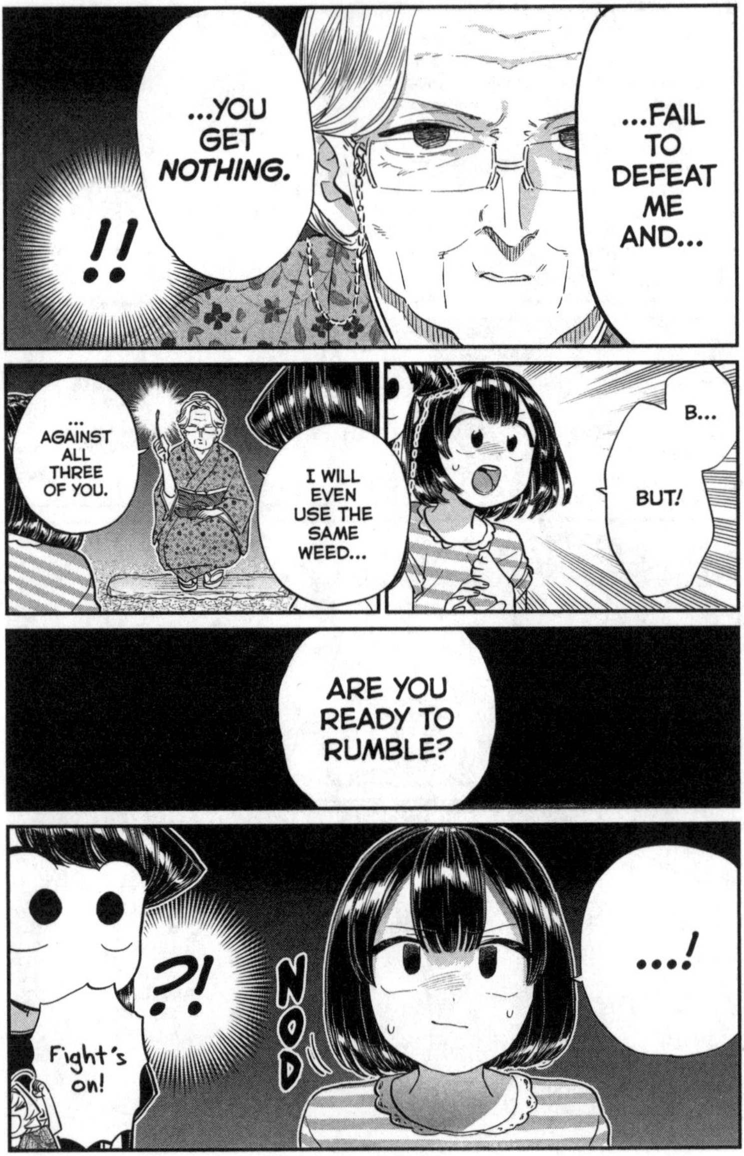
...FAIL TO DEFEAT ME AND...
...YOU GET NOTHING.
!!
B... BUT!
I WILL EVEN USE THE SAME WEED...
...AGAINST ALL THREE OF YOU.
ARE YOU READY TO RUMBLE?
...!
NOD
?!
Fight's on!

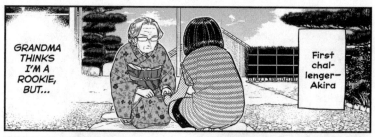

First challenger—Akira
GRANDMA THINKS I'M A ROOKIE, BUT...
...SHE UNDERESTIMATES ME!
YOU GOTTA HOLD IT TOWARD THE MIDDLE AND LET YOUR OPPONENT PULL!
THEN YOU CAN'T LOSE!!
IF I WIN... ...SHOKO WILL BE SO IMPRESSED!!
TEE HEE HEE!!
PAT PAT
SNAP
Akira loses.
Why?!
YOUR STEM WAS WEAK. NEXT!

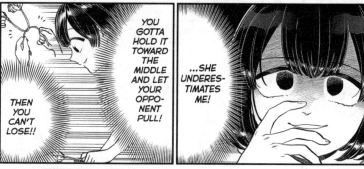

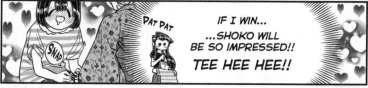

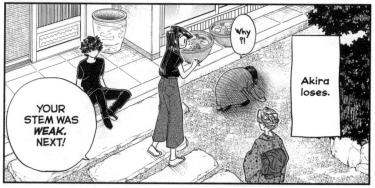

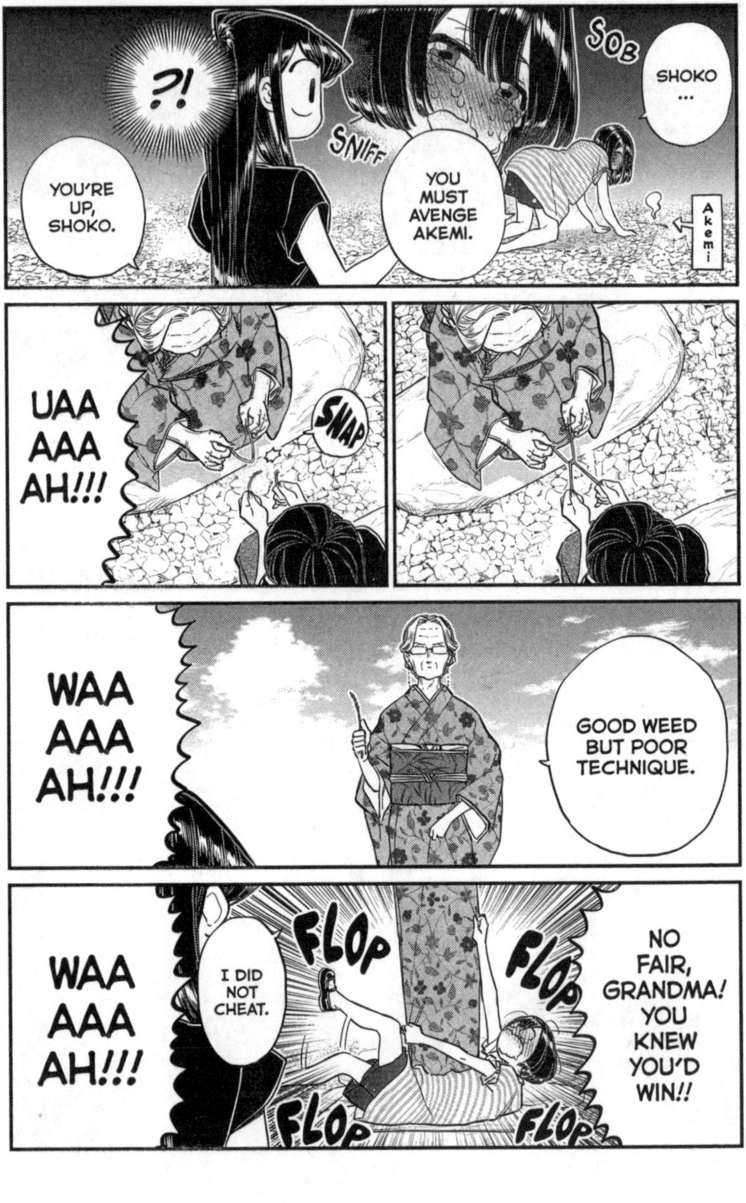
SOB
SHOKO ...
?!
SNIFF
YOU MUST AVENGE AKEMI.
Akemi
YOU'RE UP, SHOKO.
SNAP
UAA AAA AH!!!
GOOD WEED BUT POOR TECHNIQUE.
WAA AAA AH!!!
NO FAIR, GRANDMA! YOU KNEW YOU'D WIN!!
FLOP
FLOP
I DID NOT CHEAT.
FLOP
FLOP
WAA AAA AH!!!

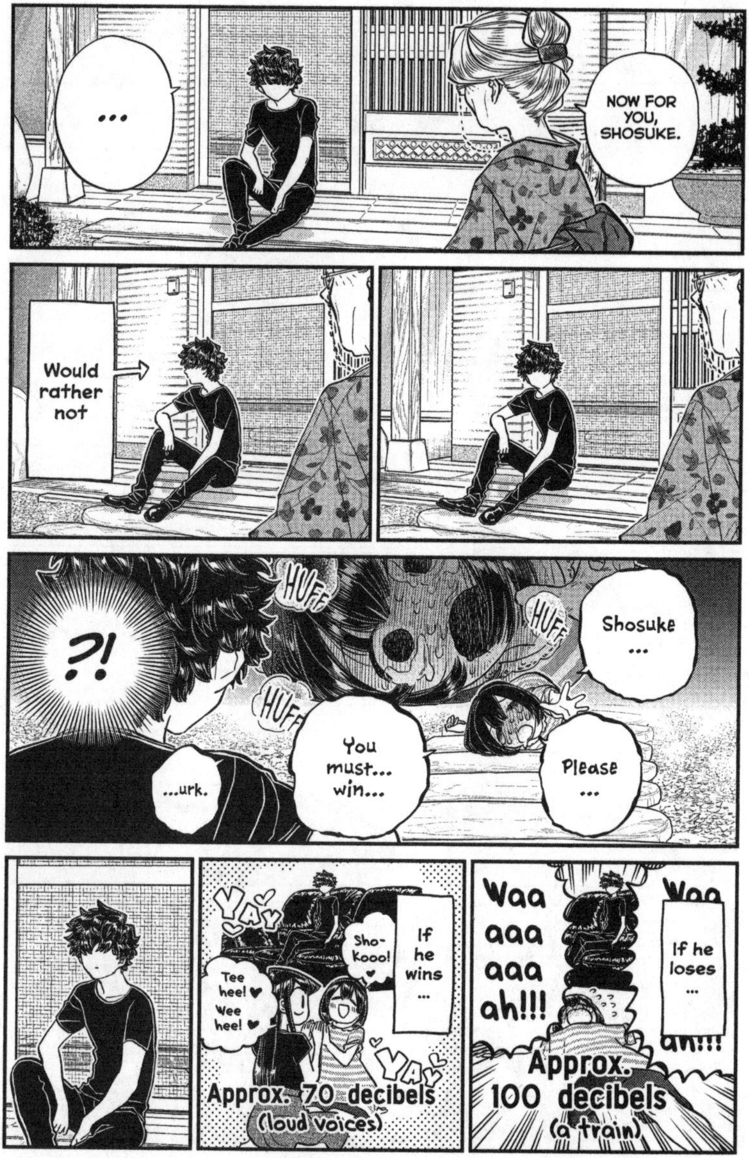
NOW FOR YOU, SHOSUKE.
...
Would rather not
Shosuke ...
HUFF
HUFF
Please ...
You must... win...
HUFF
?!
...urk.
If he loses ...
Waa aaa aaa ah!!!
Approx. 100 decibels (a train)
If he wins ...
Sho-kooo!
YAY
Tee hee! Wee hee!
YAY
Approx. 70 decibels (loud voices)

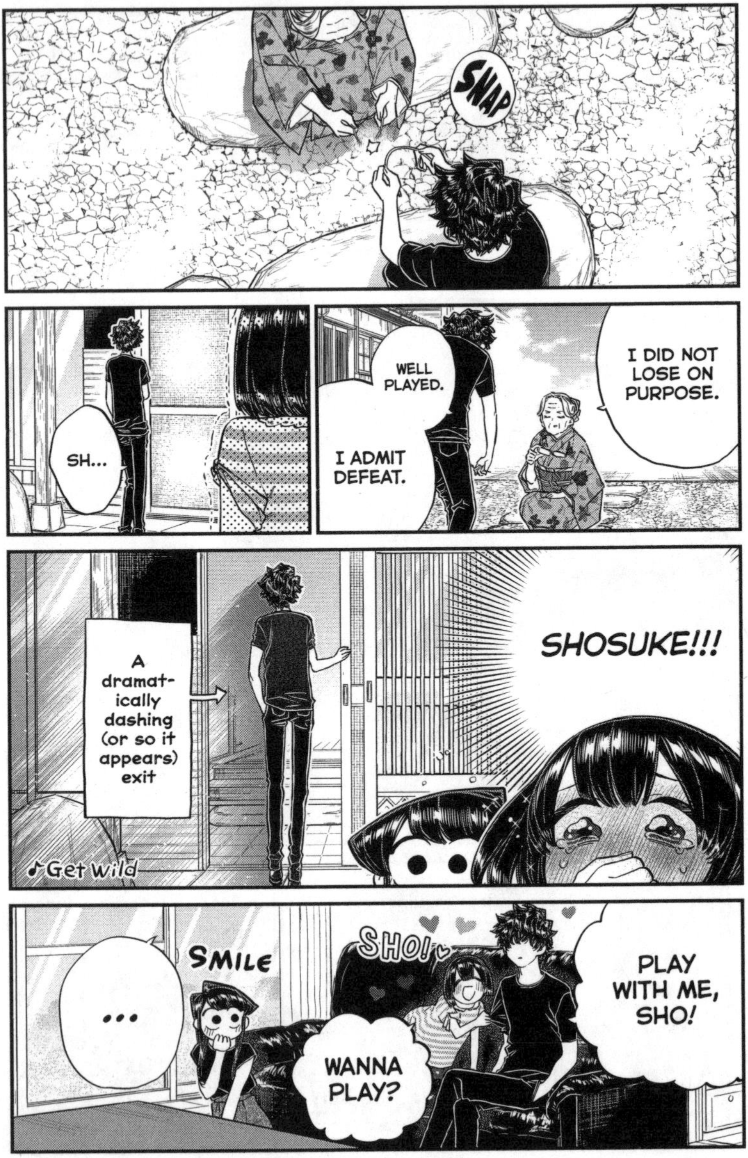
SNAP
I DID NOT LOSE ON PURPOSE.
WELL PLAYED.
I ADMIT DEFEAT.
SH...
SHOSUKE!!!
A dramatically dashing (or so it appears) exit
♪Get Wild
PLAY WITH ME, SHO!
SHO!♡
WANNA PLAY?
SMILE
...

Communication 185 — The End

Komi Can't Communicate

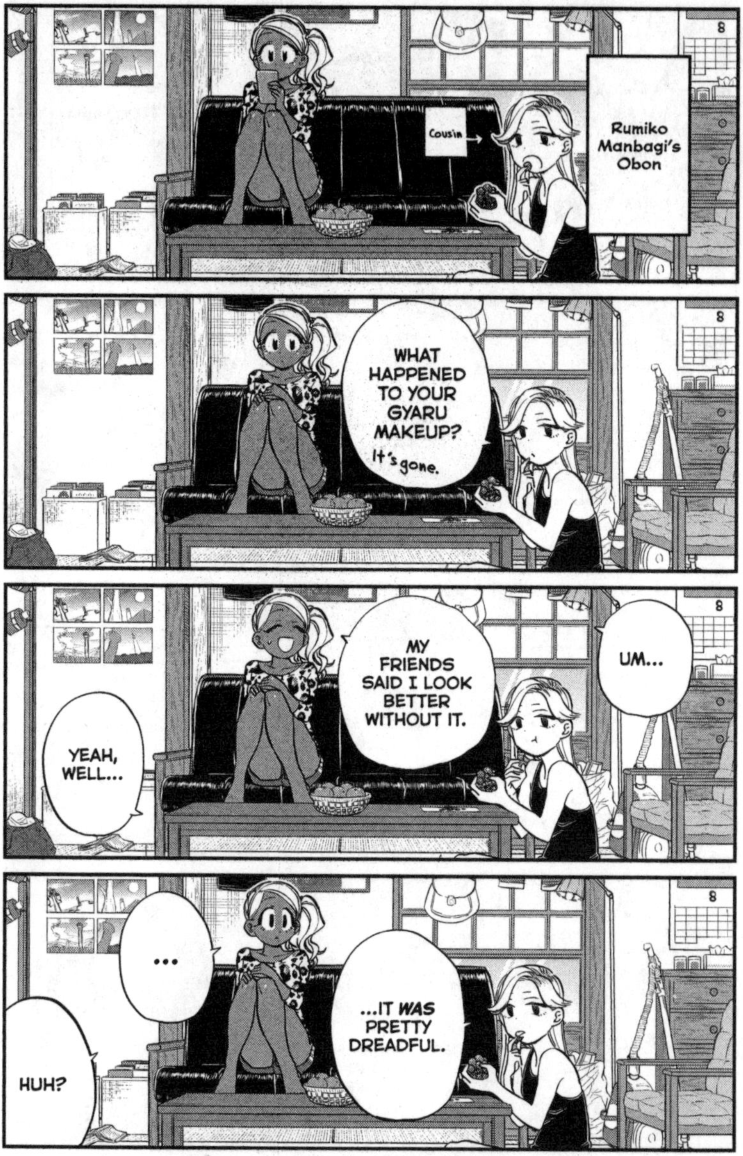
Rumiko Manbagi's Obon
Cousin
WHAT HAPPENED TO YOUR GYARU MAKEUP?
It's gone.
UM...
MY FRIENDS SAID I LOOK BETTER WITHOUT IT.
YEAH, WELL...
...IT *WAS* PRETTY DREADFUL.
...
HUH?

Communication 186: Everyone's Obon

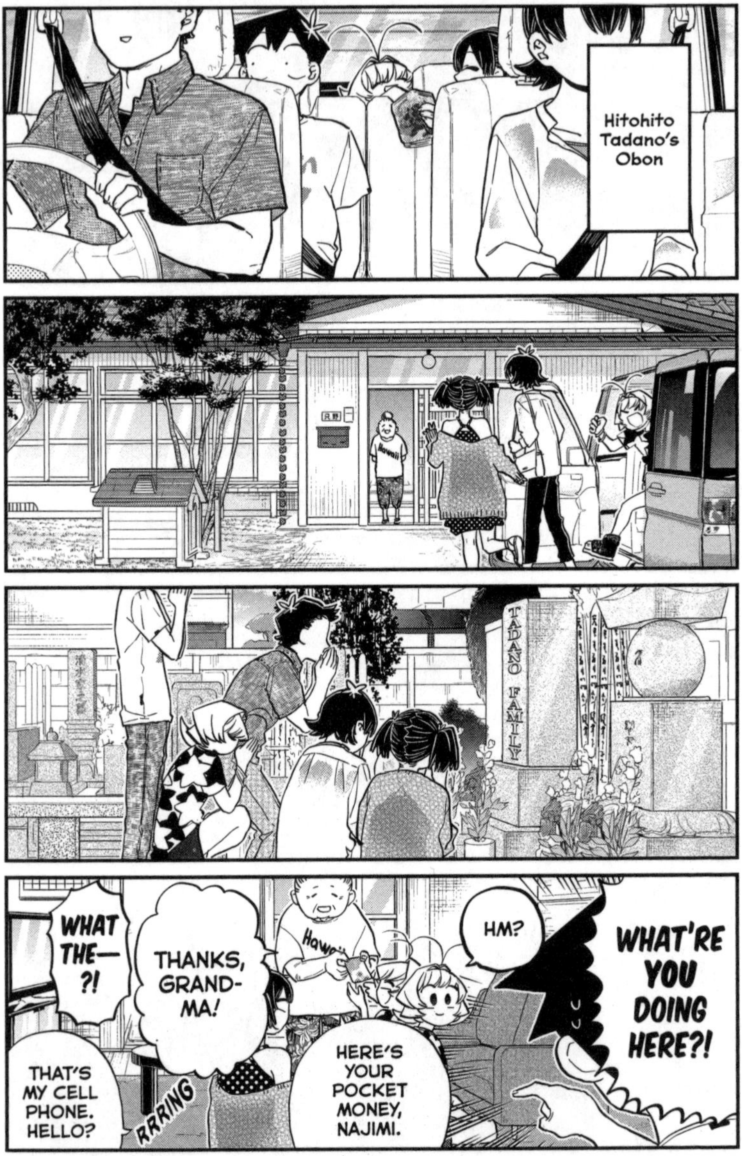
Hitohito Tadano's Obon
TADANO FAMILY
HERE'S YOUR POCKET MONEY, NAJIMI.
THANKS, GRAND-MA!
WHAT'RE YOU DOING HERE?!
HM?
WHAT THE—?!
RRRING
THAT'S MY CELL PHONE. HELLO?

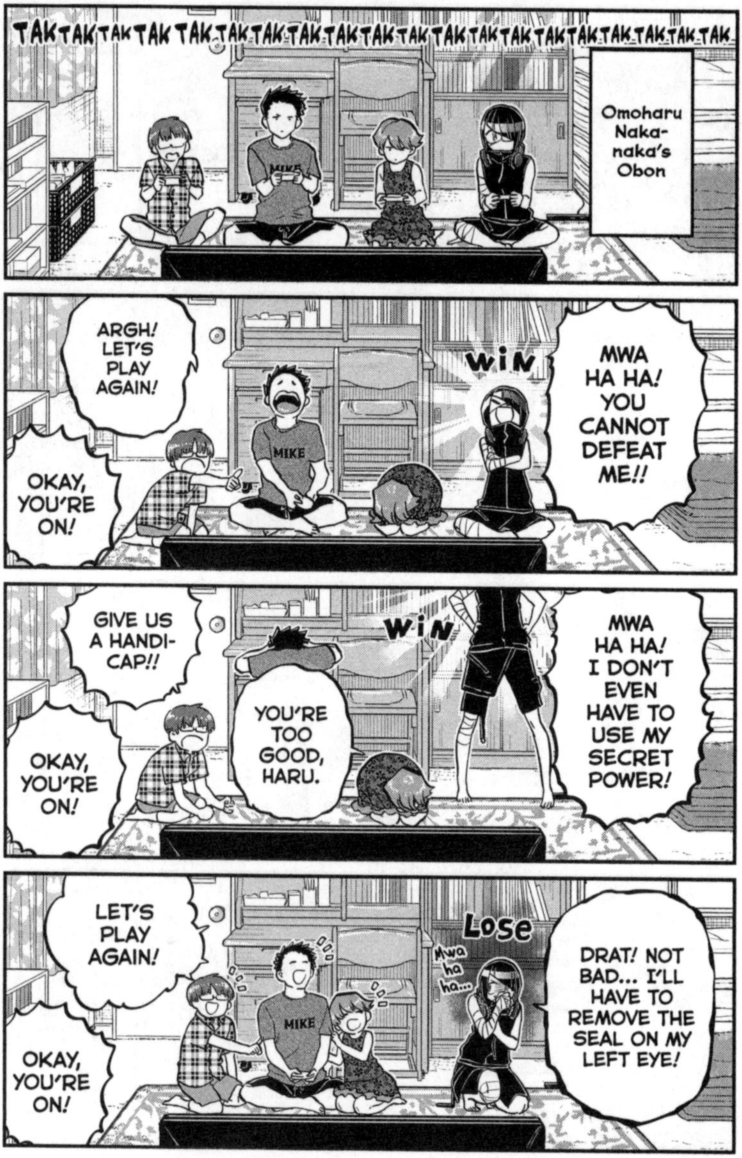
Omoharu Naka-naka's Obon
TAK TAK TAK TAK TAK TAK TAK TAK TAK TAK TAK TAK TAK TAK TAK TAK TAK TAK TAK TAK
MWA HA HA! YOU CANNOT DEFEAT ME!!
WIN
ARGH! LET'S PLAY AGAIN!
OKAY, YOU'RE ON!
MWA HA HA! I DON'T EVEN HAVE TO USE MY SECRET POWER!
WIN
GIVE US A HANDI-CAP!!
YOU'RE TOO GOOD, HARU.
OKAY, YOU'RE ON!
DRAT! NOT BAD... I'LL HAVE TO REMOVE THE SEAL ON MY LEFT EYE!
LOSE
Mwa ha ha...
LET'S PLAY AGAIN!
OKAY, YOU'RE ON!

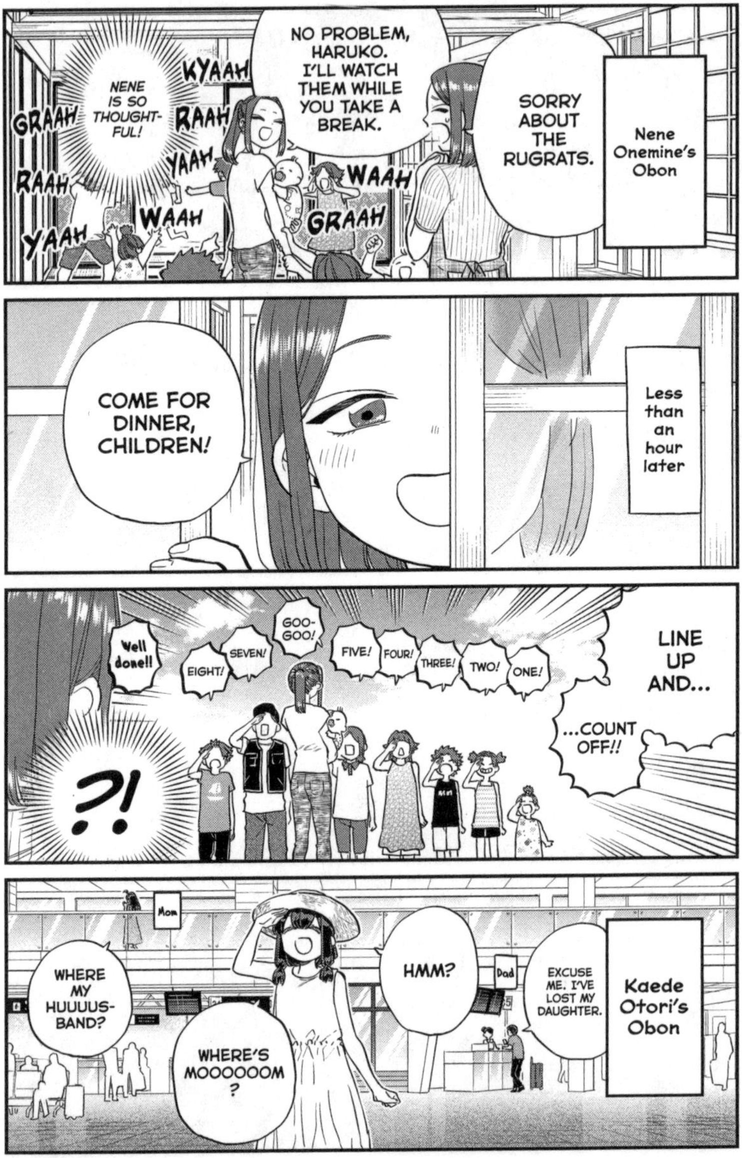
Nene Onemine's Obon
SORRY ABOUT THE RUGRATS.
NO PROBLEM, HARUKO. I'LL WATCH THEM WHILE YOU TAKE A BREAK.
KYAAH
RAAH
WAAH
GRAAH
YAAH
NENE IS SO THOUGHT-FUL!
GRAAH
RAAH
WAAH
YAAH
Less than an hour later
COME FOR DINNER, CHILDREN!
LINE UP AND...
...COUNT OFF!!
ONE!
TWO!
THREE!
FOUR!
FIVE!
GOO-GOO!
SEVEN!
EIGHT!
Well done!!
?!
Kaede Otori's Obon
EXCUSE ME. I'VE LOST MY DAUGHTER.
Dad
HMM?
Mom
WHERE'S MOOOOOOM?
WHERE MY HUUUUS-BAND?

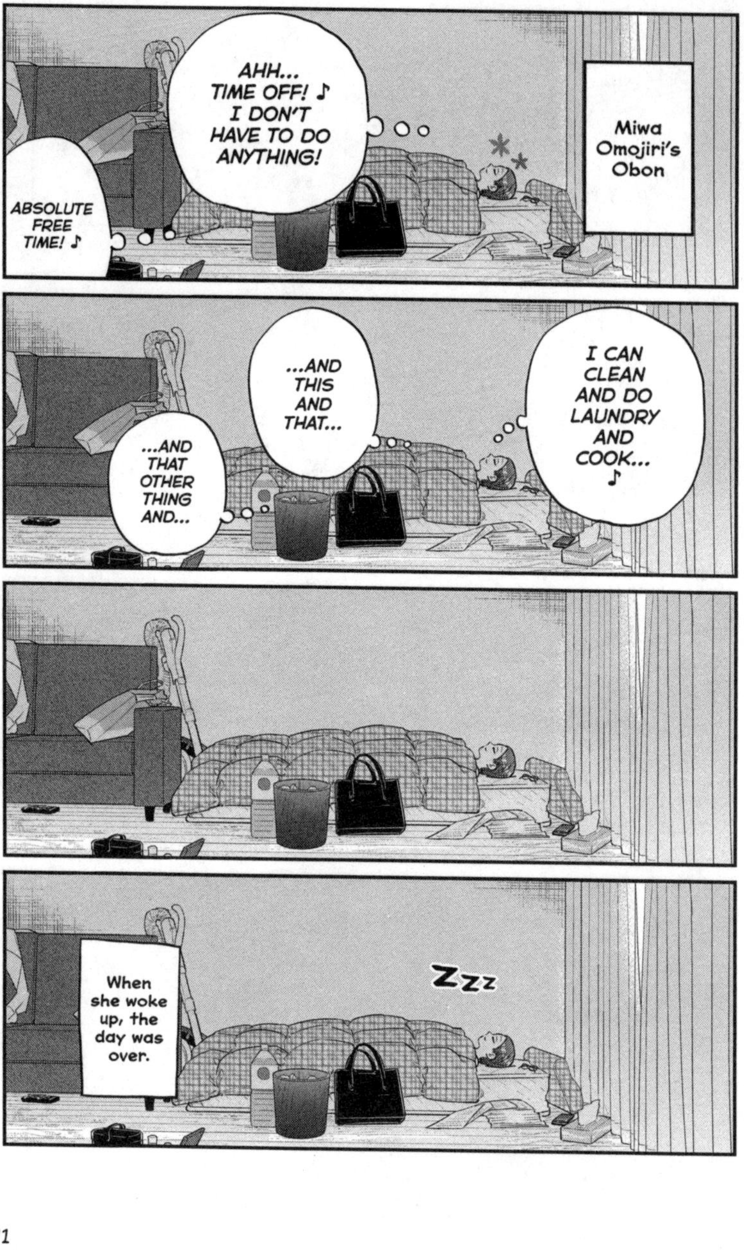
Miwa Omojiri's Obon
AHH... TIME OFF! ♪ I DON'T HAVE TO DO ANYTHING!
ABSOLUTE FREE TIME! ♪
I CAN CLEAN AND DO LAUNDRY AND COOK... ♪
...AND THIS AND THAT...
...AND THAT OTHER THING AND...
ZZZ
When she woke up, the day was over.

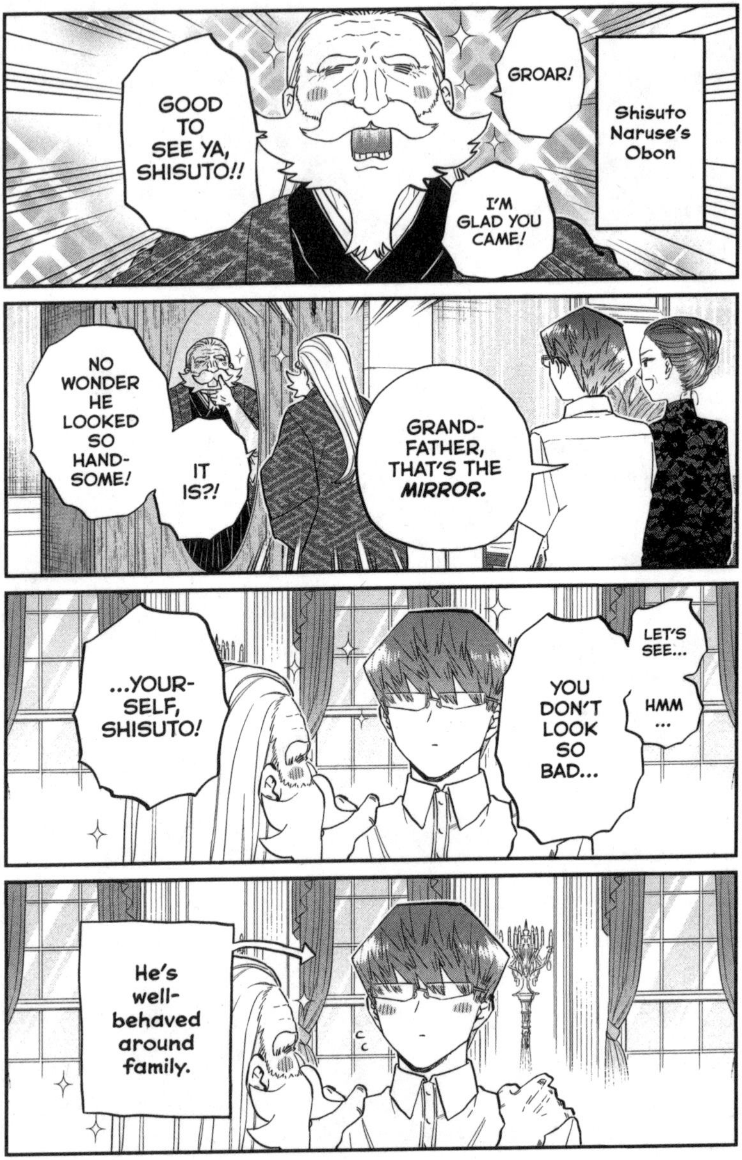
Shisuto Naruse's Obon
GROAR!
I'M GLAD YOU CAME!
GOOD TO SEE YA, SHISUTO!!
GRANDFATHER, THAT'S THE *MIRROR.*
IT IS?!
NO WONDER HE LOOKED SO HANDSOME!
LET'S SEE...
HMM...
YOU DON'T LOOK SO BAD...
...YOURSELF, SHISUTO!
He's well-behaved around family.

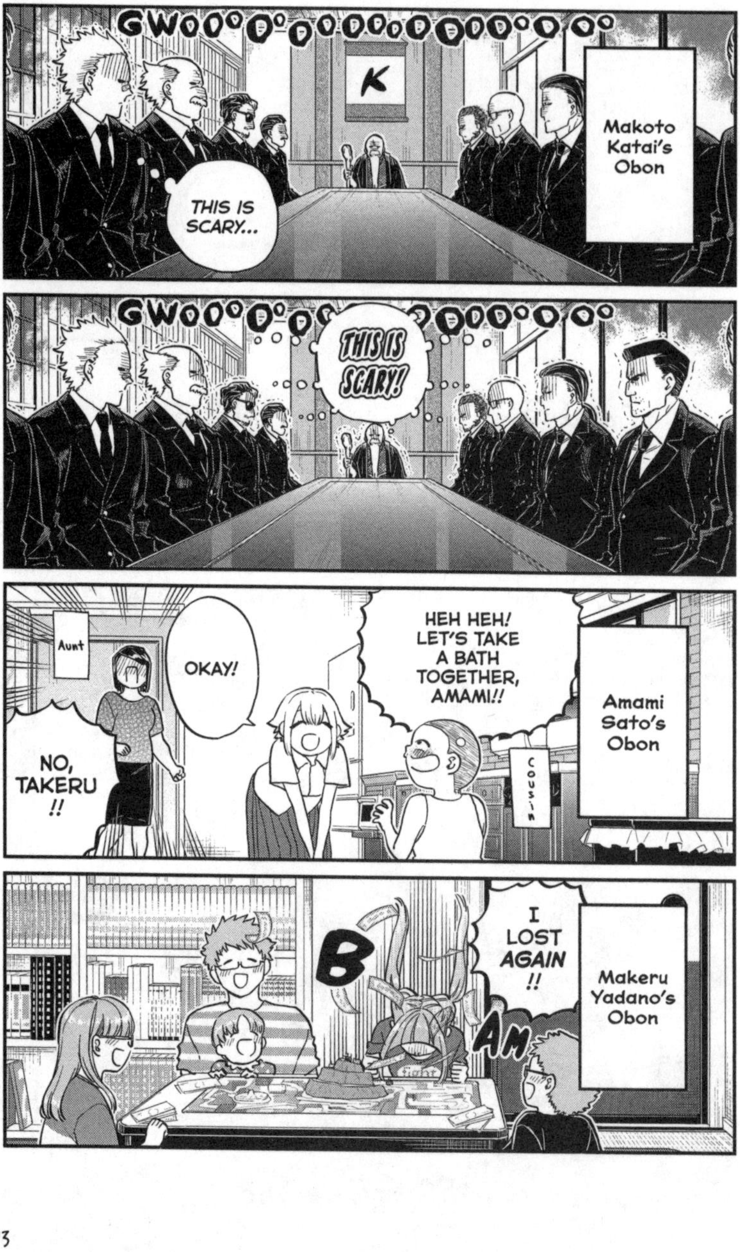
Makoto Katai's Obon
GWOOOO...
K
THIS IS SCARY...
GWOOOO...
THIS IS SCARY!
Amami Sato's Obon
HEH HEH! LET'S TAKE A BATH TOGETHER, AMAMI!!
Cousin
OKAY!
Aunt
NO, TAKERU!!
Makeru Yadano's Obon
I LOST AGAIN!!
BAM

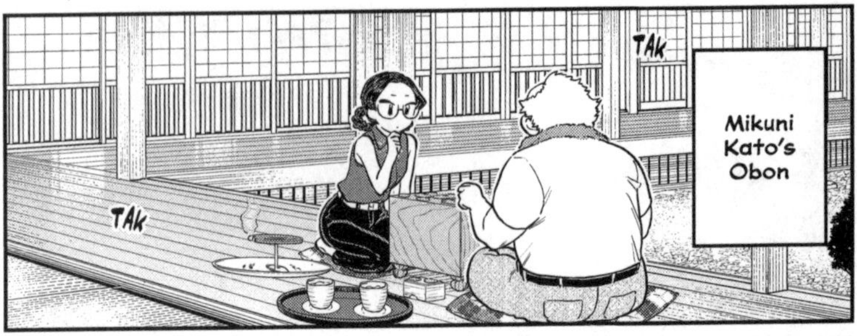
Mikuni Kato's Obon
TAK
TAK

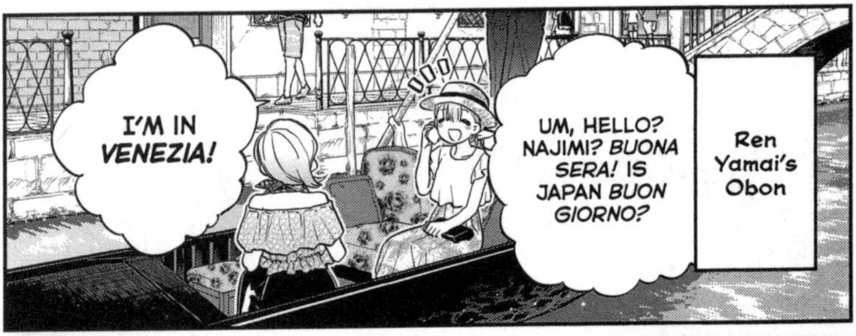
Ren Yamai's Obon
UM, HELLO? NAJIMI? *BUONA SERA!* IS JAPAN *BUON GIORNO?*
I'M IN *VENEZIA!*

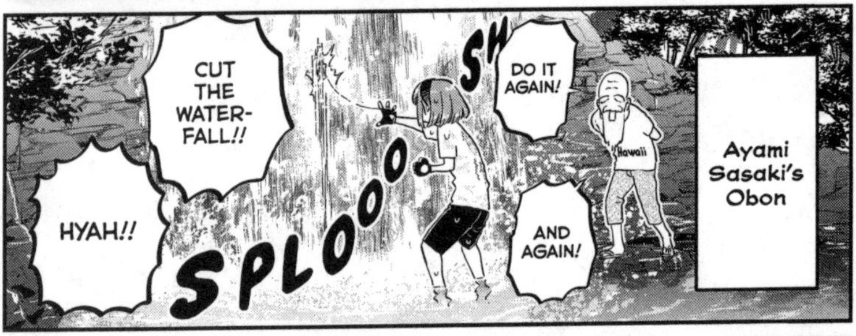
Ayami Sasaki's Obon
Hawaii
DO IT AGAIN!
SH
AND AGAIN!
CUT THE WATER-FALL!!
SPLOOO
HYAH!!

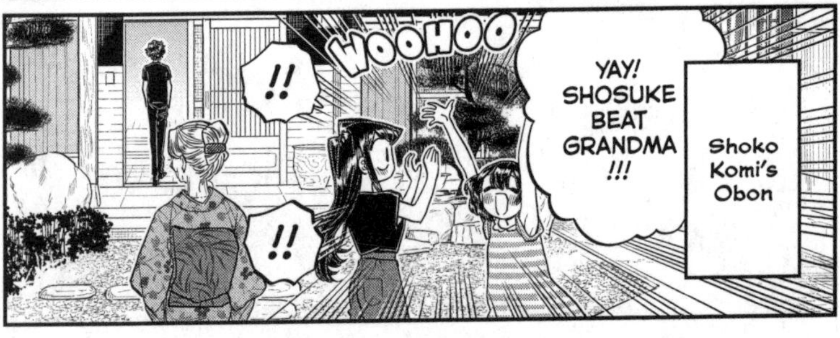
Shoko Komi's Obon
YAY! SHOSUKE BEAT GRANDMA!!!
WOOHOO
!!
!!

Communication 186 — The End

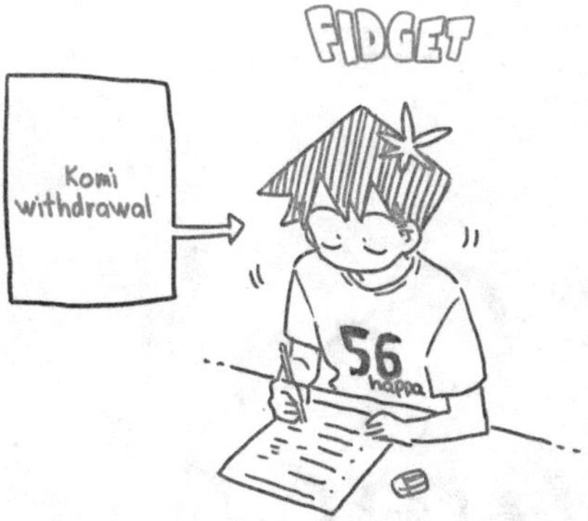
FIDGET
Komi withdrawal
56
happa

Komi Can't
Communicate

Komi Can't Communicate

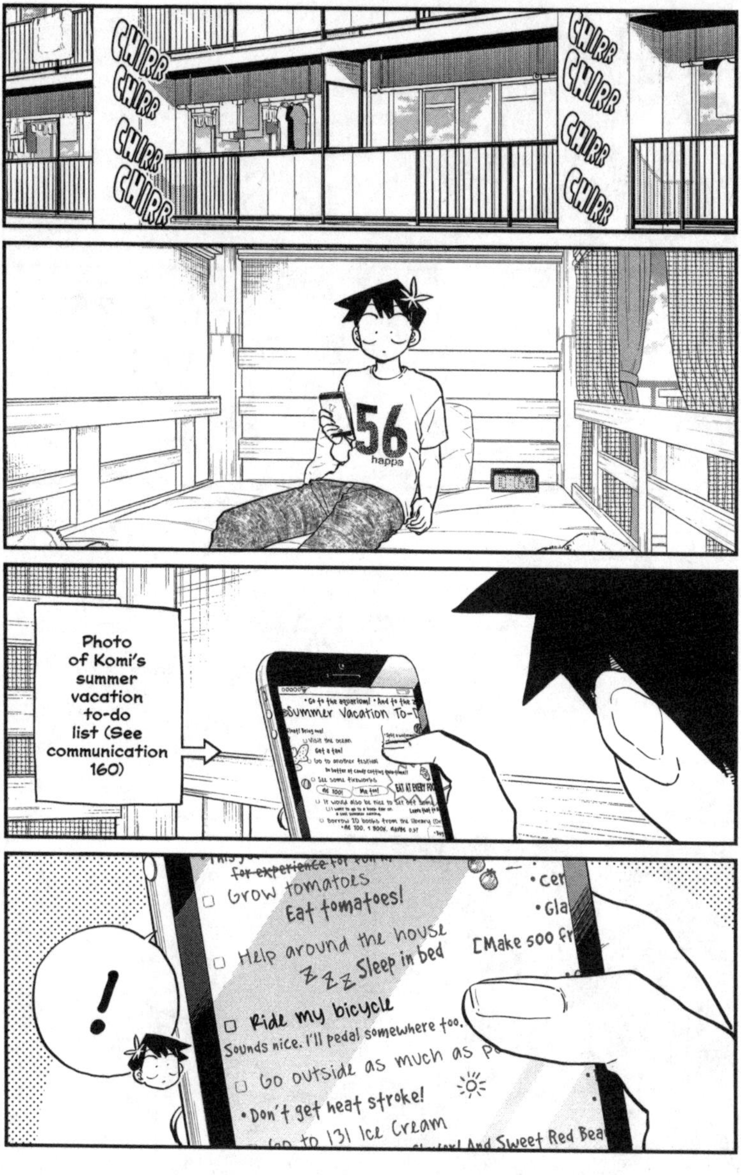
CHIRR CHIRR CHIRR CHIRR
CHIRR CHIRR CHIRR CHIRR
56
happa
Photo of Komi's summer vacation to-do list (See communication 160)
Visit the ocean
Get a tan!
See some fireworks
Me too!
Grow tomatoes
Eat tomatoes!
Help around the house
Sleep in bed
Ride my bicycle
Sounds nice. I'll pedal somewhere too.
Don't get heat stroke!
!

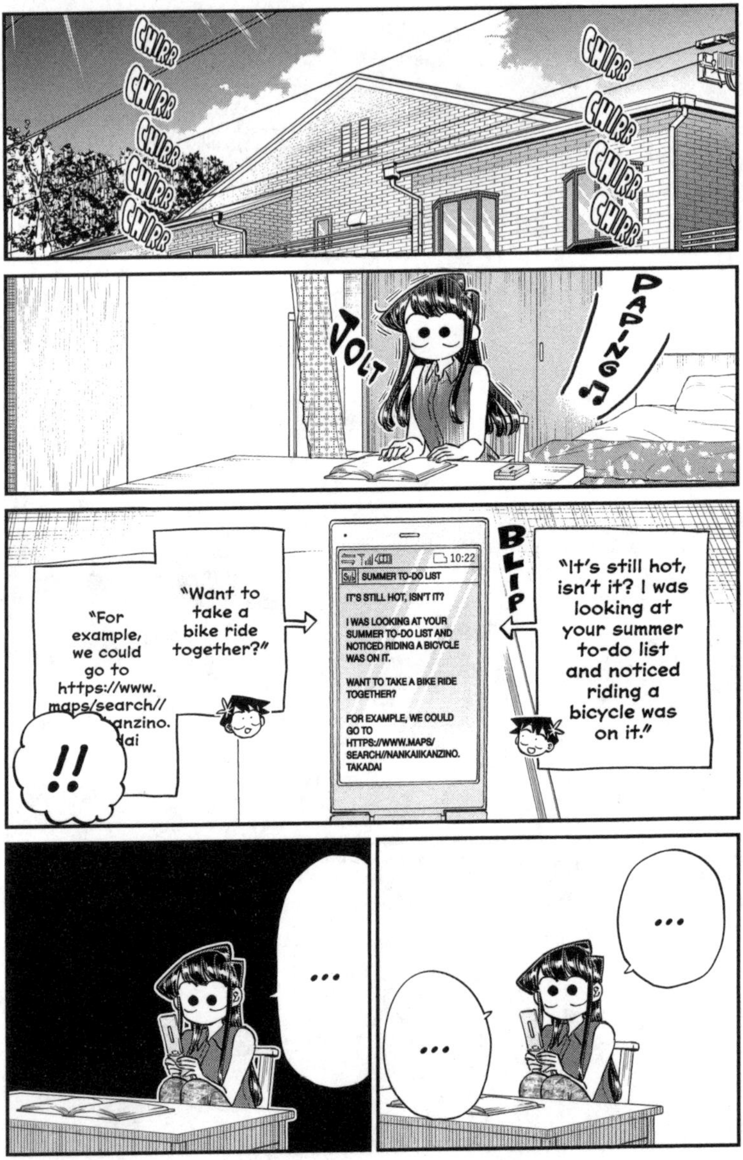

CHIRR CHIRR CHIRR CHIRR
CHIRR CHIRR CHIRR CHIRR CHIRR
DAPING♪
JOLT
BLIP
"It's still hot, isn't it? I was looking at your summer to-do list and noticed riding a bicycle was on it."
10:22
SUMMER TO-DO LIST
IT'S STILL HOT, ISN'T IT?
I WAS LOOKING AT YOUR SUMMER TO-DO LIST AND NOTICED RIDING A BICYCLE WAS ON IT.
WANT TO TAKE A BIKE RIDE TOGETHER?
FOR EXAMPLE, WE COULD GO TO HTTPS://WWW.MAPS/SEARCH//NANKAIIKANZINO.TAKADAI
"Want to take a bike ride together?"
"For example, we could go to https://www. maps/search//
!!
...
...
...

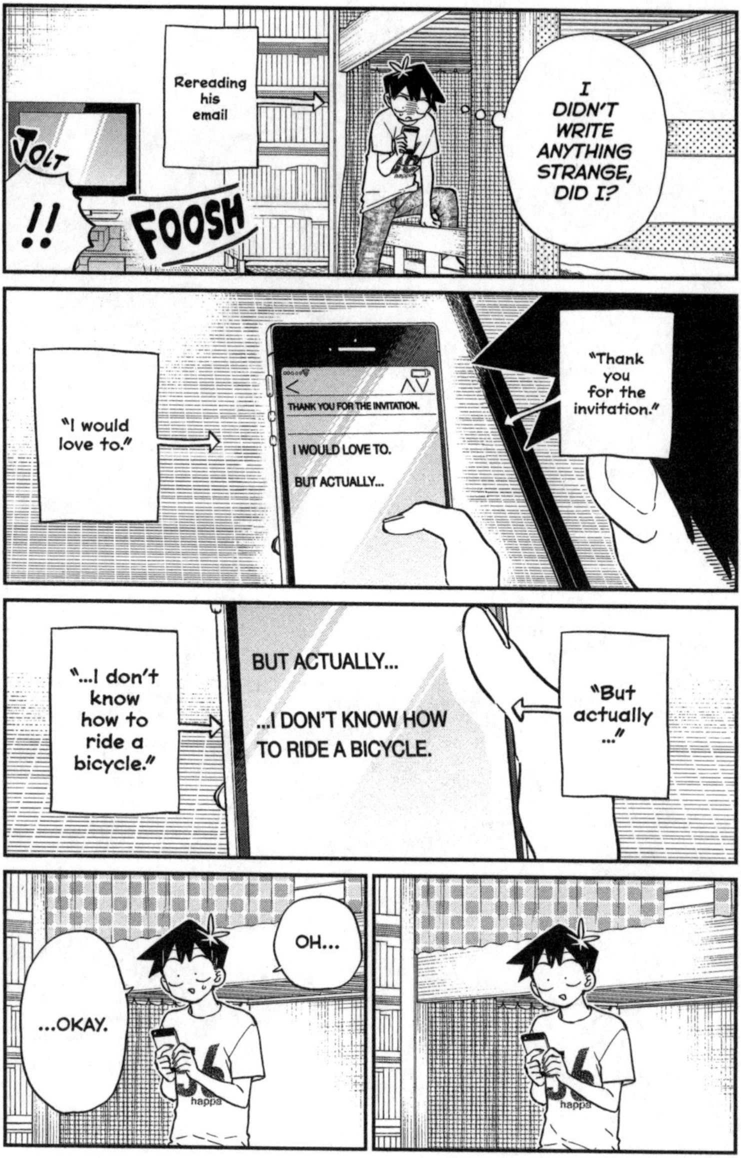
I DIDN'T WRITE ANYTHING STRANGE, DID I?
Rereading his email
JOLT
!!
FOOSH
"Thank you for the invitation."
THANK YOU FOR THE INVITATION.
I WOULD LOVE TO.
BUT ACTUALLY...
"I would love to."
"But actually ..."
BUT ACTUALLY...
...I DON'T KNOW HOW TO RIDE A BICYCLE.
"...I don't know how to ride a bicycle."
OH...
...OKAY.

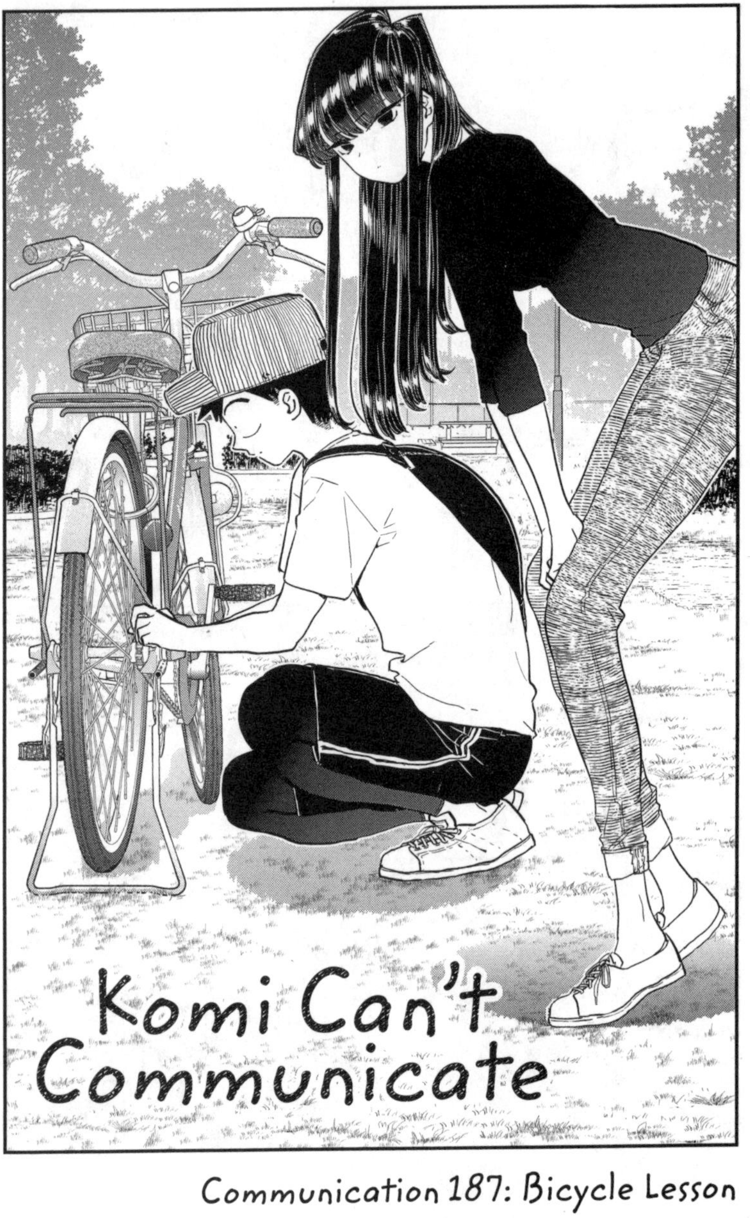
Komi Can't
Communicate

Communication 187: Bicycle Lesson

WHY DID I SAY "OKAY"?
FIDGET FIDGET FIDGET
HWOOSH
Sound of sending mail
Figures Tadano is disappointed that she can't ride a bicycle
PAPING♪
JOLT
!!
"Okay. I wasn't expecting that."
10:44
TADANO, HITOHITO
OKAY. I WASN'T EXPECTING THAT.
BUT I CAN HELP YOU LEARN.
"But I can help you learn."
!
HM? YOU WANT TO RIDE A BICYCLE?
HMPH
HMPH
YOU CAN USE THE ONE IN THE GARAGE.

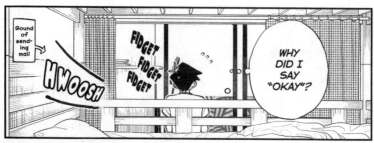

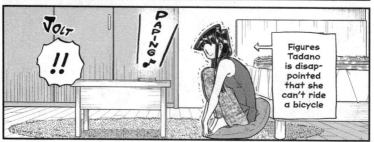

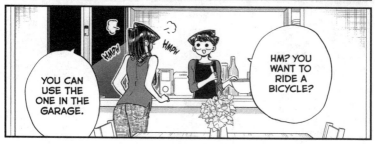

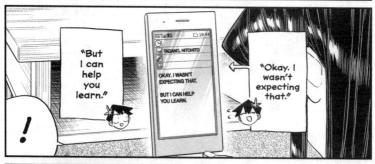

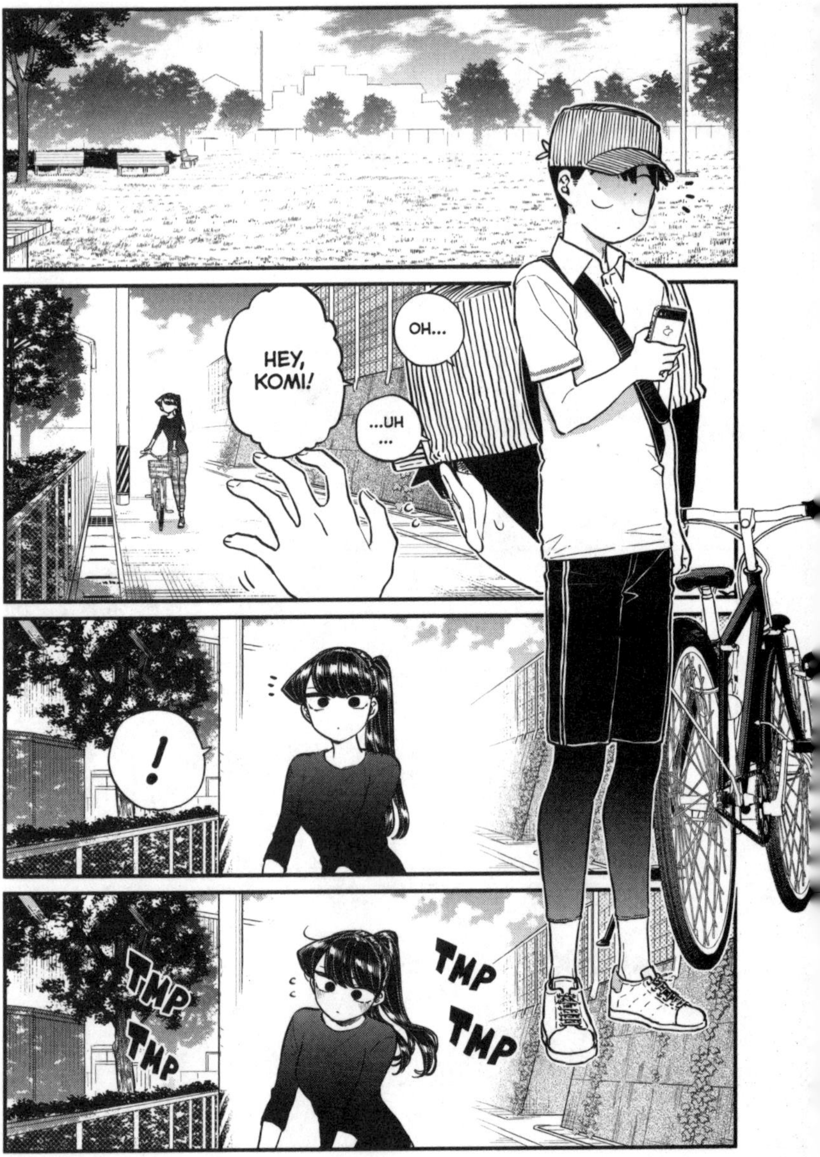
OH...
...UH ...
HEY, KOMI!
!
TMP TMP
TMP TMP

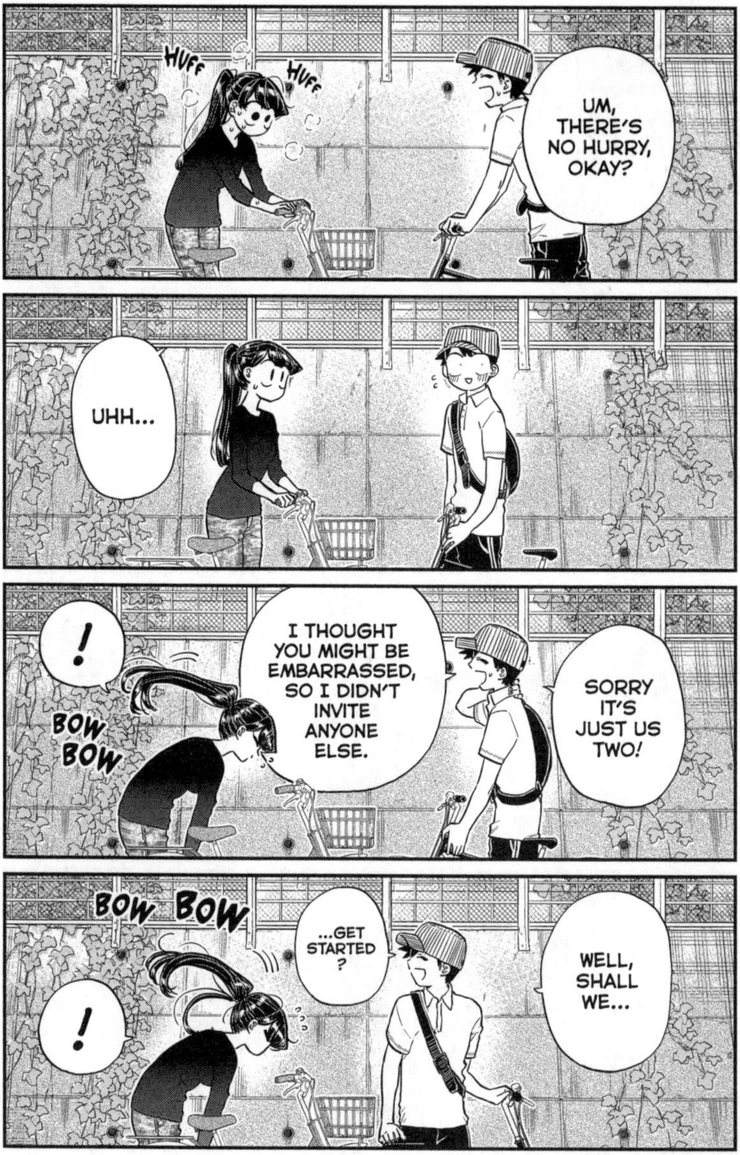
UM, THERE'S NO HURRY, OKAY?
HUFF
HUFF
UHH...
SORRY IT'S JUST US TWO!
I THOUGHT YOU MIGHT BE EMBARRASSED, SO I DIDN'T INVITE ANYONE ELSE.
!
BOW BOW
WELL, SHALL WE...
...GET STARTED?
BOW BOW
!

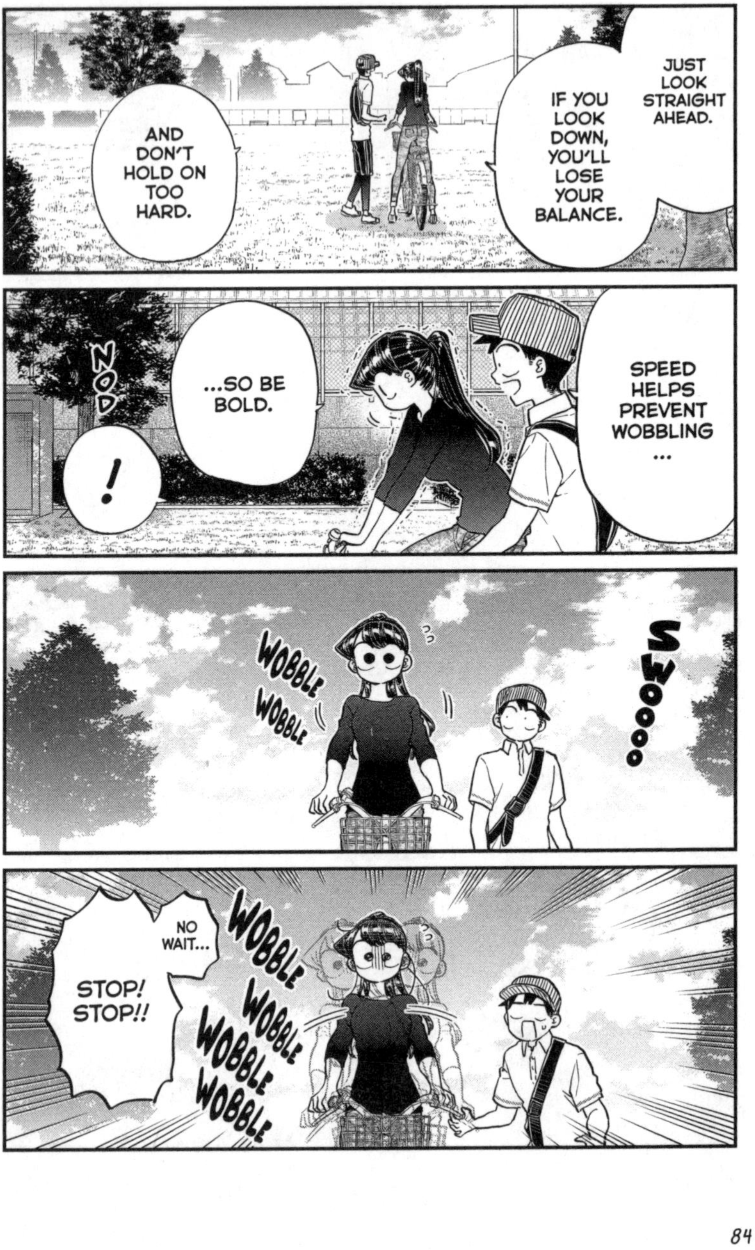
JUST LOOK STRAIGHT AHEAD.
IF YOU LOOK DOWN, YOU'LL LOSE YOUR BALANCE.
AND DON'T HOLD ON TOO HARD.
SPEED HELPS PREVENT WOBBLING...
...SO BE BOLD.
NOD
!
SWOOOO
WOBBLE WOBBLE
WOBBLE WOBBLE WOBBLE WOBBLE
NO WAIT...
STOP! STOP!!

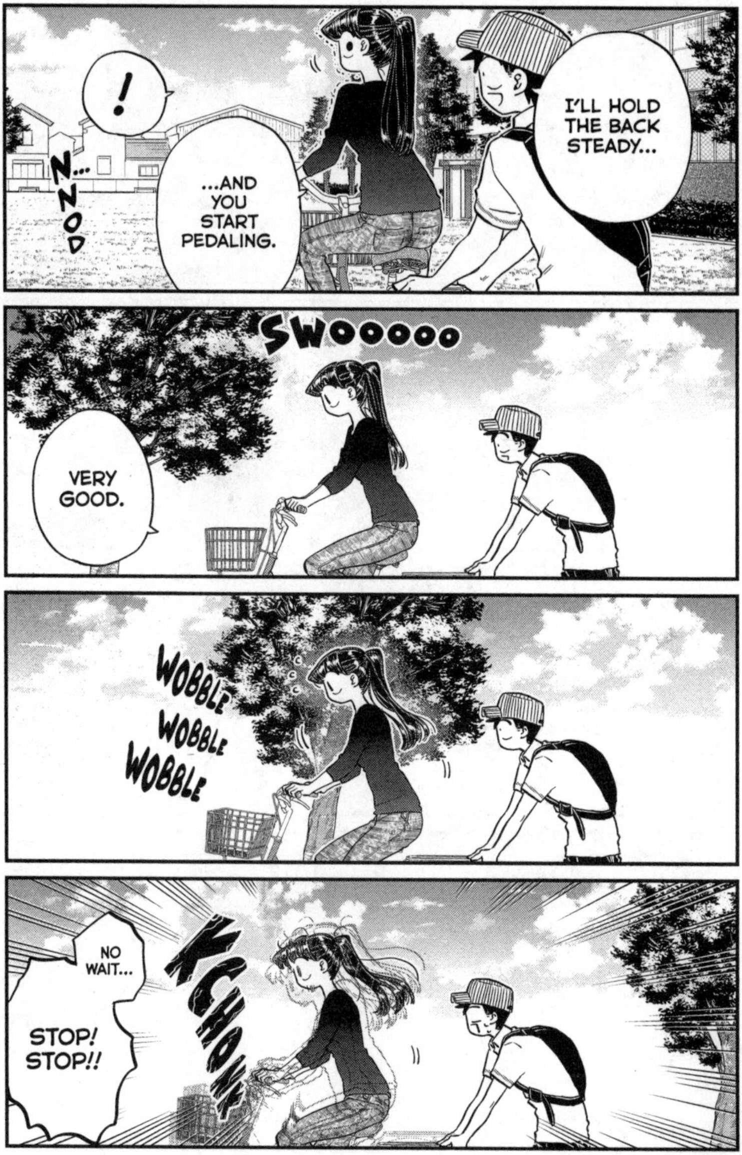
I'LL HOLD THE BACK STEADY...
...AND YOU START PEDALING.
!
N... NOD
SWOOOOO
VERY GOOD.
WOBBLE WOBBLE WOBBLE
KCHONK
NO WAIT...
STOP! STOP!!

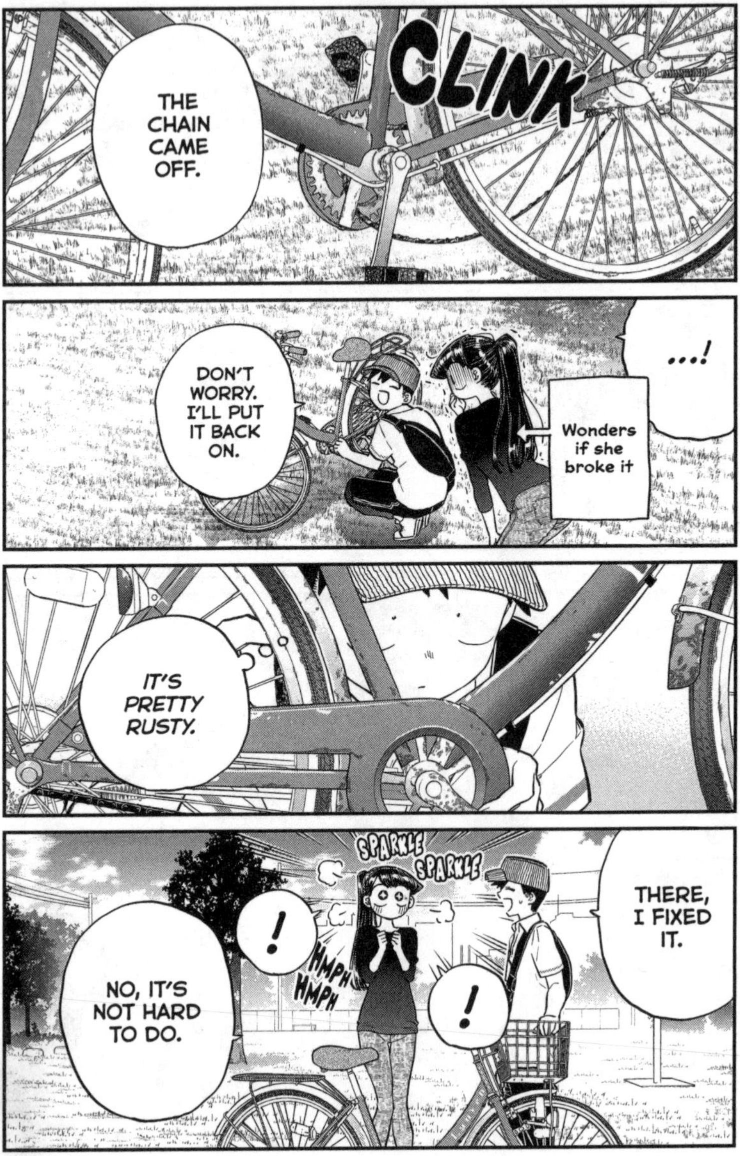
CLINK
THE CHAIN CAME OFF.
...!
Wonders if she broke it
DON'T WORRY. I'LL PUT IT BACK ON.
IT'S PRETTY RUSTY.
THERE, I FIXED IT.
SPARKLE SPARKLE
!
!
HMPH HMPH
NO, IT'S NOT HARD TO DO.

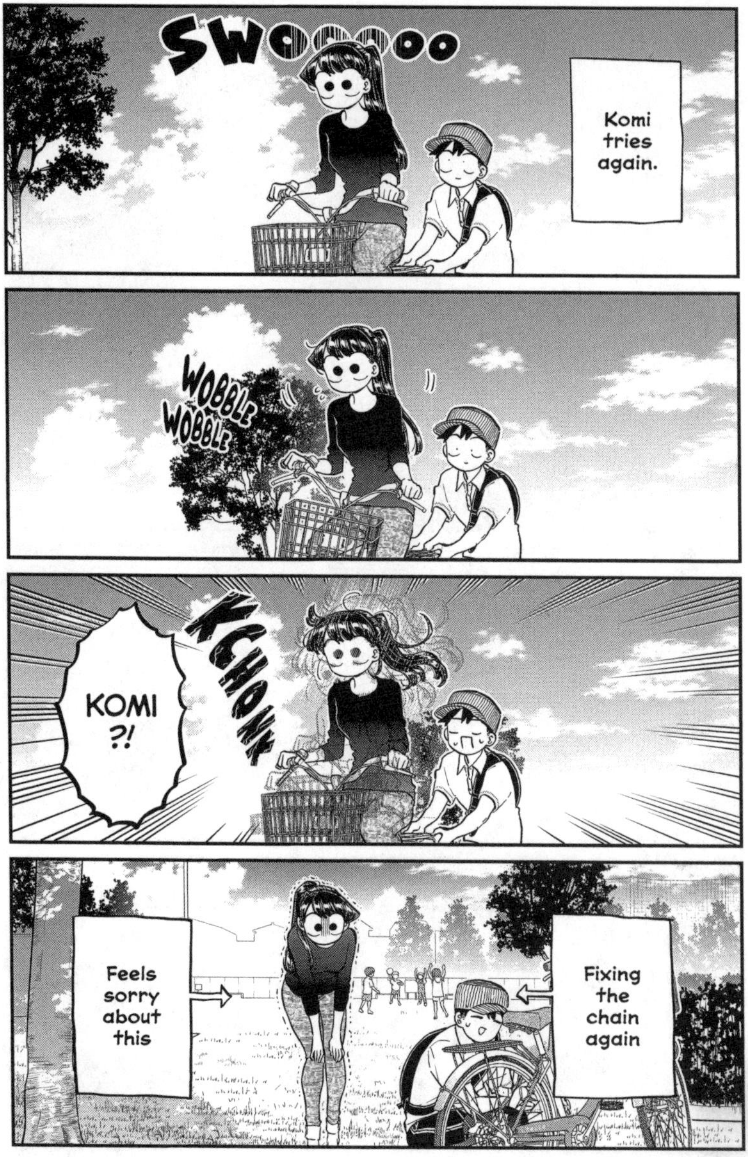
SWOOOOO
Komi tries again.
WOBBLE WOBBLE
KCHONK
KOMI ?!
Fixing the chain again
Feels sorry about this

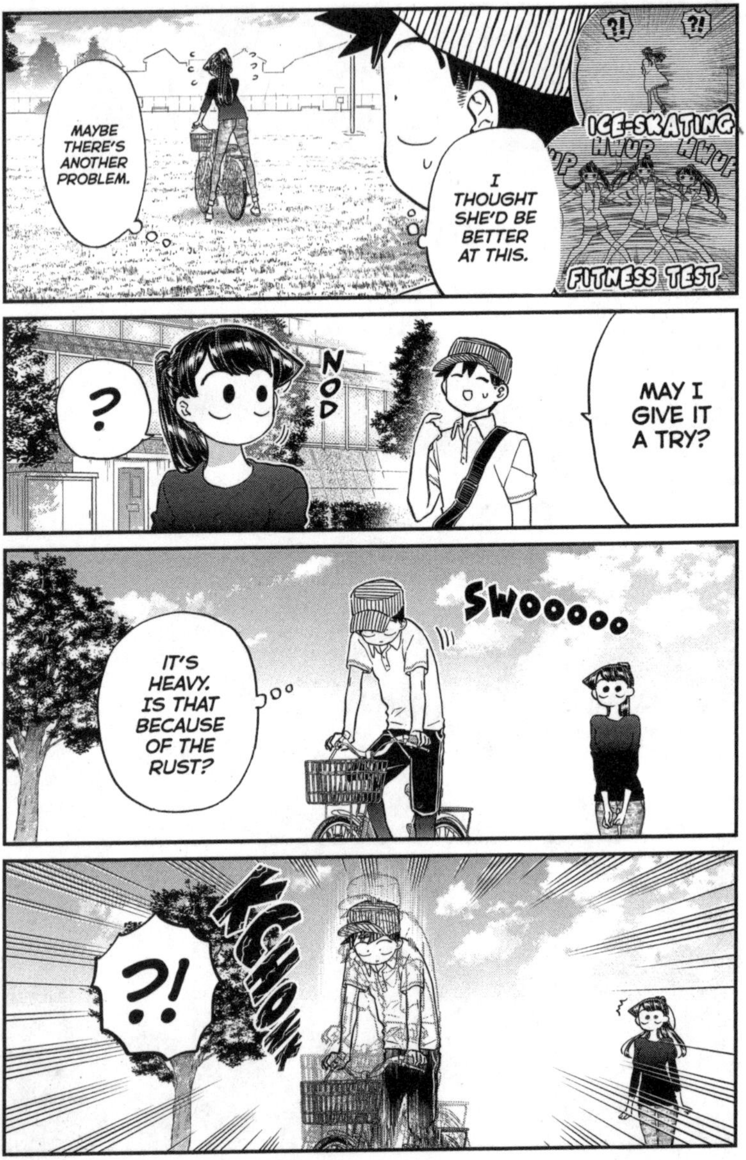
?!
?!
ICE-SKATING
HWUP HWUP HWUP
FITNESS TEST
I THOUGHT SHE'D BE BETTER AT THIS.
MAYBE THERE'S ANOTHER PROBLEM.
MAY I GIVE IT A TRY?
NOD
?
SWOOOOO
IT'S HEAVY. IS THAT BECAUSE OF THE RUST?
KCHONK
?!

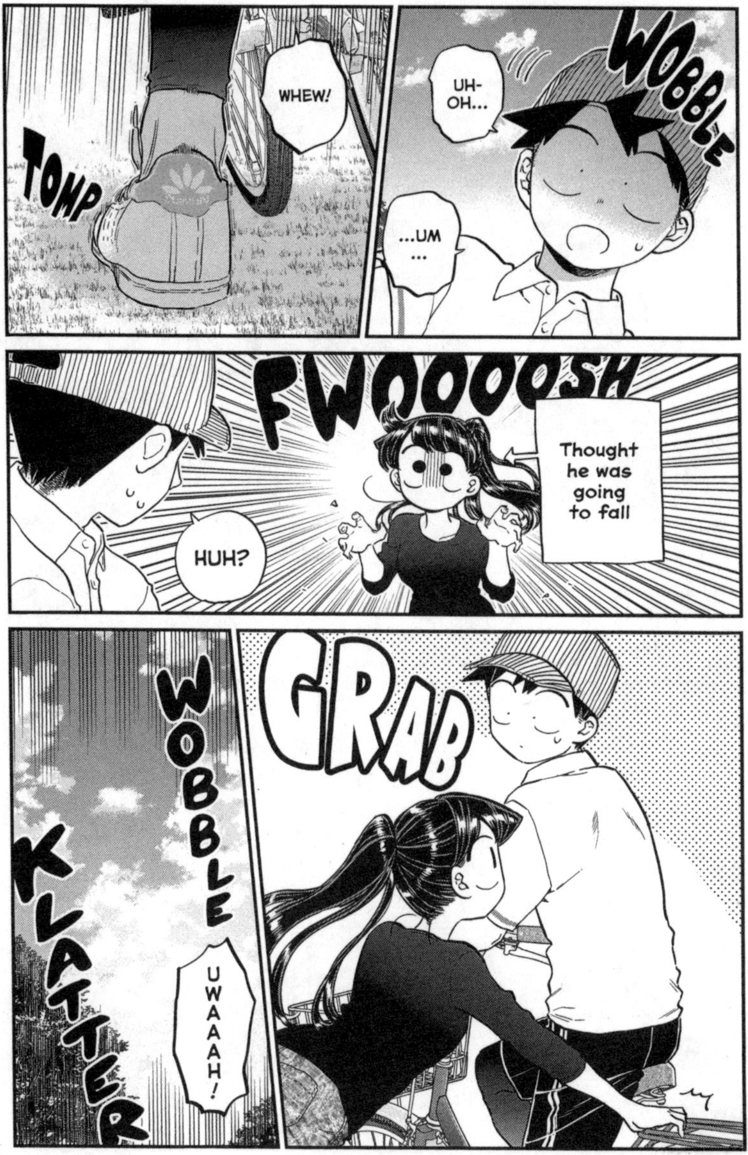
WOBBLE
UH-OH...
...UM ...
WHEW!
TOMP
FWOOOOSH
Thought he was going to fall
HUH?
GRAB
WOBBLE
UWAAAH!
KLATTER

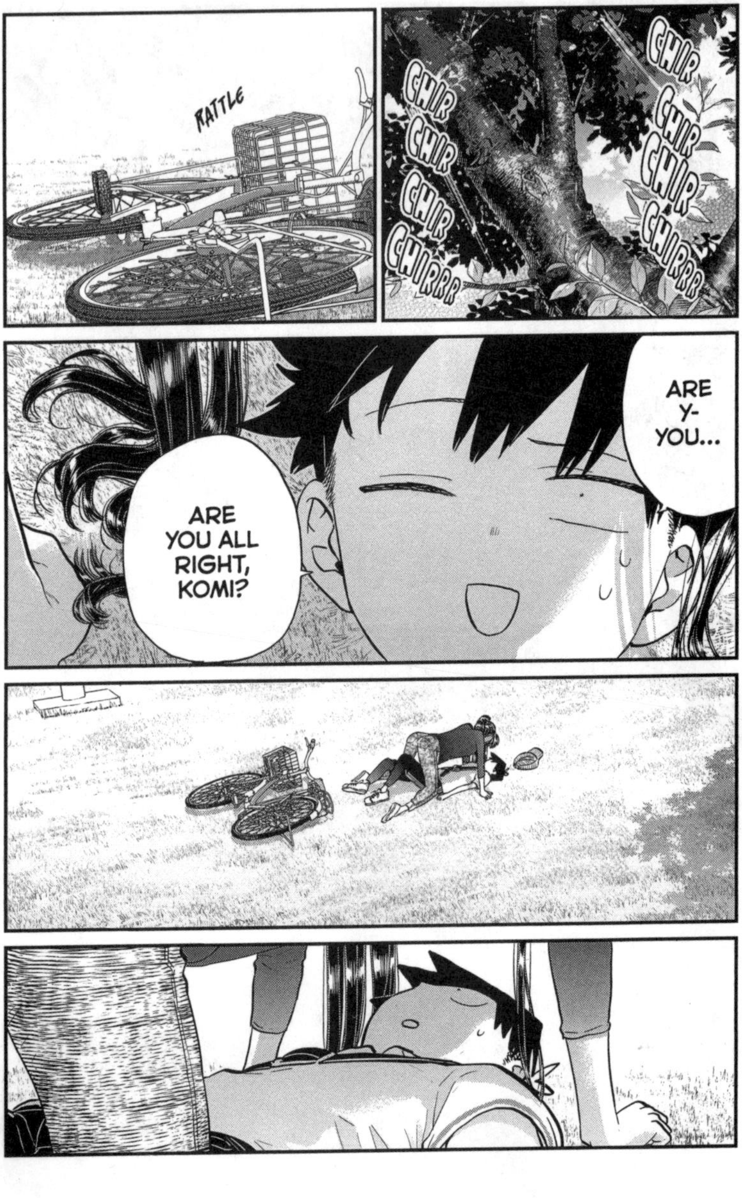
CHIR CHIR CHIR CHIRRR
CHIR CHIR CHIR CHIRRR
RATTLE
ARE Y-YOU...
ARE YOU ALL RIGHT, KOMI?

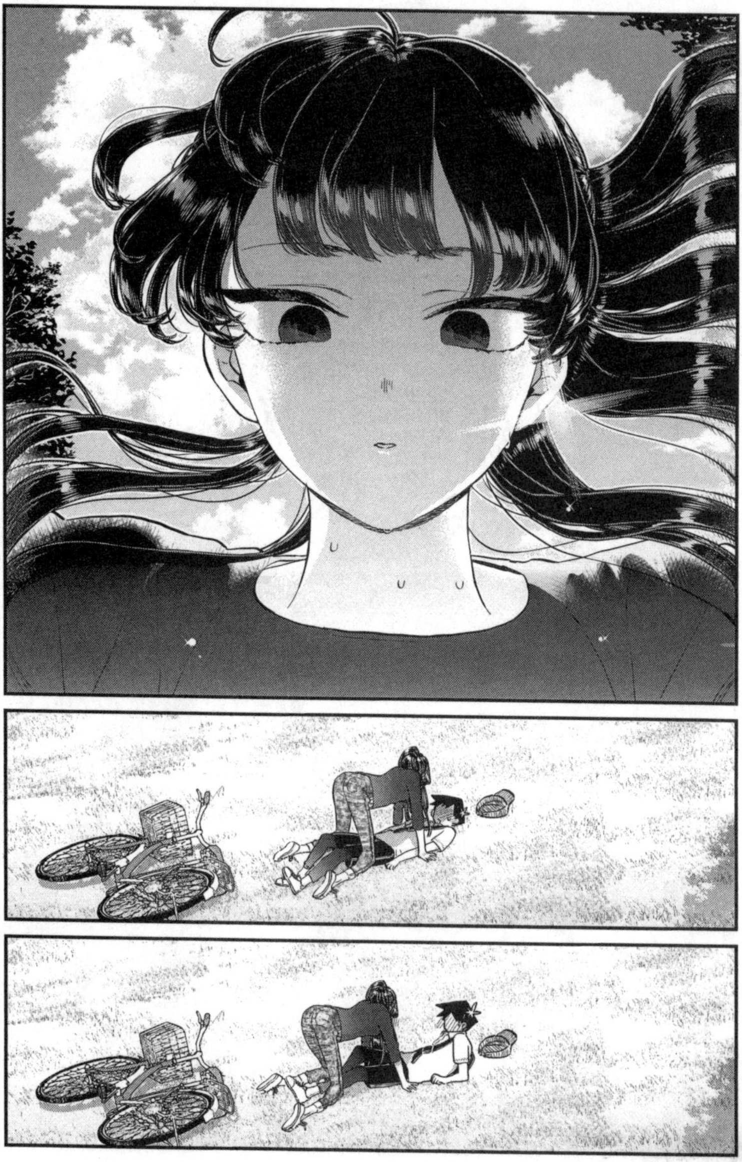

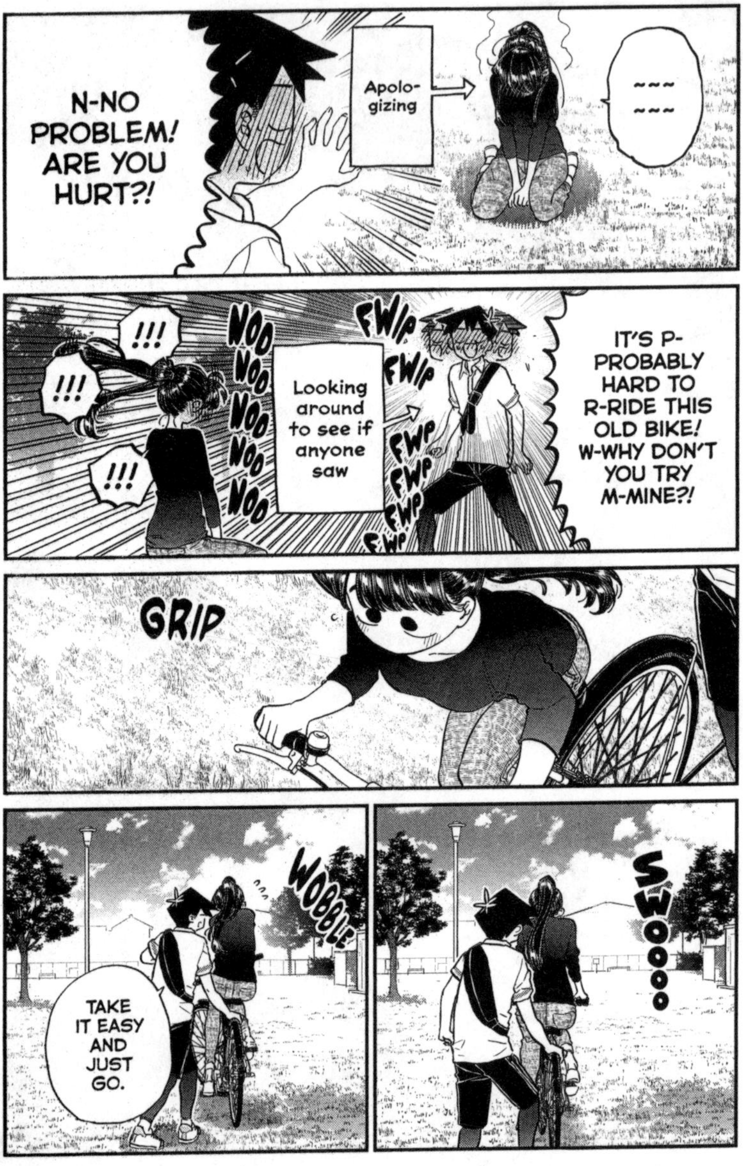

Apologizing
N-NO PROBLEM! ARE YOU HURT?!
IT'S P-PROBABLY HARD TO R-RIDE THIS OLD BIKE! W-WHY DON'T YOU TRY M-MINE?!
FWIP FWIP FWP FWP FWP FWP
Looking around to see if anyone saw
NOD NOD NOD NOD NOD NOD
!!!
!!!
!!!
GRIP
SWOOOO
WOBBLE
TAKE IT EASY AND JUST GO.

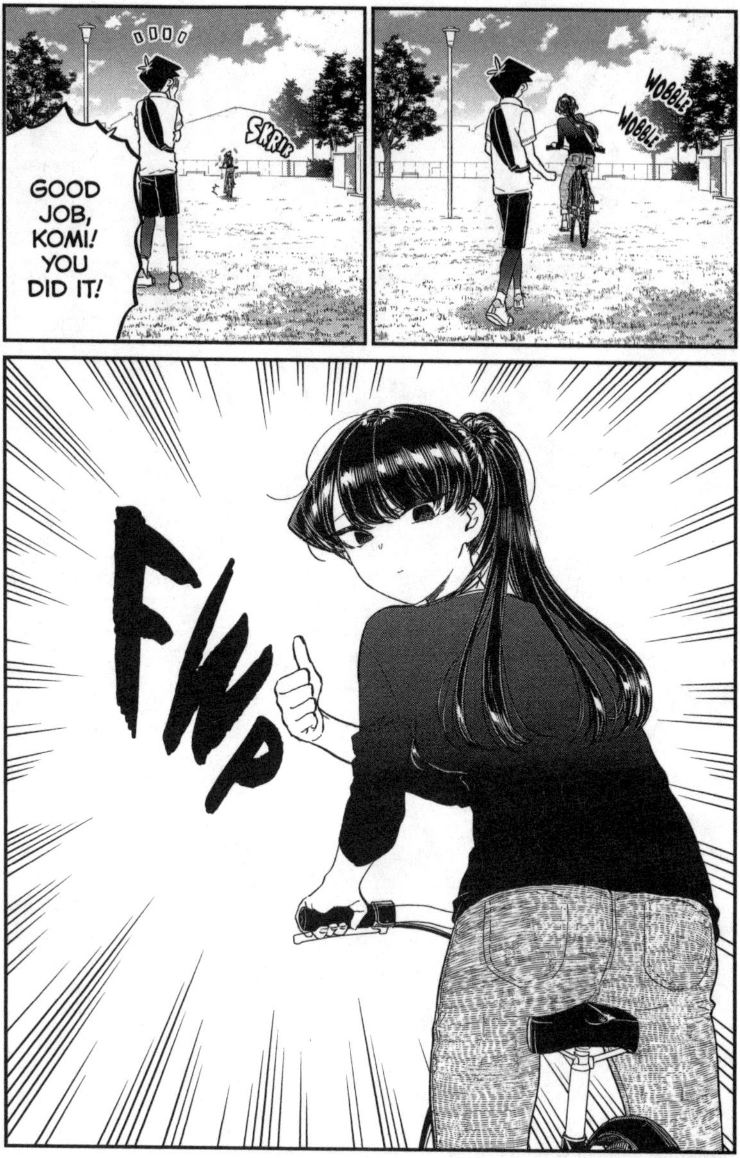
WOBBLE
WOBBLE
SKRIK
GOOD JOB, KOMI! YOU DID IT!
FWP

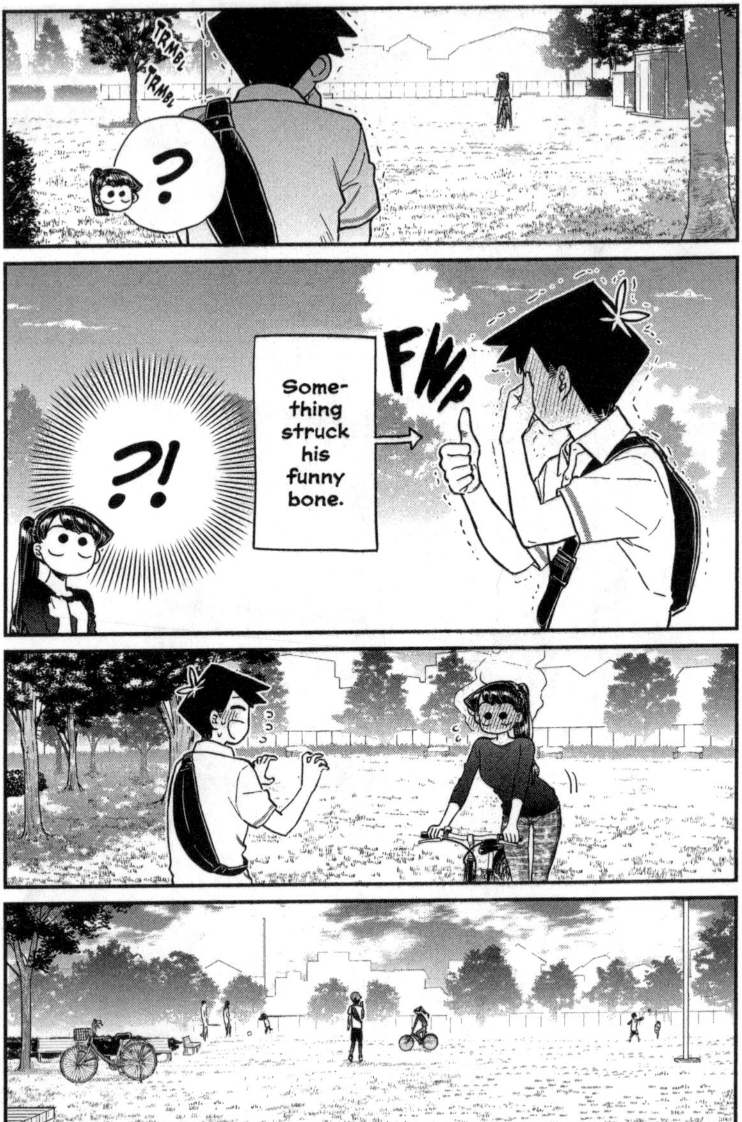
TRMBL
TRMBL
?
FWP
Something struck his funny bone.
?!

Communication 187 — The End

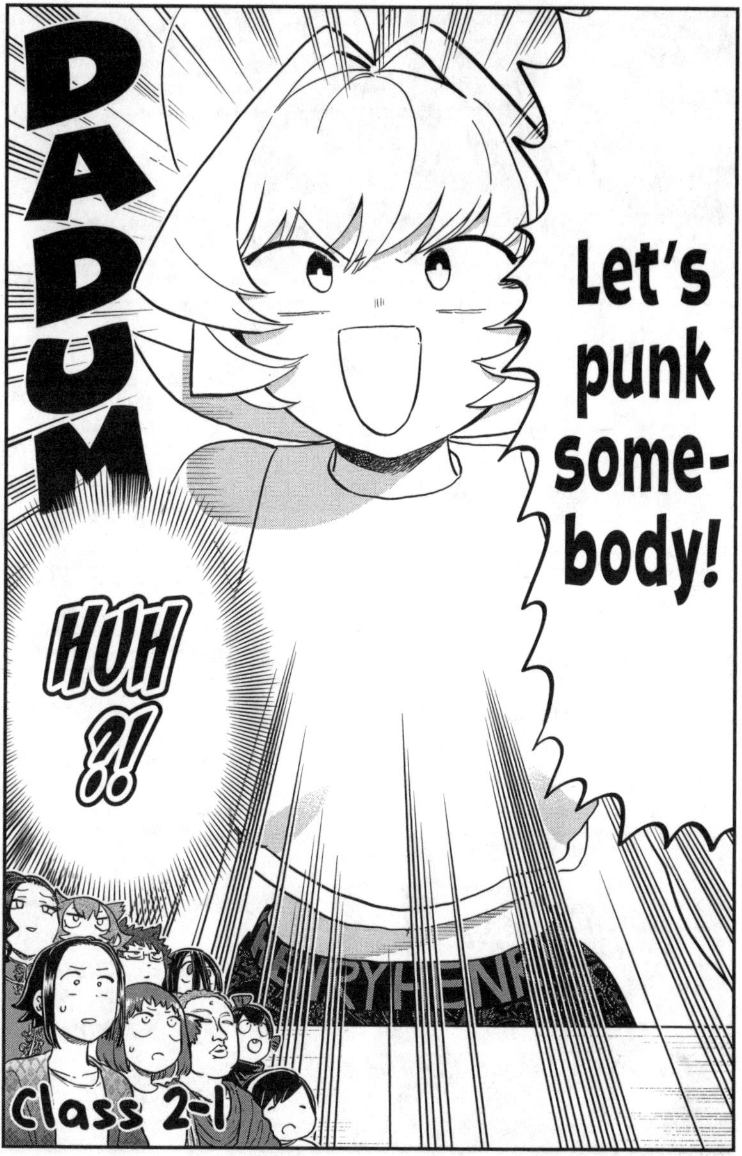
Let's punk some-body!
DADUM
HUH?!
Class 2-1

Communication 188: The Class 2-1 Social

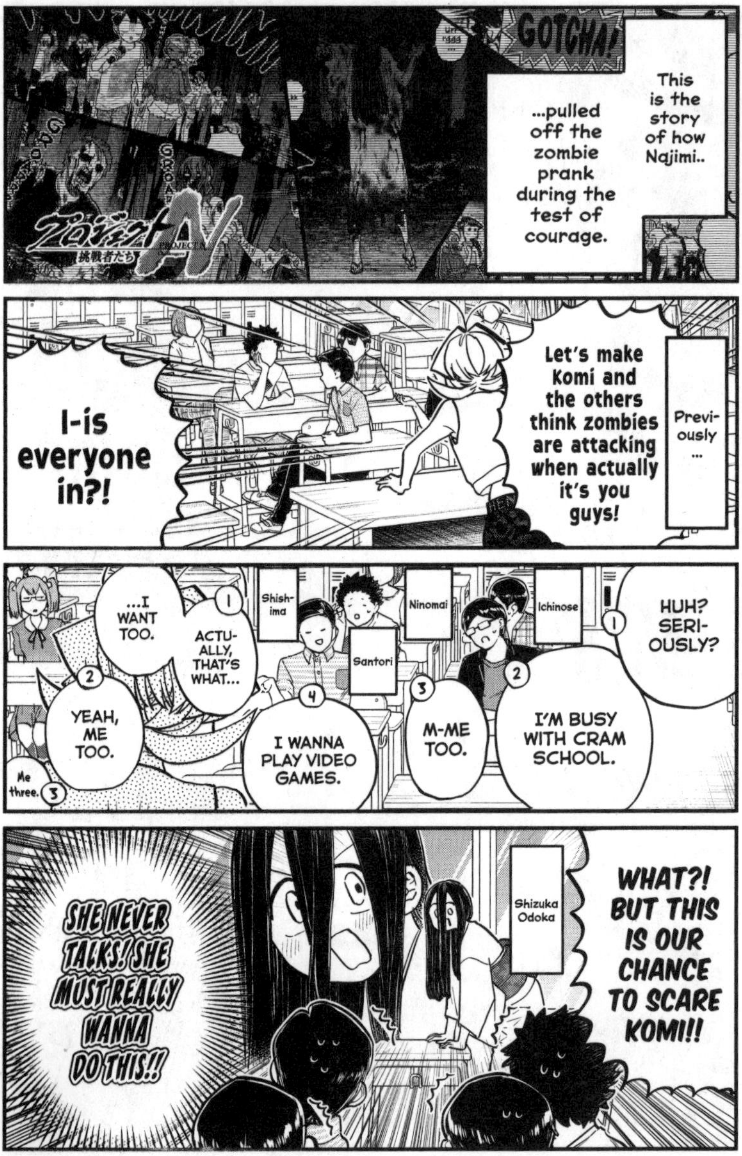
GOTCHA!
This is the story of how Najimi..
...pulled off the zombie prank during the test of courage.
Previ-ously ...
Let's make Komi and the others think zombies are attacking when actually it's you guys!
I-is everyone in?!
HUH? SERI-OUSLY?
Ichinose
I'M BUSY WITH CRAM SCHOOL.
Ninomai
M-ME TOO.
Santori
I WANNA PLAY VIDEO GAMES.
Shish-ima
ACTU-ALLY, THAT'S WHAT...
...I WANT TOO.
YEAH, ME TOO.
Me three.
WHAT?! BUT THIS IS OUR CHANCE TO SCARE KOMI!!
Shizuka Odoka
SHE NEVER TALKS! SHE MUST REALLY WANNA DO THIS!!

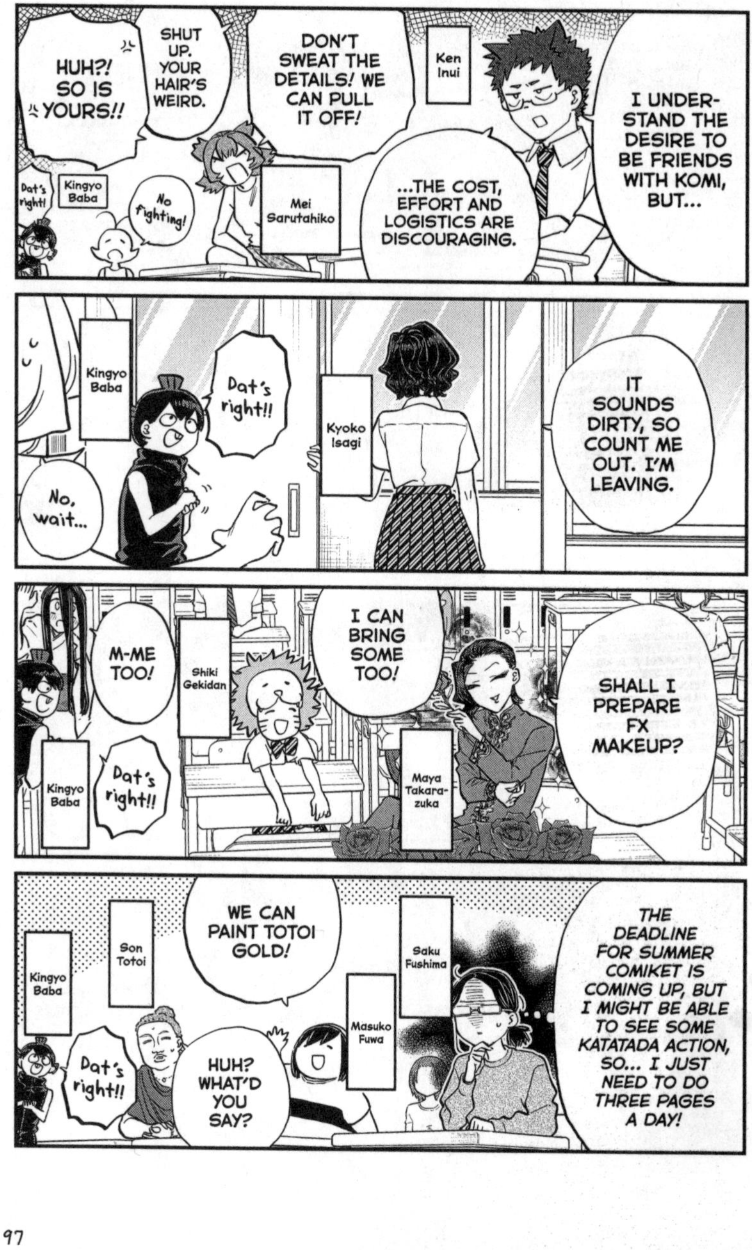
I UNDERSTAND THE DESIRE TO BE FRIENDS WITH KOMI, BUT...
Ken Inui
...THE COST, EFFORT AND LOGISTICS ARE DISCOURAGING.
DON'T SWEAT THE DETAILS! WE CAN PULL IT OFF!
Mei Sarutahiko
SHUT UP. YOUR HAIR'S WEIRD.
HUH?! SO IS YOURS!!
No fighting!
Kingyo Baba
Dat's right!
IT SOUNDS DIRTY, SO COUNT ME OUT. I'M LEAVING.
Kyoko Isagi
Dat's right!!
Kingyo Baba
No, wait...
SHALL I PREPARE FX MAKEUP?
Maya Takarazuka
I CAN BRING SOME TOO!
Shiki Gekidan
M-ME TOO!
Dat's right!!
Kingyo Baba
THE DEADLINE FOR SUMMER COMIKET IS COMING UP, BUT I MIGHT BE ABLE TO SEE SOME KATATADA ACTION, SO... I JUST NEED TO DO THREE PAGES A DAY!
Saku Fushima
Masuko Fuwa
WE CAN PAINT TOTOI GOLD!
HUH? WHAT'D YOU SAY?
Son Totoi
Dat's right!!
Kingyo Baba

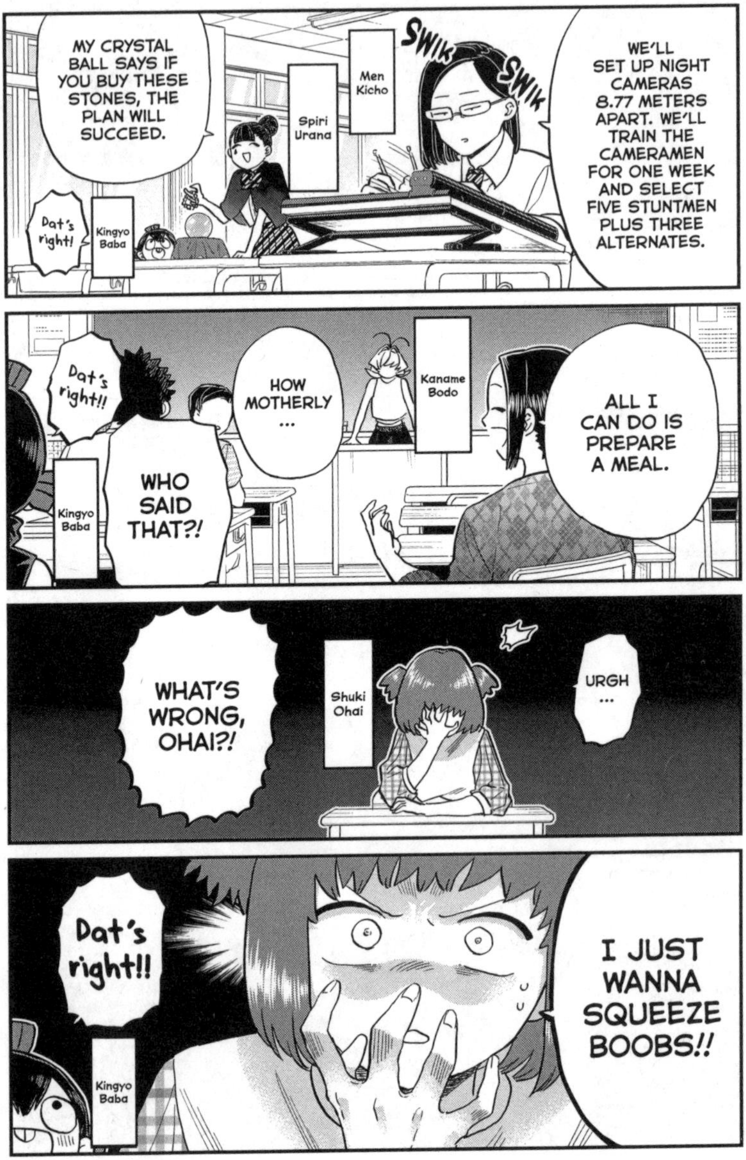
SWIK SWIK
WE'LL SET UP NIGHT CAMERAS 8.77 METERS APART. WE'LL TRAIN THE CAMERAMEN FOR ONE WEEK AND SELECT FIVE STUNTMEN PLUS THREE ALTERNATES.
Men Kicho
Spiri Urana
MY CRYSTAL BALL SAYS IF YOU BUY THESE STONES, THE PLAN WILL SUCCEED.
Kingyo Baba
Dat's right!
ALL I CAN DO IS PREPARE A MEAL.
Kaname Bodo
HOW MOTHERLY...
WHO SAID THAT?!
Dat's right!!
Kingyo Baba
URGH...
Shuki Ohai
WHAT'S WRONG, OHAI?!
I JUST WANNA SQUEEZE BOOBS!!
Dat's right!!
Kingyo Baba

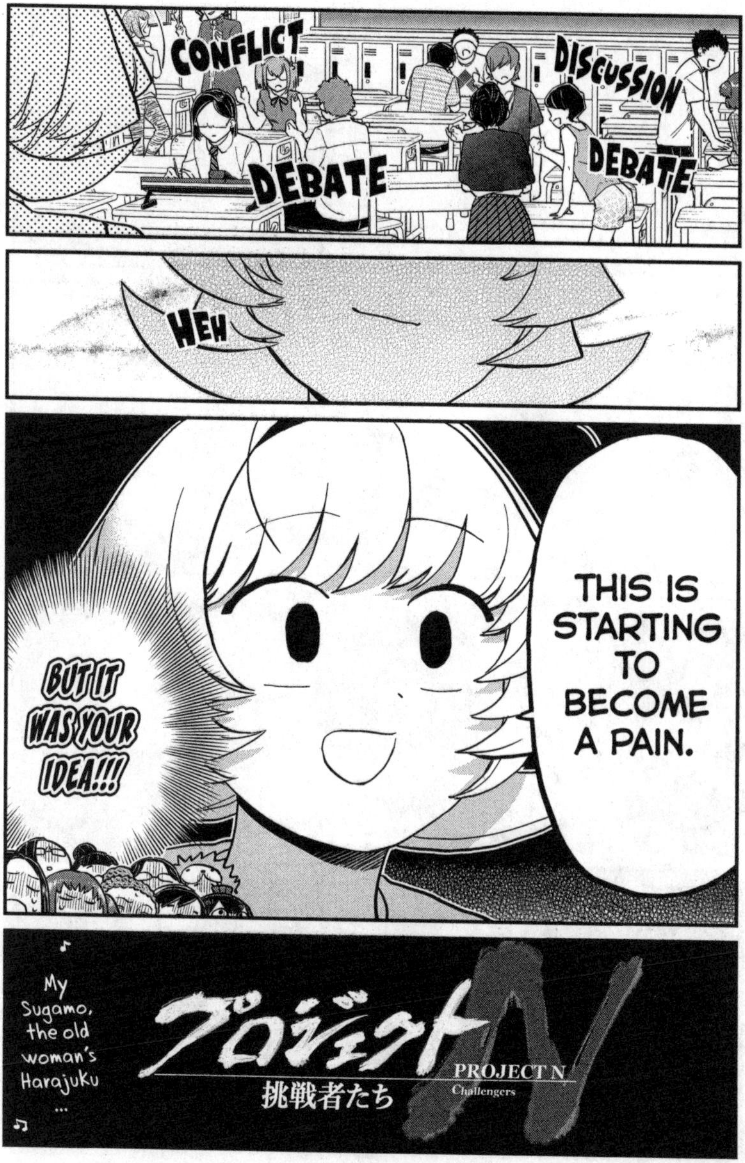
DISCUSSION
DEBATE
CONFLICT
DEBATE
HEH
THIS IS STARTING TO BECOME A PAIN.
BUT IT WAS YOUR IDEA!!!
プロジェクトN
PROJECT N
挑戦者たち
Challengers
My Sugamo, the old woman's Harajuku ...

Communication 188 — The End

Komi Can't Communicate

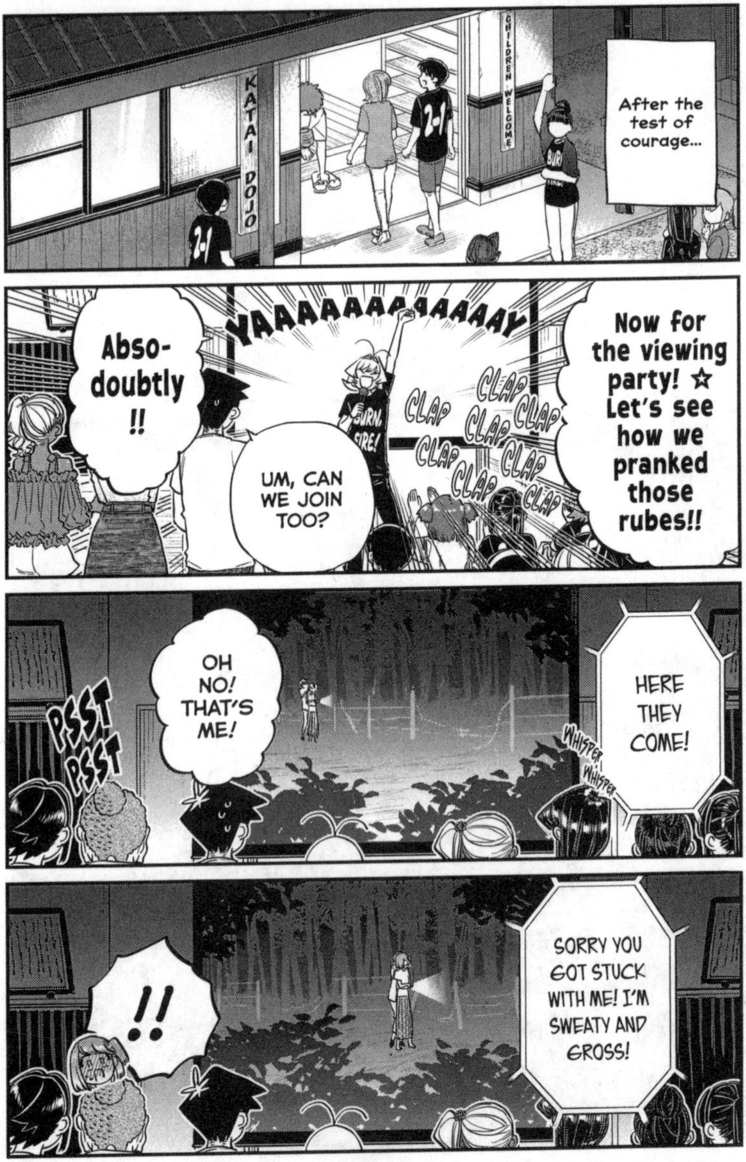
After the test of courage...
CHILDREN WELCOME
KATAI DOJO
Now for the viewing party! ☆ Let's see how we pranked those rubes!!
CLAP CLAP CLAP CLAP CLAP CLAP CLAP CLAP
YAAAAAAAAAAAAY
UM, CAN WE JOIN TOO?
Abso-doubtly!!
HERE THEY COME!
WHISPER WHISPER
OH NO! THAT'S ME!
PSST PSST
SORRY YOU GOT STUCK WITH ME! I'M SWEATY AND GROSS!
!!

Communication 189: After the Test of Courage

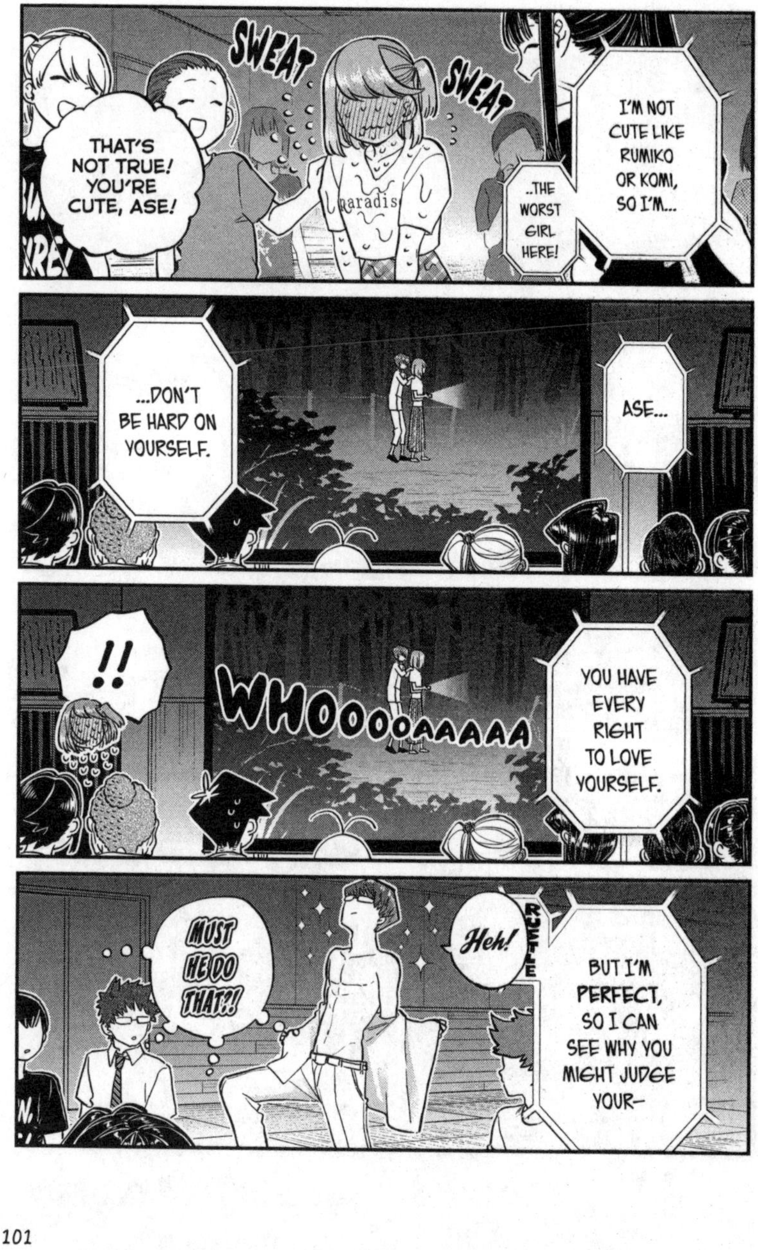

I'M NOT CUTE LIKE RUMIKO OR KOMI, SO I'M...
..THE WORST GIRL HERE!
SWEAT
SWEAT
THAT'S NOT TRUE! YOU'RE CUTE, ASE!
ASE...
...DON'T BE HARD ON YOURSELF.
YOU HAVE EVERY RIGHT TO LOVE YOURSELF.
WHOOOOOAAAAA
!!
BUT I'M PERFECT, SO I CAN SEE WHY YOU MIGHT JUDGE YOUR–
RUSTLE
Heh!
MUST HE DO THAT?!

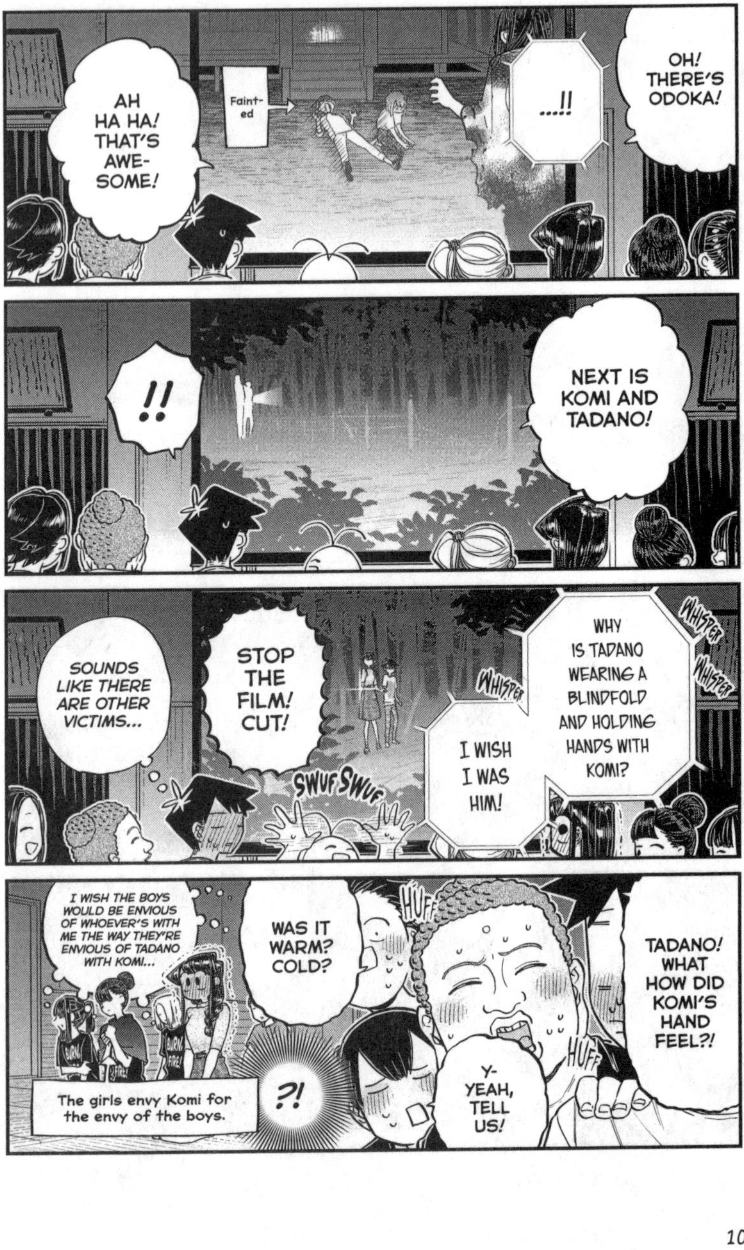
OH! THERE'S ODOKA!
...!!
Faint-ed
AH HA HA! THAT'S AWESOME!
NEXT IS KOMI AND TADANO!
!!
WHISPER
WHISPER
WHY IS TADANO WEARING A BLINDFOLD AND HOLDING HANDS WITH KOMI?
WHISPER
I WISH I WAS HIM!
SWUF SWUF
STOP THE FILM! CUT!
SOUNDS LIKE THERE ARE OTHER VICTIMS...
TADANO! WHAT HOW DID KOMI'S HAND FEEL?!
HUFF
HUFF
Y-YEAH, TELL US!
WAS IT WARM? COLD?
?!
I WISH THE BOYS WOULD BE ENVIOUS OF WHOEVER'S WITH ME THE WAY THEY'RE ENVIOUS OF TADANO WITH KOMI...
The girls envy Komi for the envy of the boys.

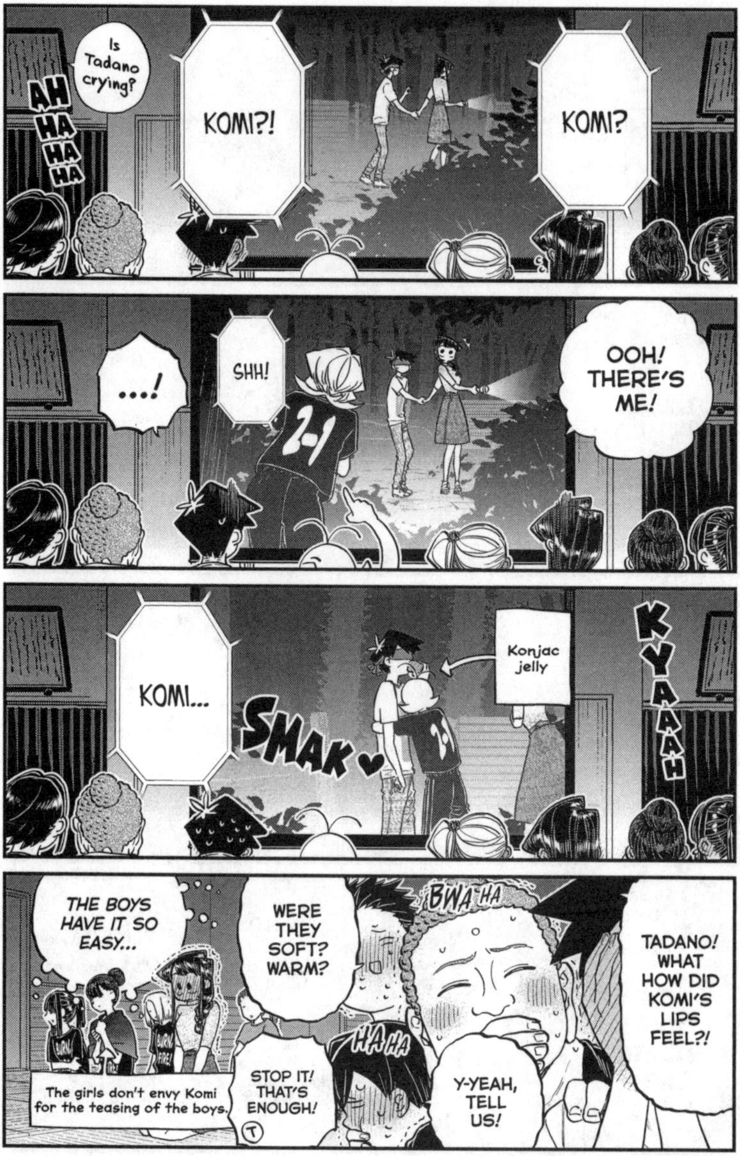
KOMI?
KOMI?!
Is Tadano crying?
AH HA HA HA
OOH! THERE'S ME!
SHH!
...!
KYAAAAH
Konjac jelly
SMAK
KOMI...
TADANO! WHAT HOW DID KOMI'S LIPS FEEL?!
BWA HA
Y-YEAH, TELL US!
HA HA
WERE THEY SOFT? WARM?
STOP IT! THAT'S ENOUGH!
THE BOYS HAVE IT SO EASY...
The girls don't envy Komi for the teasing of the boys.

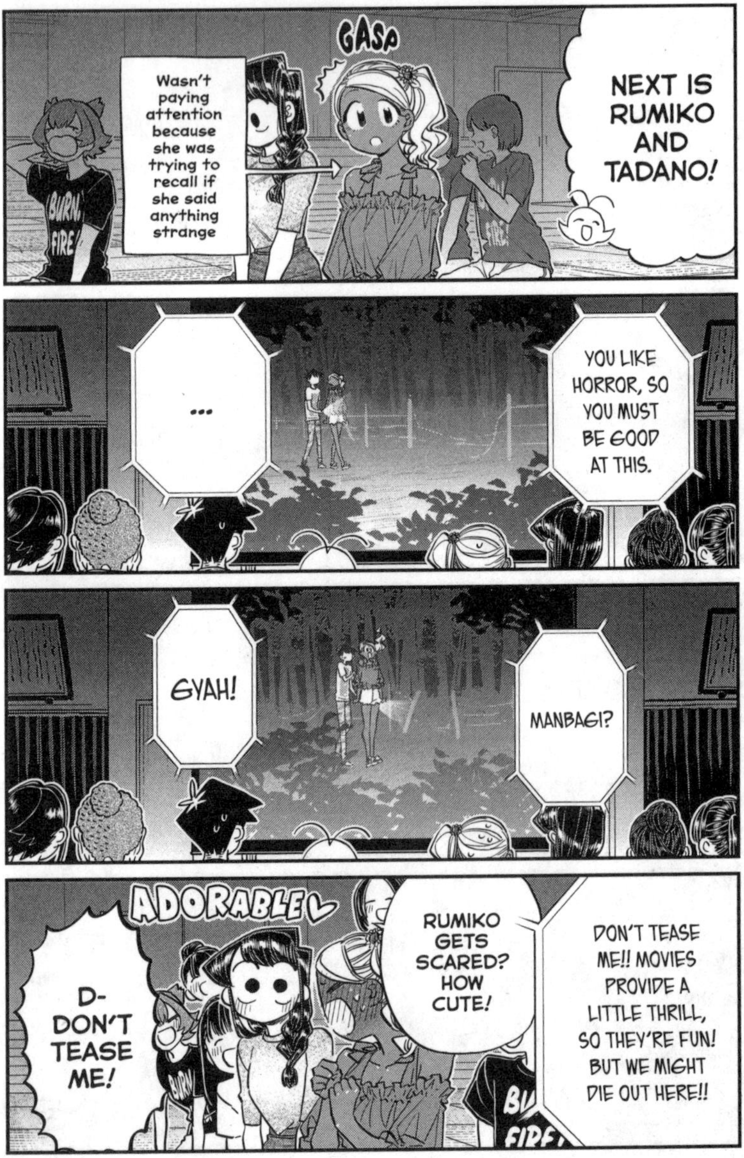
NEXT IS RUMIKO AND TADANO!
GASP
Wasn't paying attention because she was trying to recall if she said anything strange
YOU LIKE HORROR, SO YOU MUST BE GOOD AT THIS.
...
MANBAGI?
GYAH!
DON'T TEASE ME!! MOVIES PROVIDE A LITTLE THRILL, SO THEY'RE FUN! BUT WE MIGHT DIE OUT HERE!!
RUMIKO GETS SCARED? HOW CUTE!
ADORABLE♥
D-DON'T TEASE ME!

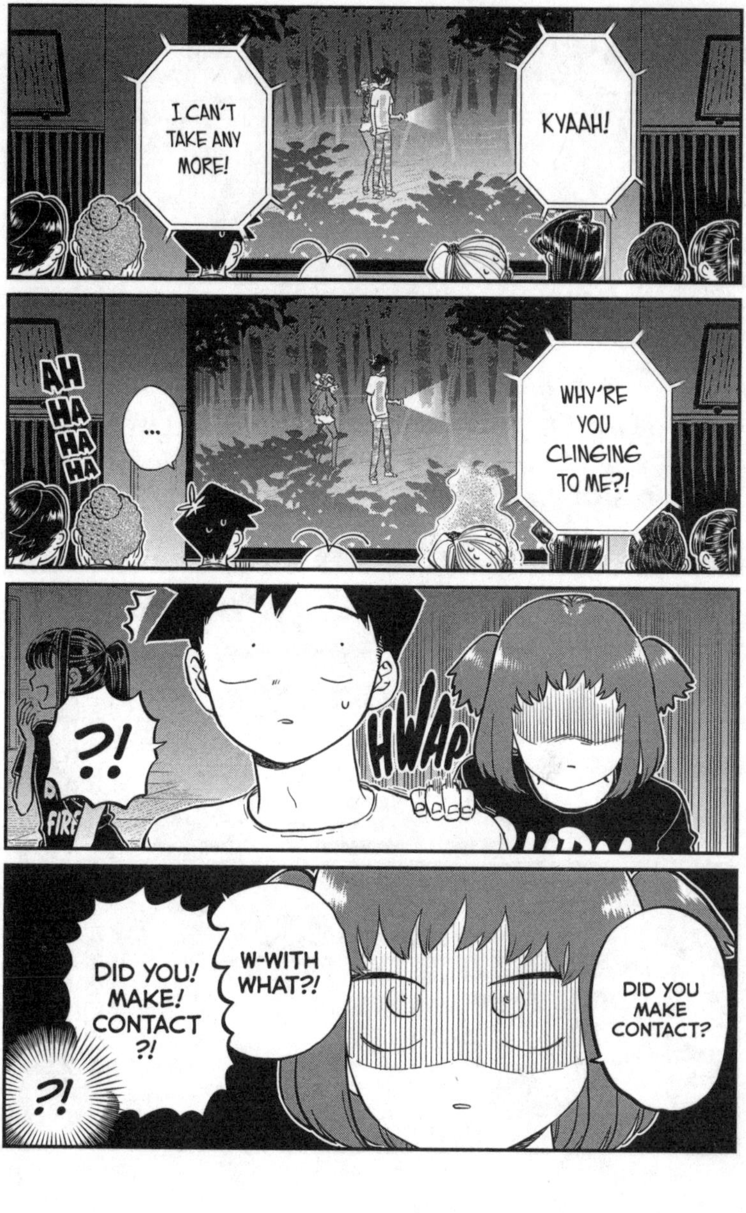
KYAAH!
I CAN'T TAKE ANY MORE!
WHY'RE YOU CLINGING TO ME?!
...
AH HA HA HA HA
HWAP
?!
DID YOU MAKE CONTACT?
W-WITH WHAT?!
DID YOU! MAKE! CONTACT ?!
?!

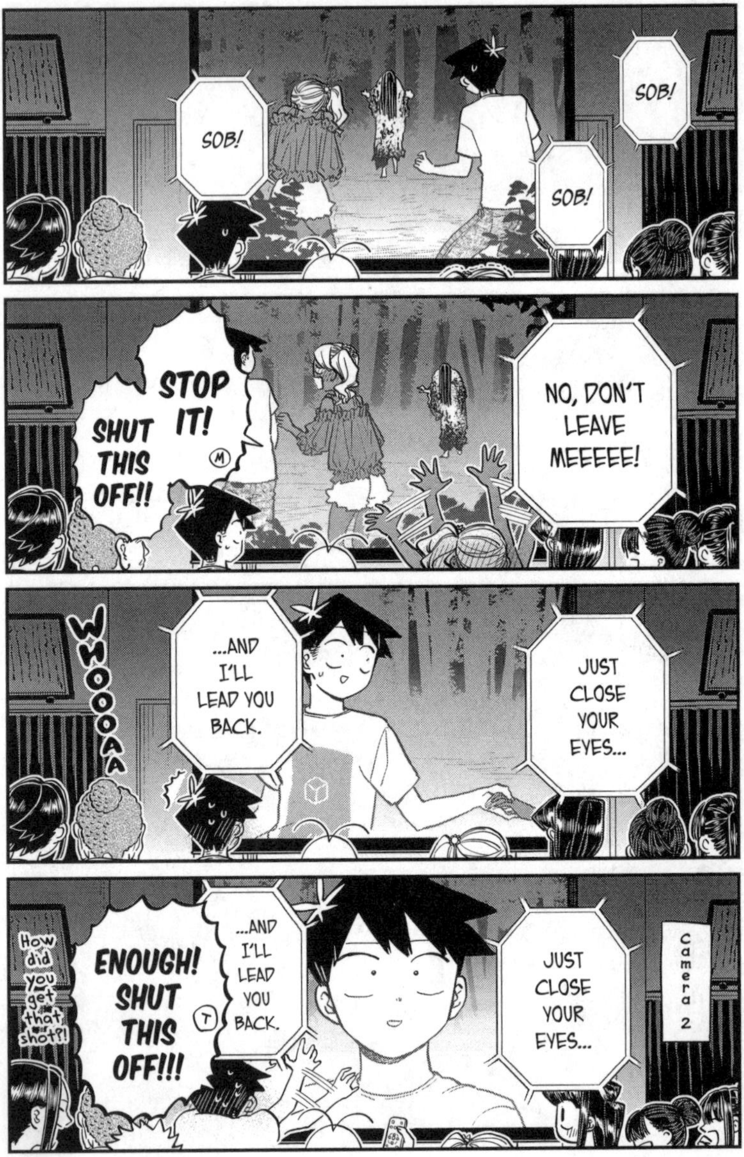
SOB!
SOB!
SOB!
NO, DON'T LEAVE MEEEEE!
STOP IT!
SHUT THIS OFF!!
JUST CLOSE YOUR EYES...
...AND I'LL LEAD YOU BACK.
WHOOOOAA
Camera 2
JUST CLOSE YOUR EYES...
...AND I'LL LEAD YOU BACK.
ENOUGH! SHUT THIS OFF!!!
How did you get that shot?!

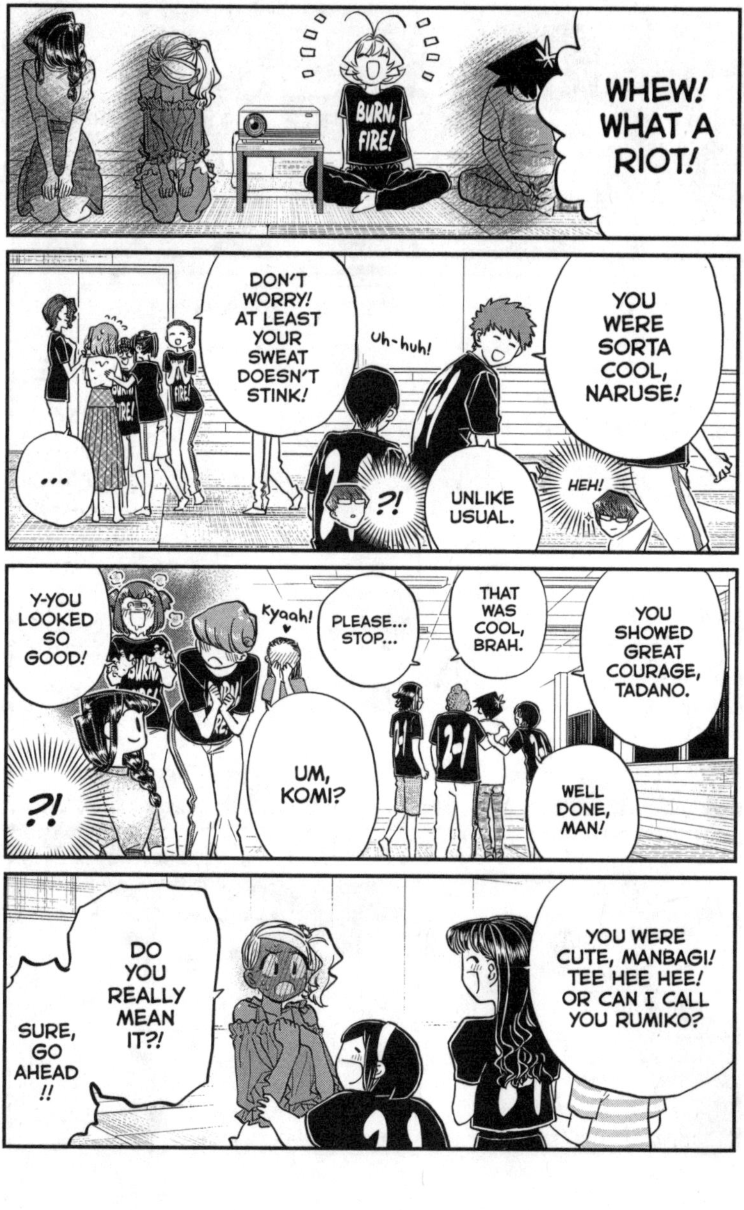
WHEW! WHAT A RIOT!
YOU WERE SORTA COOL, NARUSE!
HEH!
UNLIKE USUAL.
?!
Uh-huh!
DON'T WORRY! AT LEAST YOUR SWEAT DOESN'T STINK!
...
YOU SHOWED GREAT COURAGE, TADANO.
WELL DONE, MAN!
THAT WAS COOL, BRAH.
PLEASE... STOP...
Kyaah!
UM, KOMI?
Y-YOU LOOKED SO GOOD!
?!
YOU WERE CUTE, MANBAGI! TEE HEE HEE! OR CAN I CALL YOU RUMIKO?
DO YOU REALLY MEAN IT?!
SURE, GO AHEAD!!

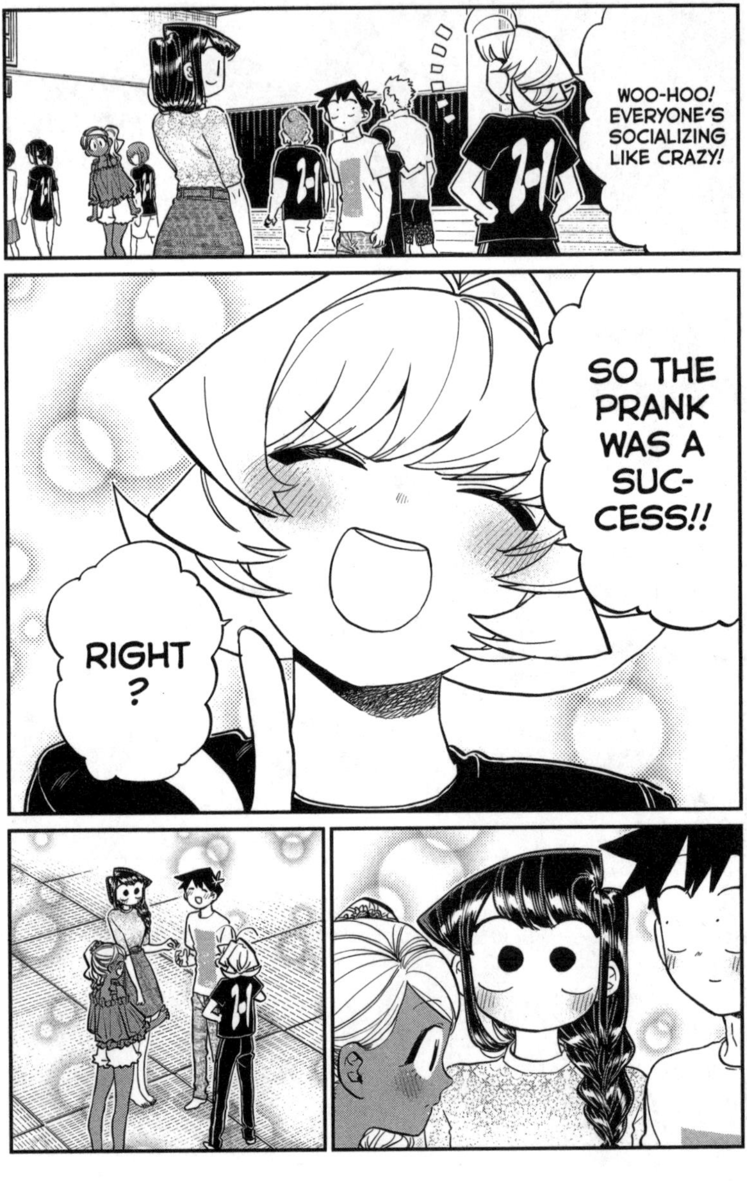
WOO-HOO! EVERYONE'S SOCIALIZING LIKE CRAZY!
SO THE PRANK WAS A SUC-CESS!!
RIGHT ?

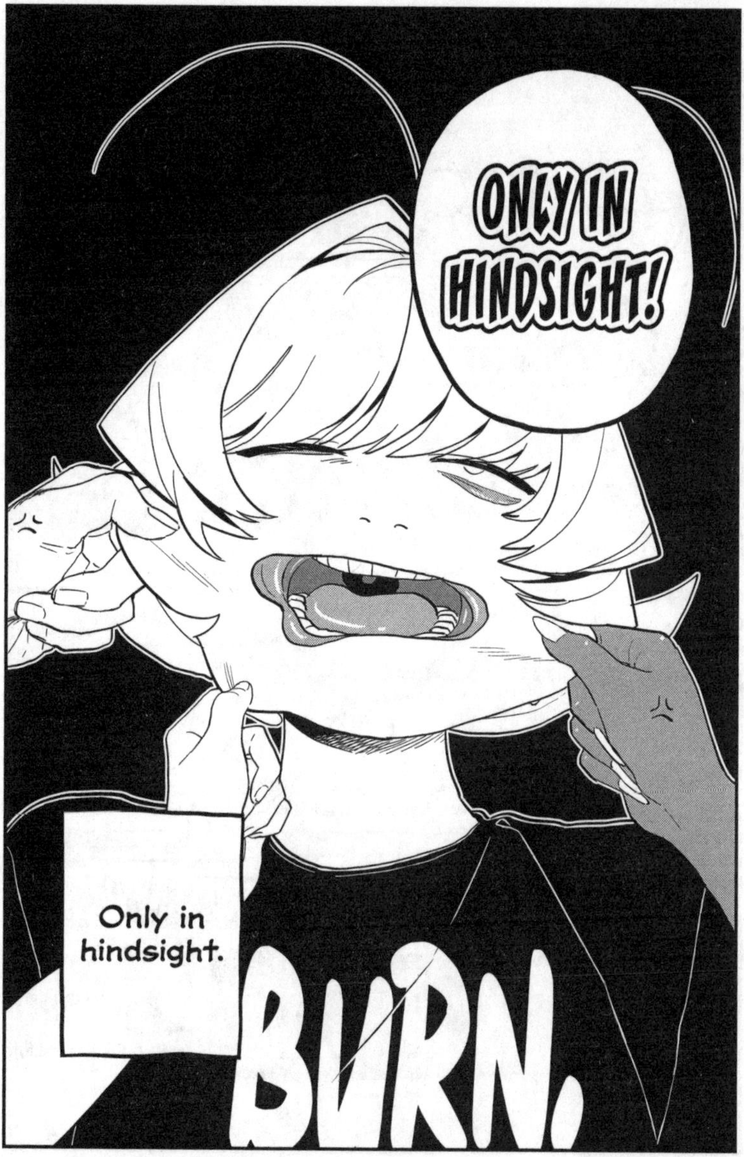
ONLY IN HINDSIGHT!
Only in hindsight.
BURN.

Communication 189 — The End

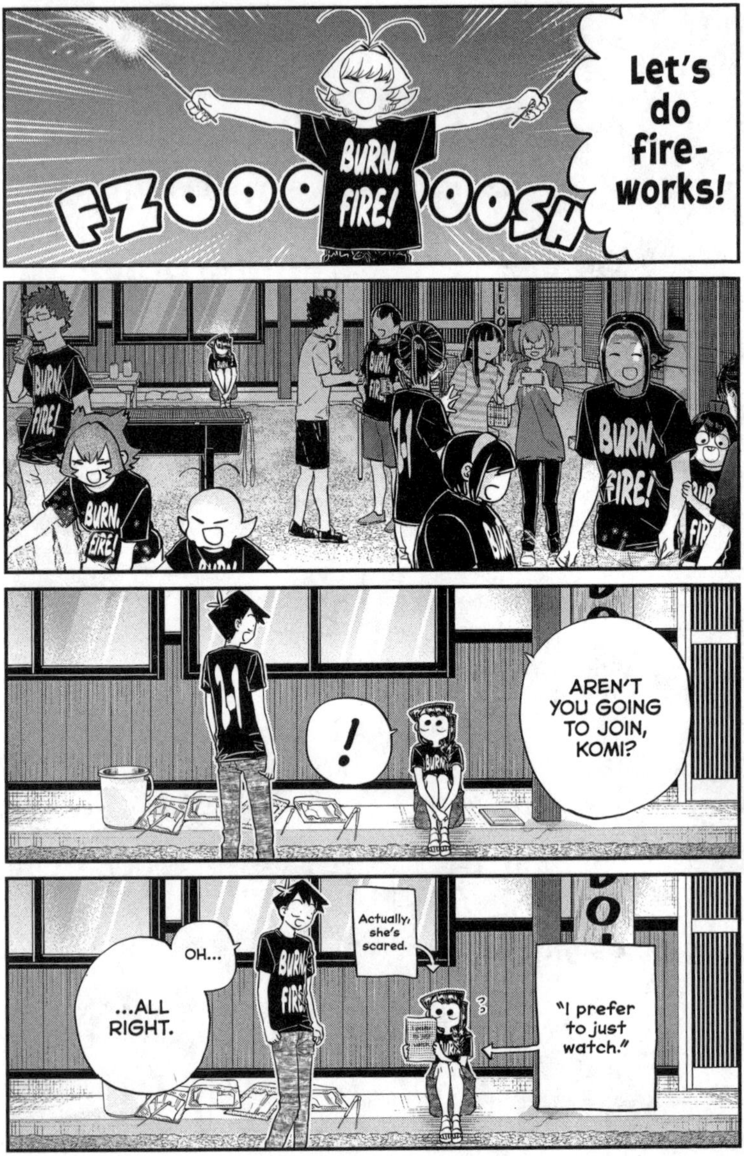
Let's do fire-works!
FZOOO OOSH
BURN, FIRE!
AREN'T YOU GOING TO JOIN, KOMI?
!
"I prefer to just watch."
Actually, she's scared.
OH...
...ALL RIGHT.

Communication 190: Sparklers

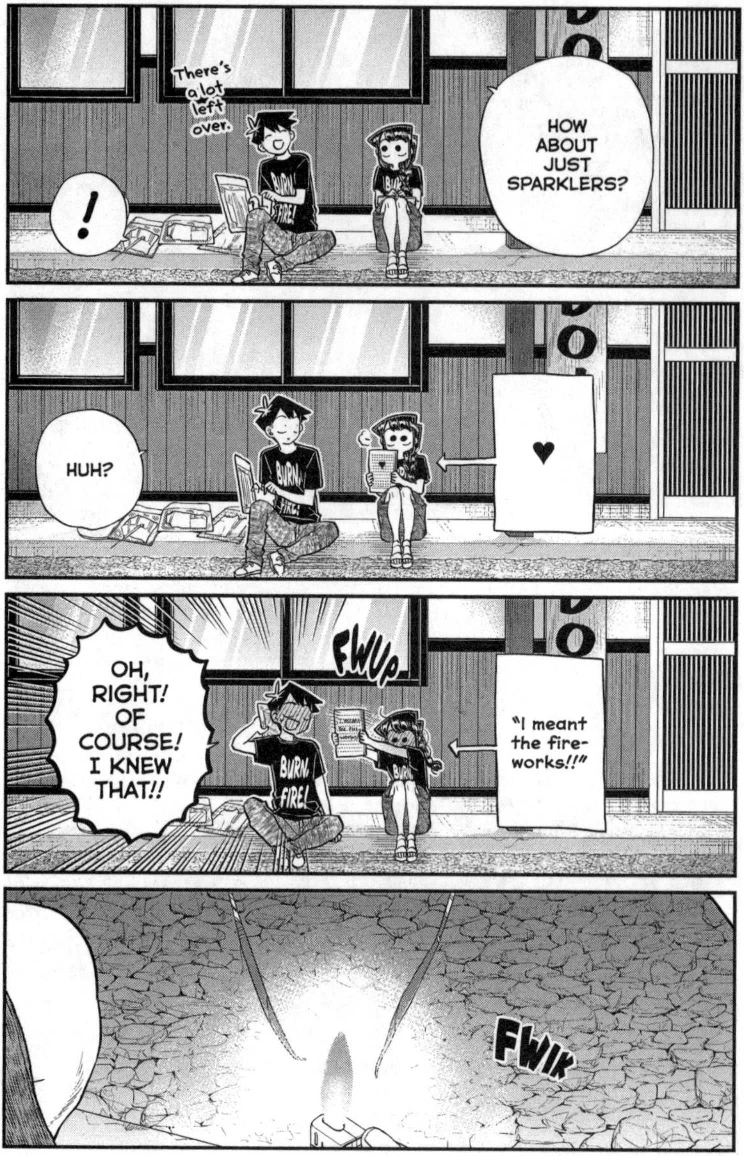
HOW ABOUT JUST SPARKLERS?
There's a lot left over.
!
♥
HUH?
"I meant the fire-works!!"
FWUP
OH, RIGHT! OF COURSE! I KNEW THAT!!
FWIK

THOSE TWO ARE SO CLOSE!!

Communication 190 — The End

Komi Can't Communicate

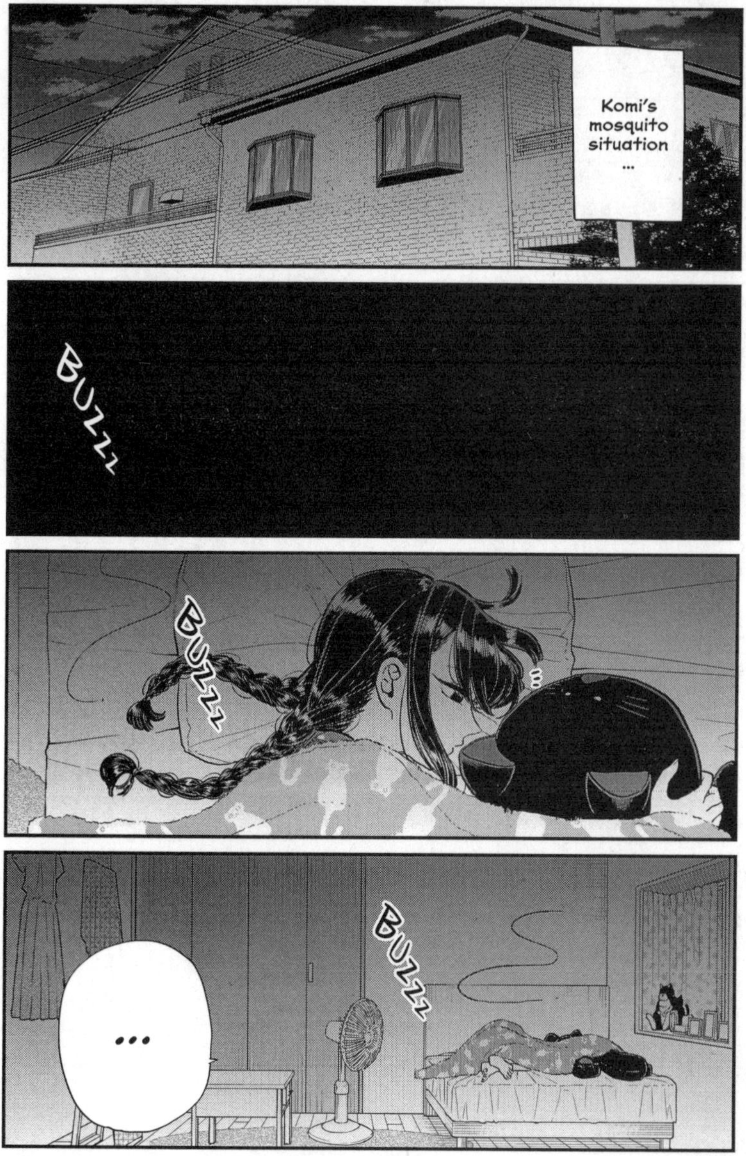
Komi's mosquito situation ...
BUZZZ
BUZZZ
BUZZZ
...

Communication 191: Mosquitoes

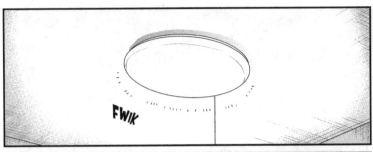

FWIK

Vapo (electric mosquito repellant)

KTUNK

...

GLANCE GLANCE

GASP

!!

Buzzzzzz

NOD NOD

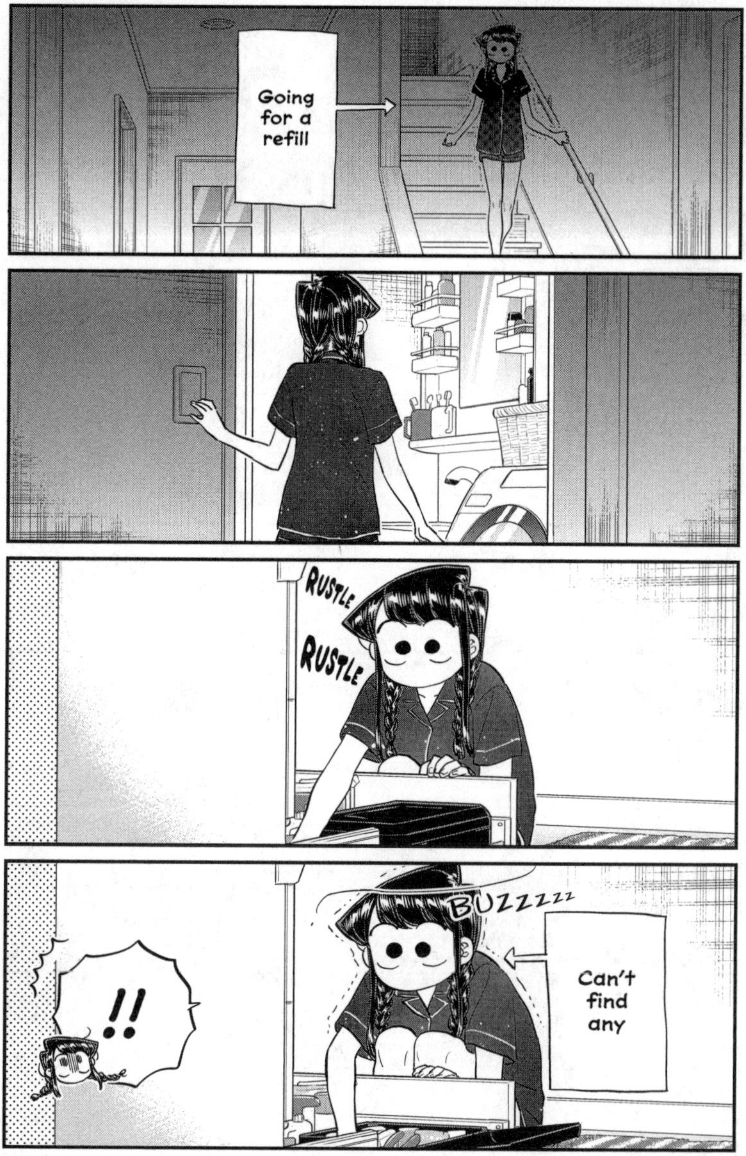
Going for a refill
RUSTLE
RUSTLE
Can't find any
BUZZzzz
!!

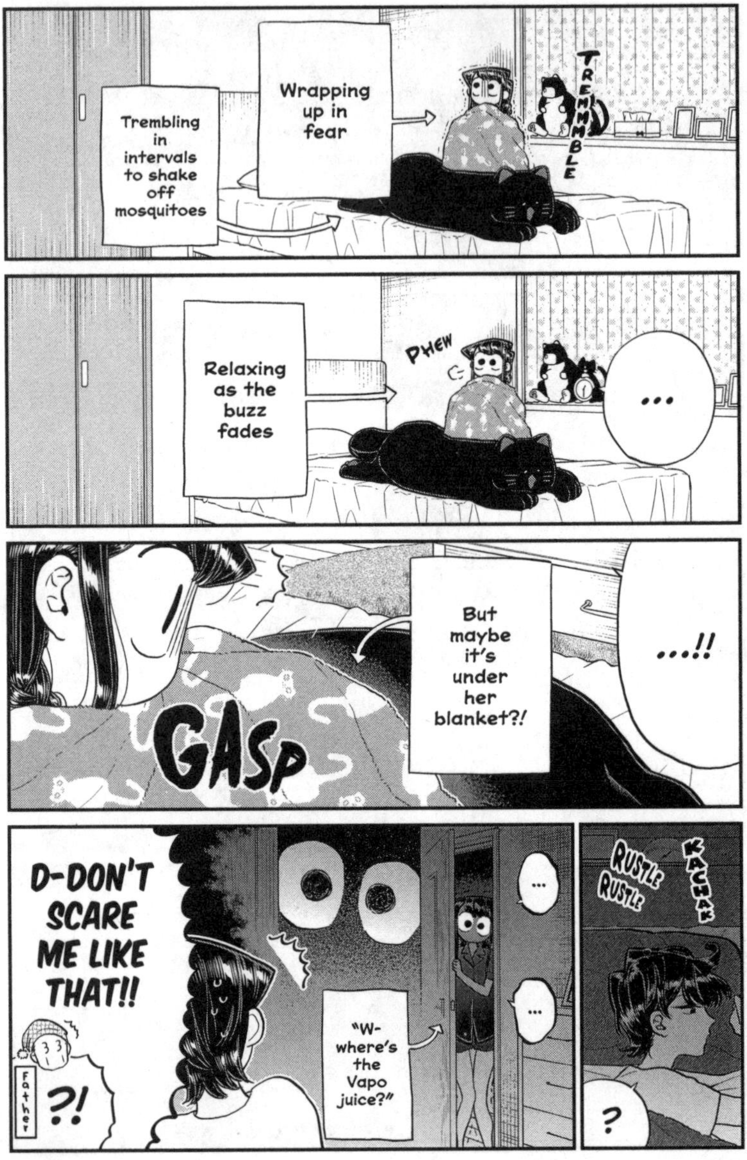
TREMMMBLE
Wrapping up in fear
Trembling in intervals to shake off mosquitoes
...
PHEW
Relaxing as the buzz fades
...!!
But maybe it's under her blanket?!
GASP
KACHAK
RUSTLE RUSTLE
?
...
...
"W-where's the Vapo juice?"
D-DON'T SCARE ME LIKE THAT!!
?!
Father

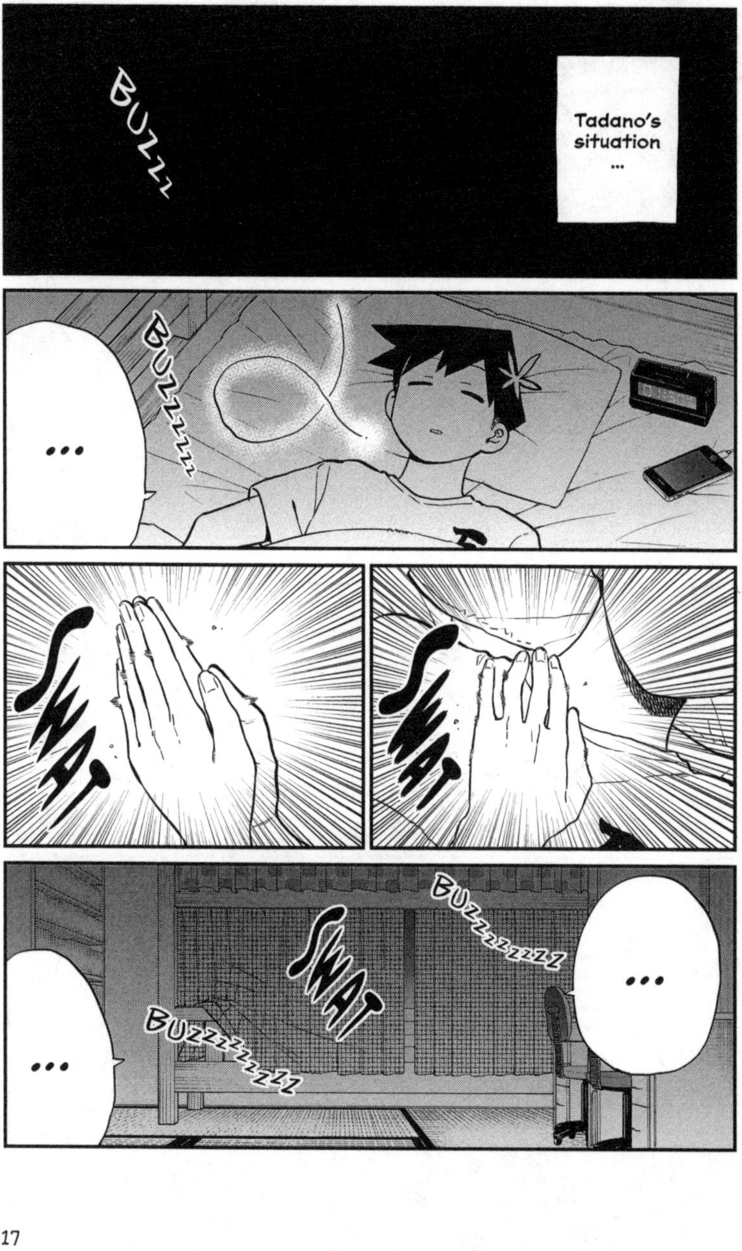
Tadano's situation
...
BUZZZ
BUZZZZZZZ
...
SWAT
SWAT
...
BUZZZZZZZZZ
SWAT
BUZZZZZZZZZ
...

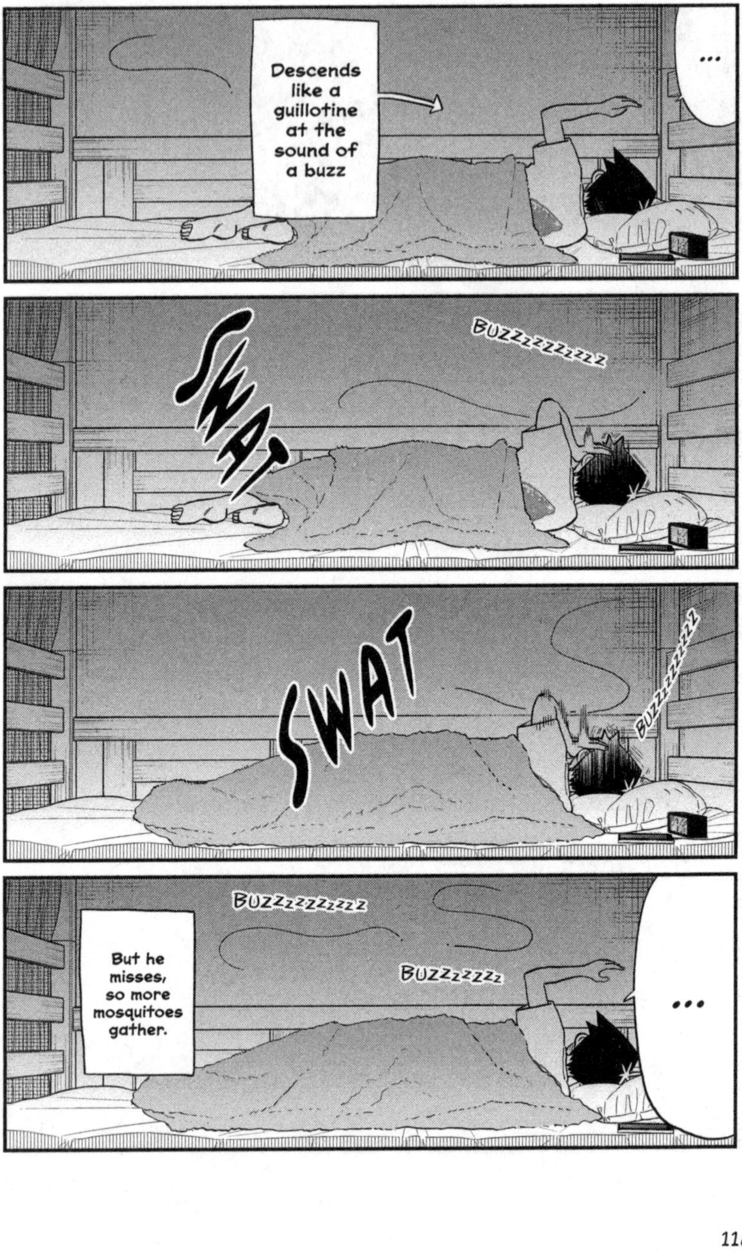
...
Descends like a guillotine at the sound of a buzz
BUZZzzzzzzzz
SWAT
BUZZzzzzzzzz
SWAT
...
BUZZzzzzzzzz
BUZZzzzz
But he misses, so more mosquitoes gather.

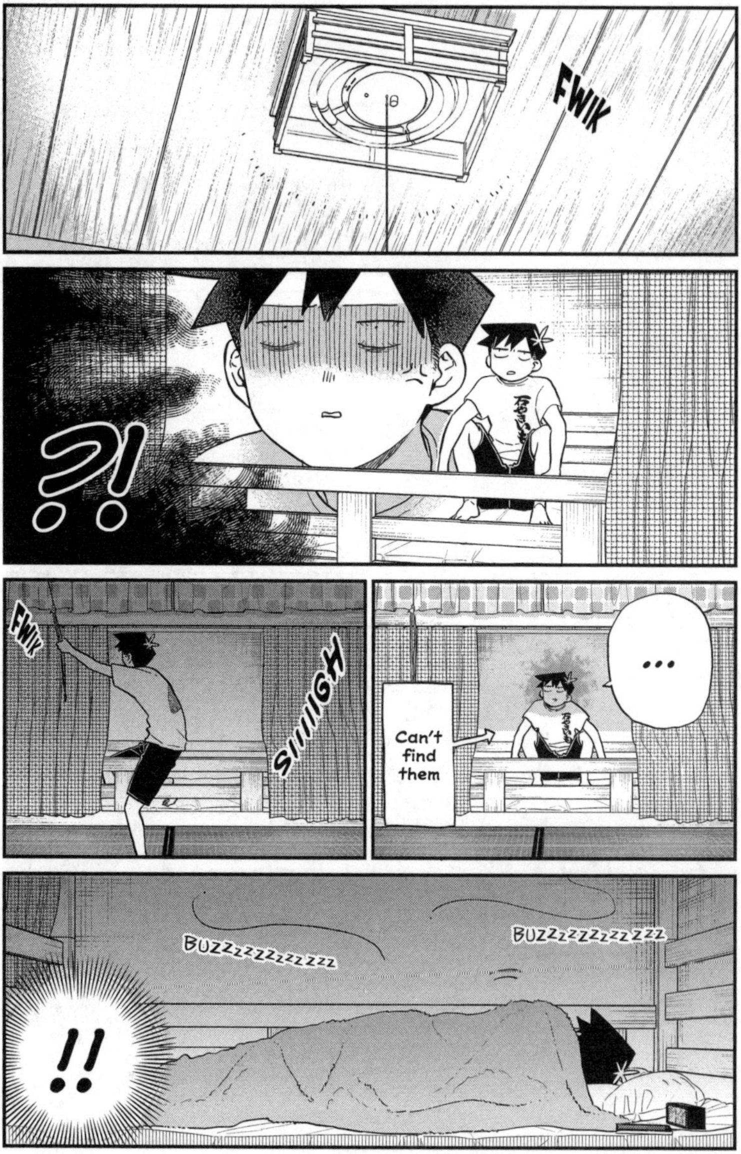
FWIK
?!
...
Can't find them
SIIIIGH
FWIK
BUZZzzzzzzzzzz
BUZZzzzzzzzzzz
!!

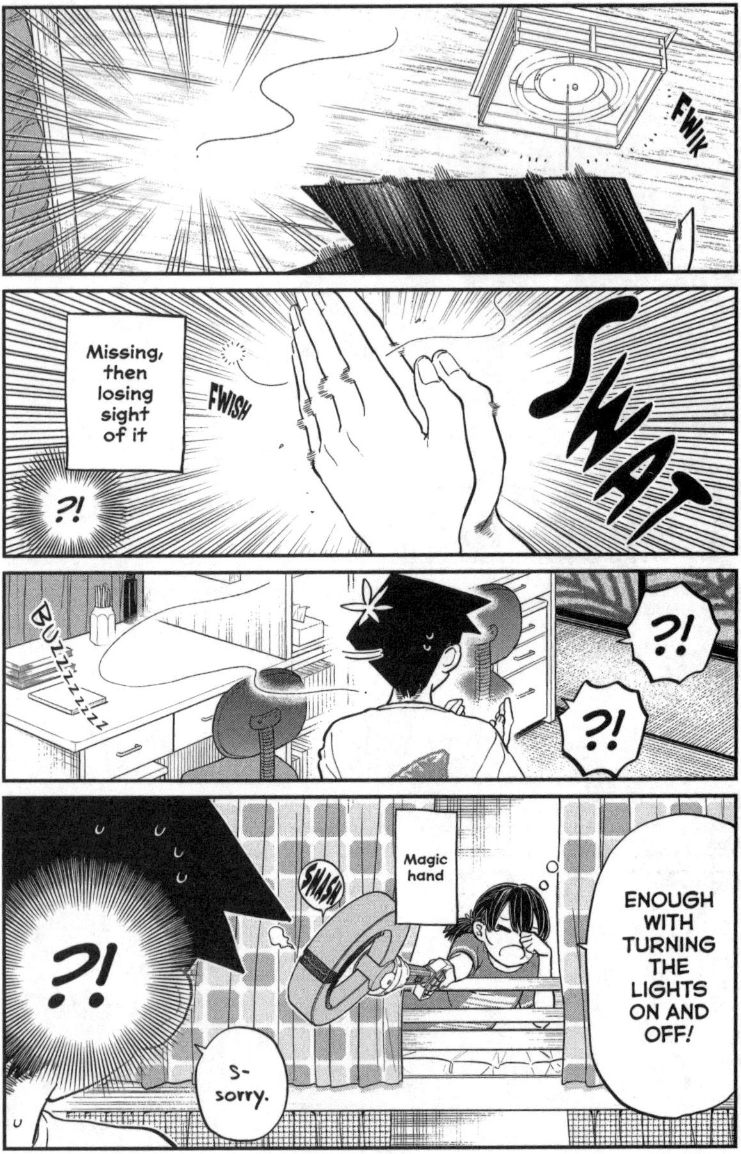
FWIK
SWAT
Missing, then losing sight of it
FWISH
?!
?!
?!
BUZZZZZZZ
ENOUGH WITH TURNING THE LIGHTS ON AND OFF!
Magic hand
SMASH
?!
S-sorry.

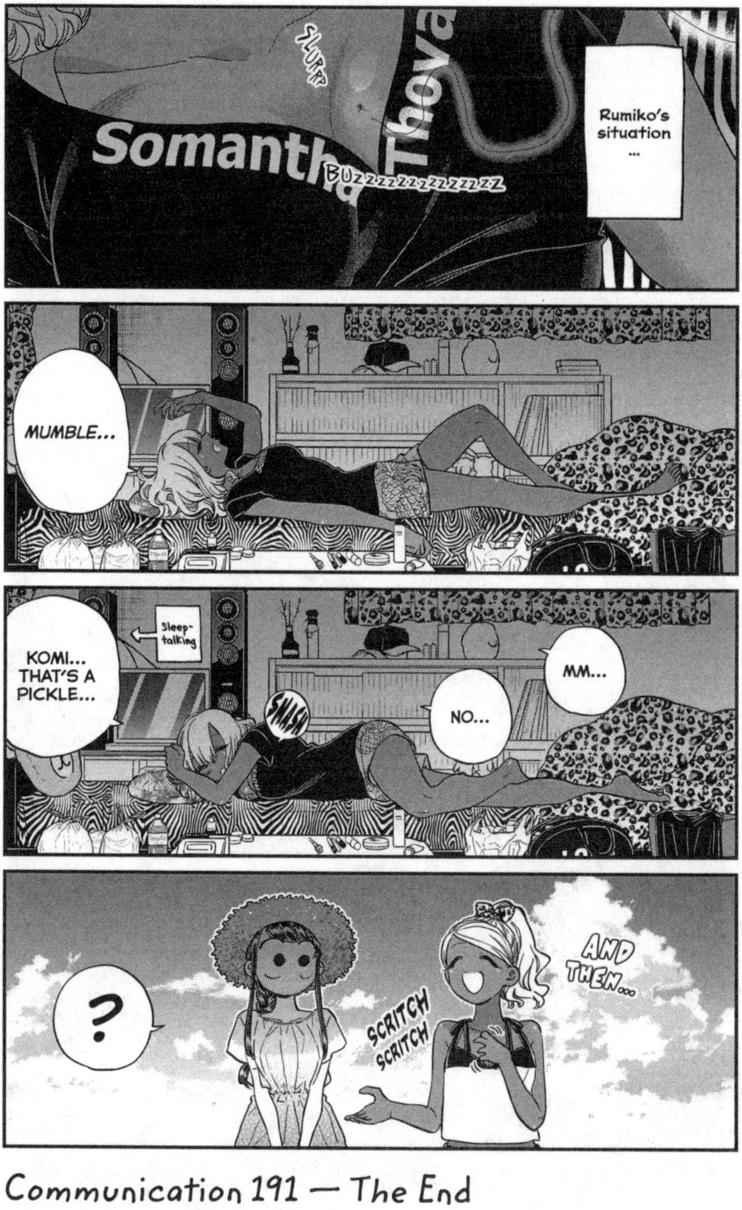
Rumiko's situation ...
SLURP
Somantha Thoya
BUZZZZZZZZZZZZZZ
MUMBLE...
MM...
NO...
SMASH
Sleep-talking
KOMI... THAT'S A PICKLE...
AND THEN...
SCRITCH SCRITCH
?

Communication 191 — The End

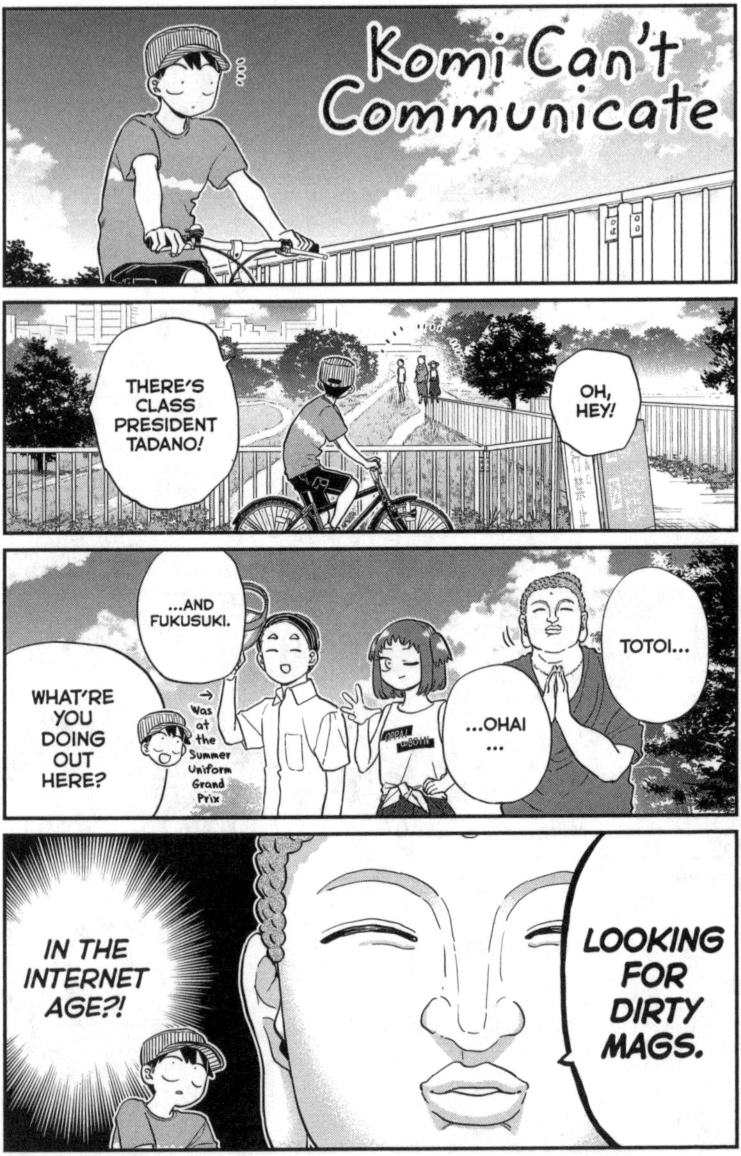
Komi Can't Communicate
OH, HEY!
THERE'S CLASS PRESIDENT TADANO!
TOTOI...
...OHAI ...
...AND FUKUSUKI.
WHAT'RE YOU DOING OUT HERE?
→ Was at the Summer Uniform Grand Prix
LOOKING FOR DIRTY MAGS.
IN THE INTERNET AGE?!

Communication 192: The Riverside Magazine Hunters Club

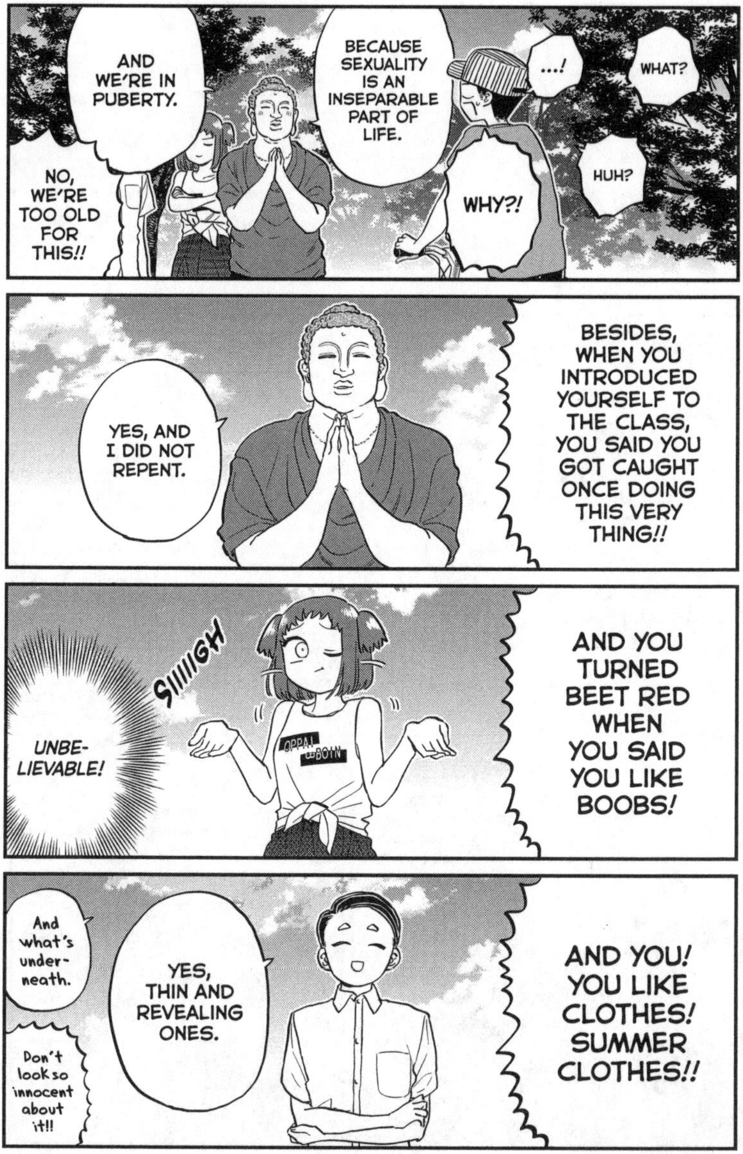
WHAT?
...!
HUH?
WHY?!
BECAUSE SEXUALITY IS AN INSEPARABLE PART OF LIFE.
AND WE'RE IN PUBERTY.
NO, WE'RE TOO OLD FOR THIS!!
BESIDES, WHEN YOU INTRODUCED YOURSELF TO THE CLASS, YOU SAID YOU GOT CAUGHT ONCE DOING THIS VERY THING!!
YES, AND I DID NOT REPENT.
AND YOU TURNED BEET RED WHEN YOU SAID YOU LIKE BOOBS!
SIIIIIGH
OPPAI
BOIN
UNBE-LIEVABLE!
AND YOU! YOU LIKE CLOTHES! SUMMER CLOTHES!!
YES, THIN AND REVEALING ONES.
And what's under-neath.
Don't look so innocent about it!!

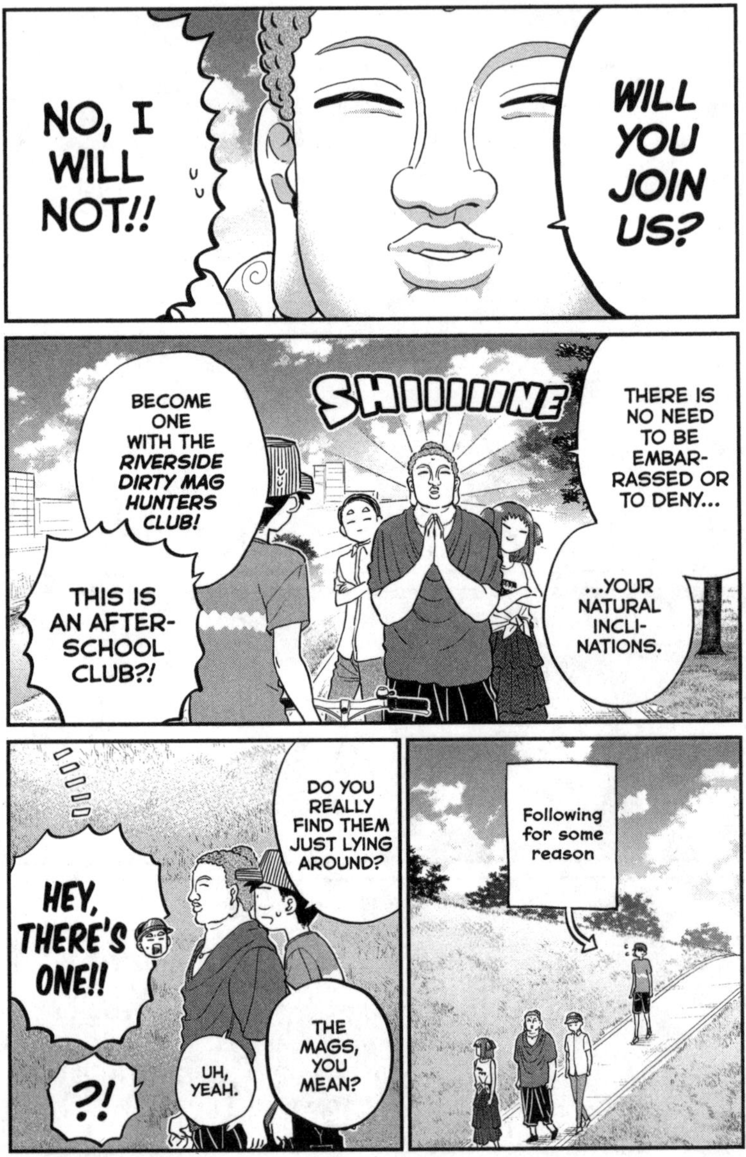
WILL YOU JOIN US?
NO, I WILL NOT!!
THERE IS NO NEED TO BE EMBARRASSED OR TO DENY...
...YOUR NATURAL INCLINATIONS.
SHIIIIIINE
BECOME ONE WITH THE *RIVERSIDE DIRTY MAG HUNTERS CLUB!*
THIS IS AN AFTER-SCHOOL CLUB?!
Following for some reason
DO YOU REALLY FIND THEM JUST LYING AROUND?
THE MAGS, YOU MEAN?
UH, YEAH.
HEY, THERE'S ONE!!
?!

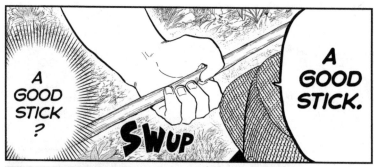

A GOOD STICK.
A GOOD STICK ?
SWUP
They equipped them-selves.
IS THIS SOMETHING HIGH SCHOOLERS DO?
YOU ASKED ME IF DIRTY MAGS ...
...ARE FOUND JUST LYING AROUND.
YEAH, AND?
SIMPLY DISCARDING DIRTY MAGS IS NOT ENCOUR-AGED...
... BECAUSE THAT'S LIT-TERING.
SOME FIND THEM OFFENSIVE. AND THEY AREN'T MEANT...
...FOR UNDERAGE INDIVID-UALS.
that girl that time
THUS, WE HAVE A DUTY TO ATTEMPT TO FIND AND RECLAIM THEM...
...TO PROMOTE WORLD PEACE.
ACTUALLY, WE'RE UNDERAGE TOO.

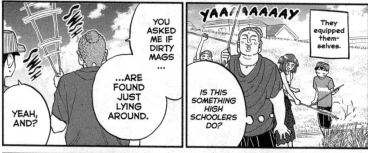

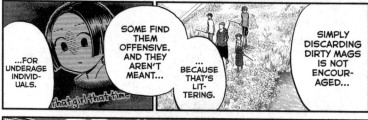

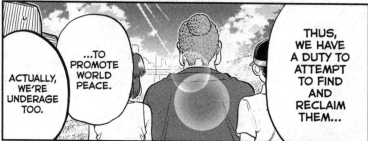

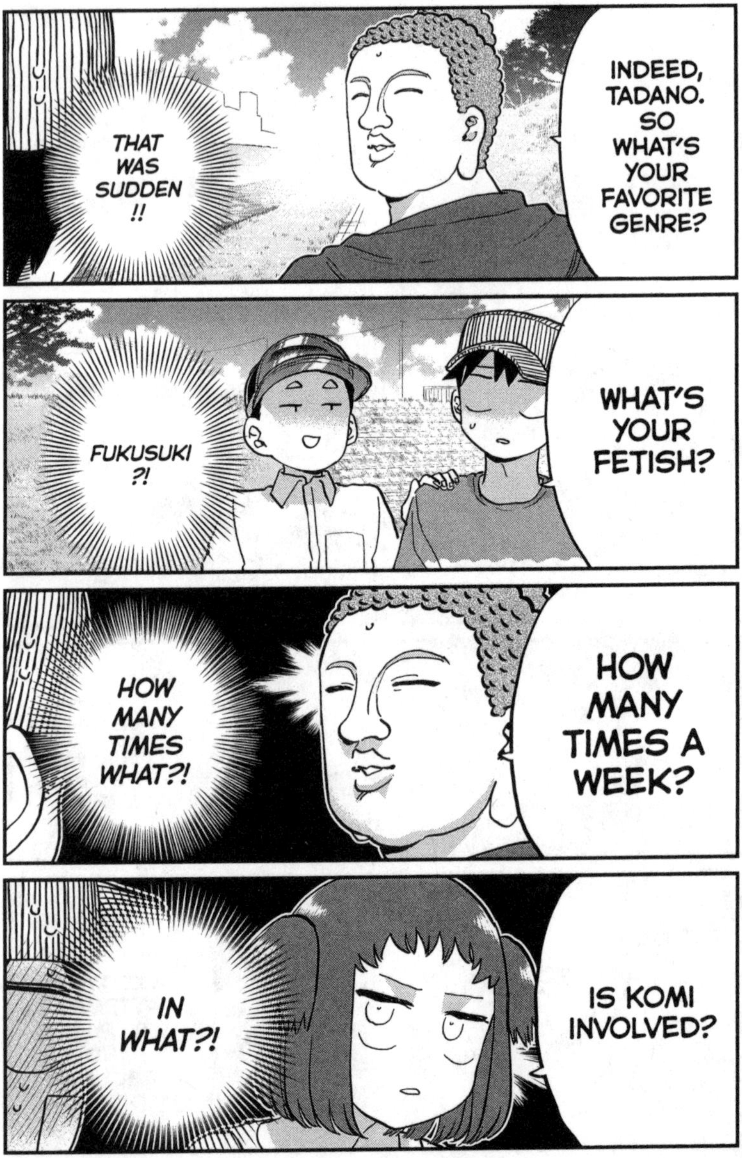
INDEED, TADANO. SO WHAT'S YOUR FAVORITE GENRE?
THAT WAS SUDDEN !!
WHAT'S YOUR FETISH?
FUKUSUKI ?!
HOW MANY TIMES A WEEK?
HOW MANY TIMES WHAT?!
IS KOMI INVOLVED?
IN WHAT?!

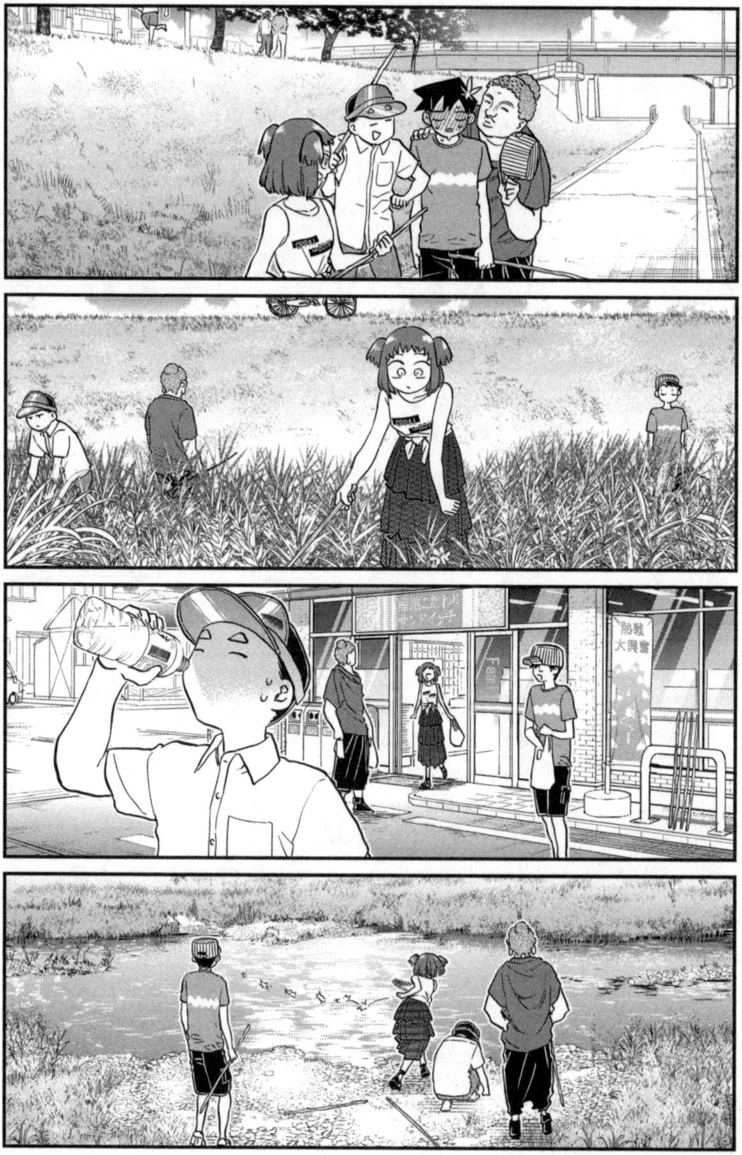

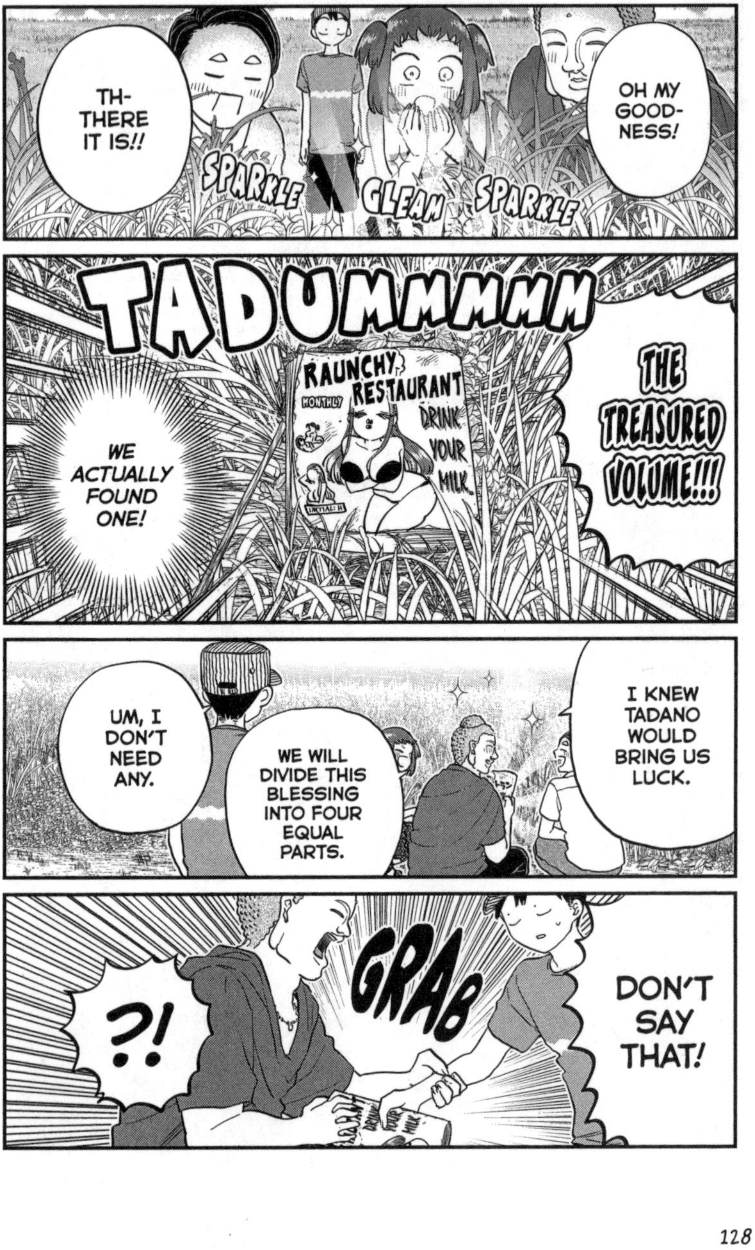
OH MY GOOD-NESS!
TH-THERE IT IS!!
SPARKLE
GLEAM
SPARKLE
TADUMMMMM
THE TREASURED VOLUME!!!
RAUNCHY RESTAURANT
MONTHLY
DRINK YOUR MILK
WE ACTUALLY FOUND ONE!
I KNEW TADANO WOULD BRING US LUCK.
WE WILL DIVIDE THIS BLESSING INTO FOUR EQUAL PARTS.
UM, I DON'T NEED ANY.
DON'T SAY THAT!
GRAB
?!

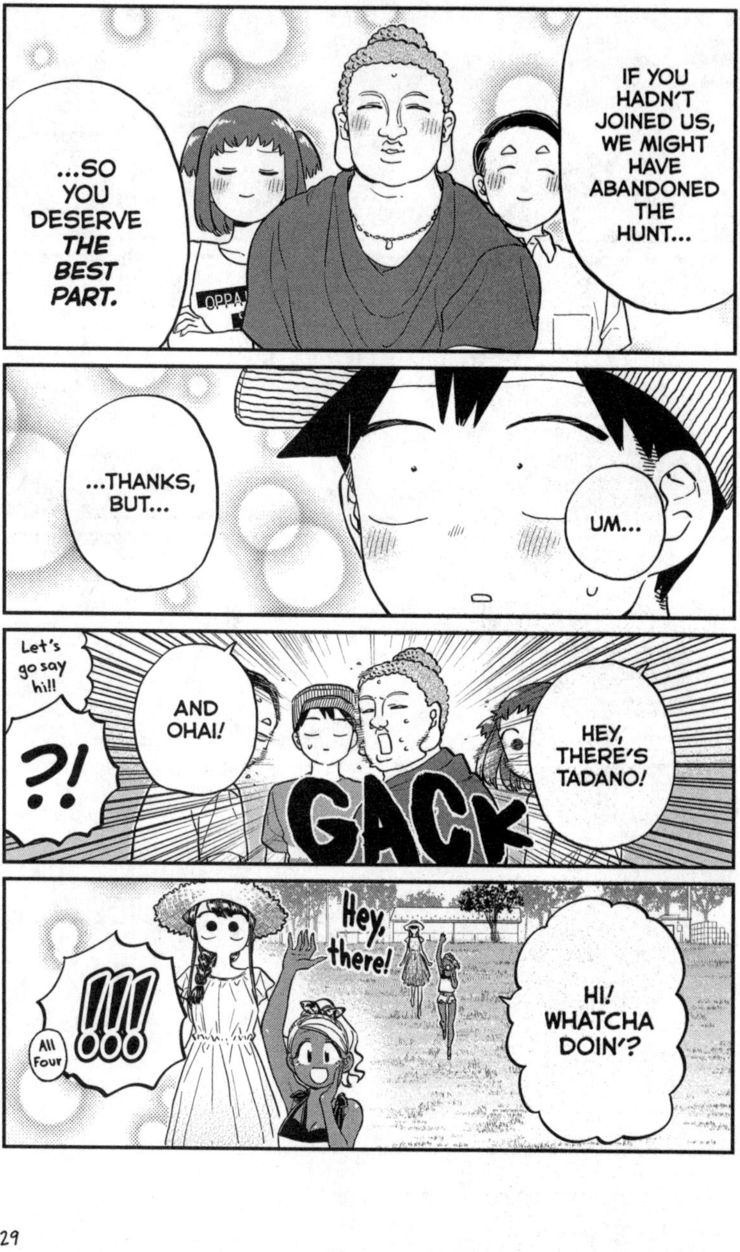
IF YOU HADN'T JOINED US, WE MIGHT HAVE ABANDONED THE HUNT...
...SO YOU DESERVE THE BEST PART.
UM...
...THANKS, BUT...
HEY, THERE'S TADANO!
GACK
AND OHAI!
?!
Let's go say hi!!
HI! WHATCHA DOIN'?
Hey, there!
!!!!
All Four

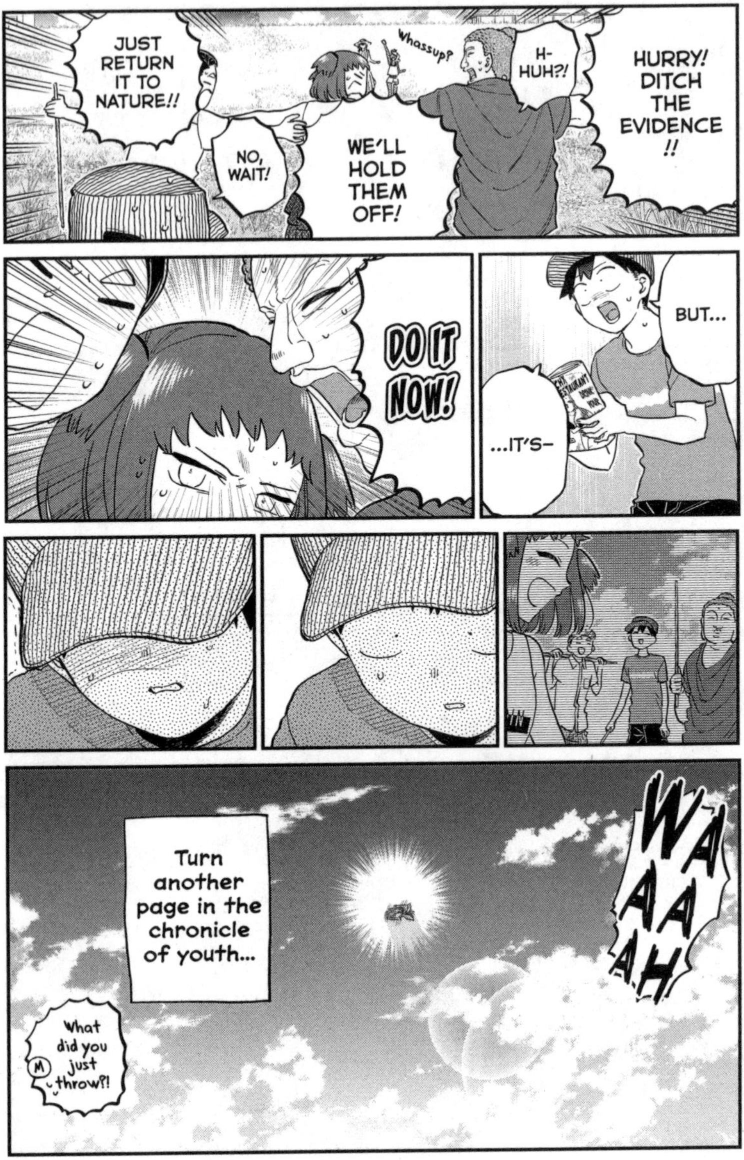
HURRY! DITCH THE EVIDENCE!!
H-HUH?!
Whassup?
WE'LL HOLD THEM OFF!
JUST RETURN IT TO NATURE!!
NO, WAIT!
BUT...
...IT'S—
DO IT NOW!
WAAAAAH
Turn another page in the chronicle of youth...
What did you just throw?!

Communication 192 — The End

Komi Can't Communicate

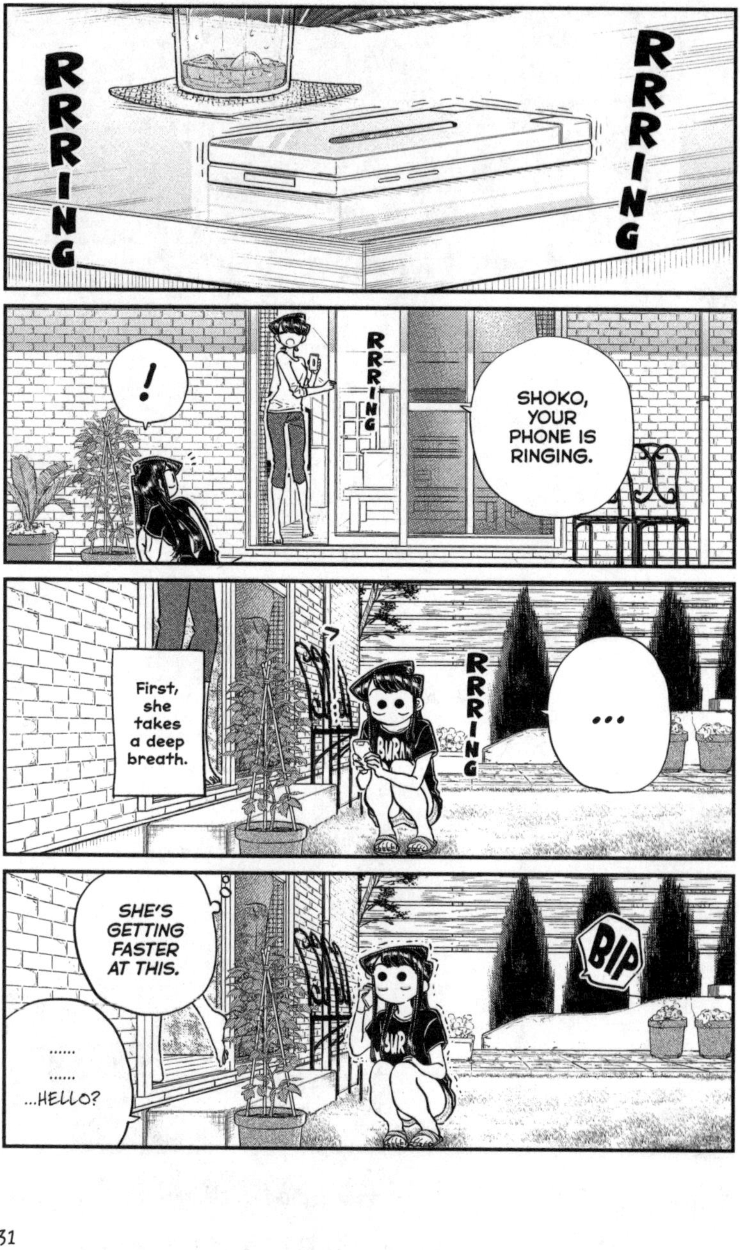
RRRING
RRRING
SHOKO, YOUR PHONE IS RINGING.
RRRING
!
...
RRRING
First, she takes a deep breath.
BIP
SHE'S GETTING FASTER AT THIS.
......
......
...HELLO?

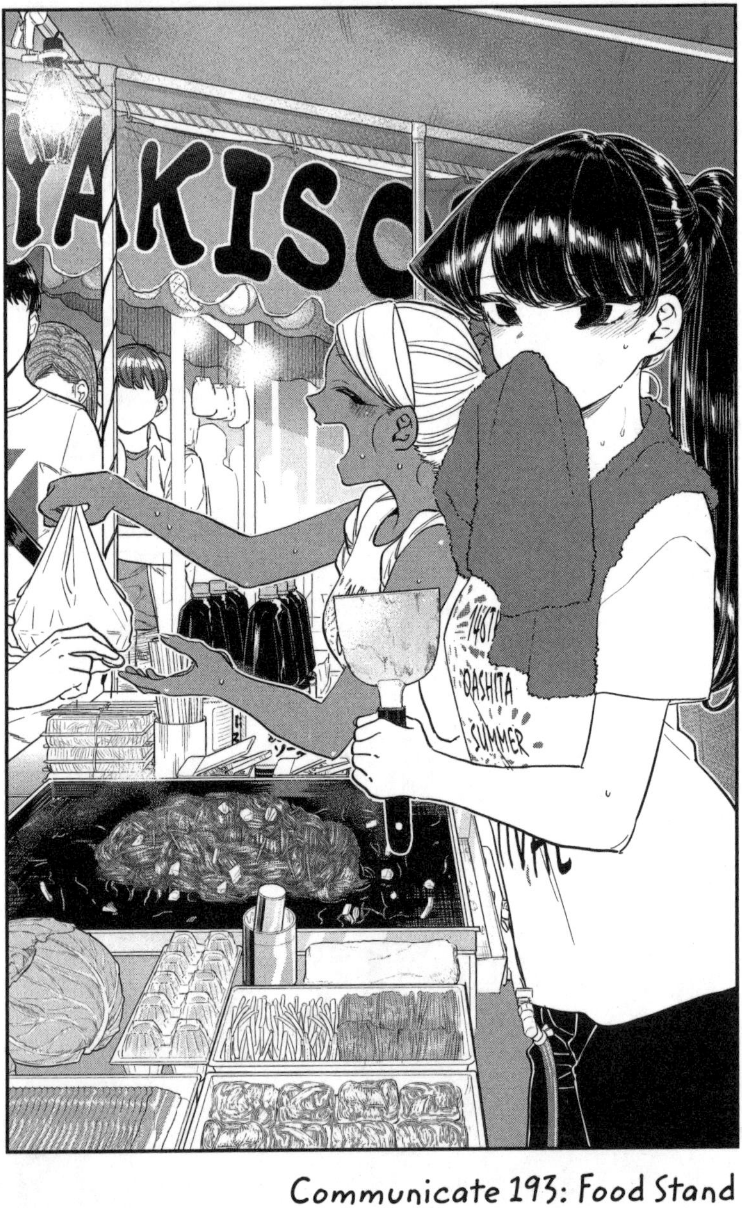
YAKISO
OASHITA
SUMMER

Communicate 193: Food Stand

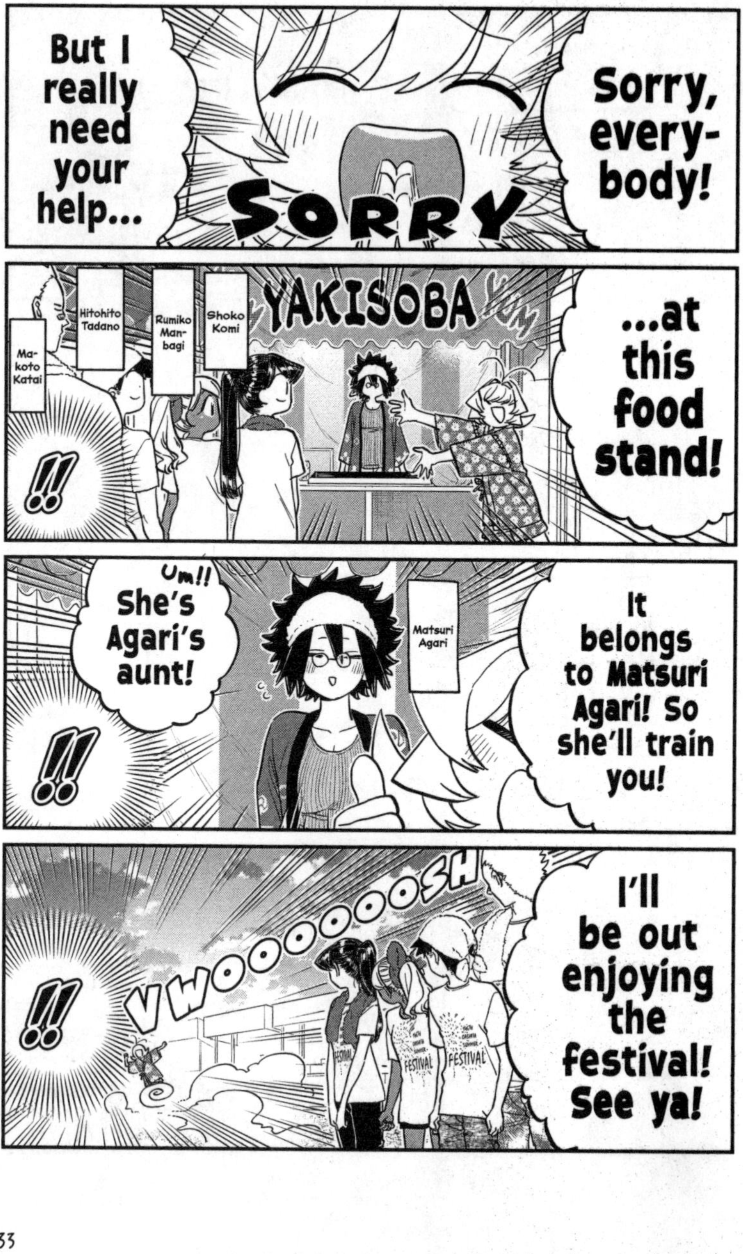

Sorry, every-body!
SORRY
But I really need your help...
...at this food stand!
YAKISOBA
Shoko Komi
Rumiko Man-bagi
Hitohito Tadano
Ma-koto Katai
!!
It belongs to Matsuri Agari! So she'll train you!
Matsuri Agari
Um!!
She's Agari's aunt!
!!
I'll be out enjoying the festival! See ya!
VWOOOOOOOSH
FESTIVAL
FESTIVAL
FESTIVAL
!!

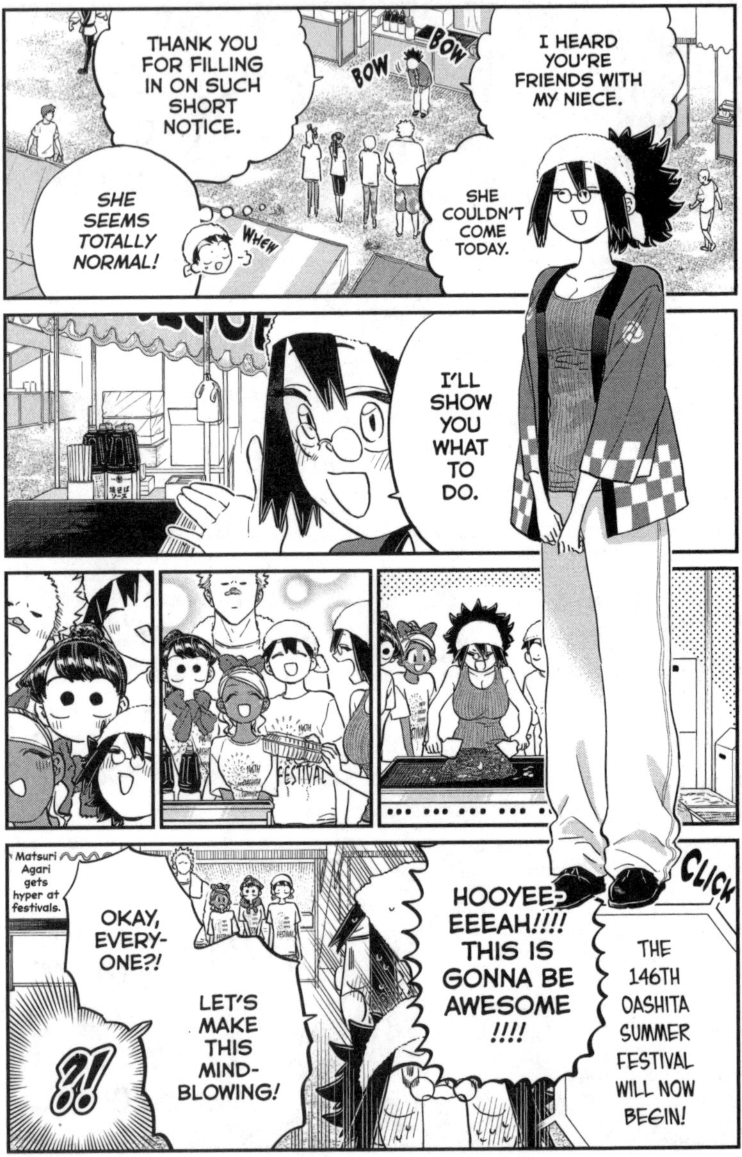
I HEARD YOU'RE FRIENDS WITH MY NIECE.
BOW BOW
THANK YOU FOR FILLING IN ON SUCH SHORT NOTICE.
SHE COULDN'T COME TODAY.
WHEW
SHE SEEMS TOTALLY NORMAL!
I'LL SHOW YOU WHAT TO DO.
THE 146TH OASHITA SUMMER FESTIVAL WILL NOW BEGIN!
CLICK
HOOYEE-EEEAH!!!! THIS IS GONNA BE AWESOME!!!!
OKAY, EVERY-ONE?!
LET'S MAKE THIS MIND-BLOWING!
?!
Matsuri Agari gets hyper at festivals.

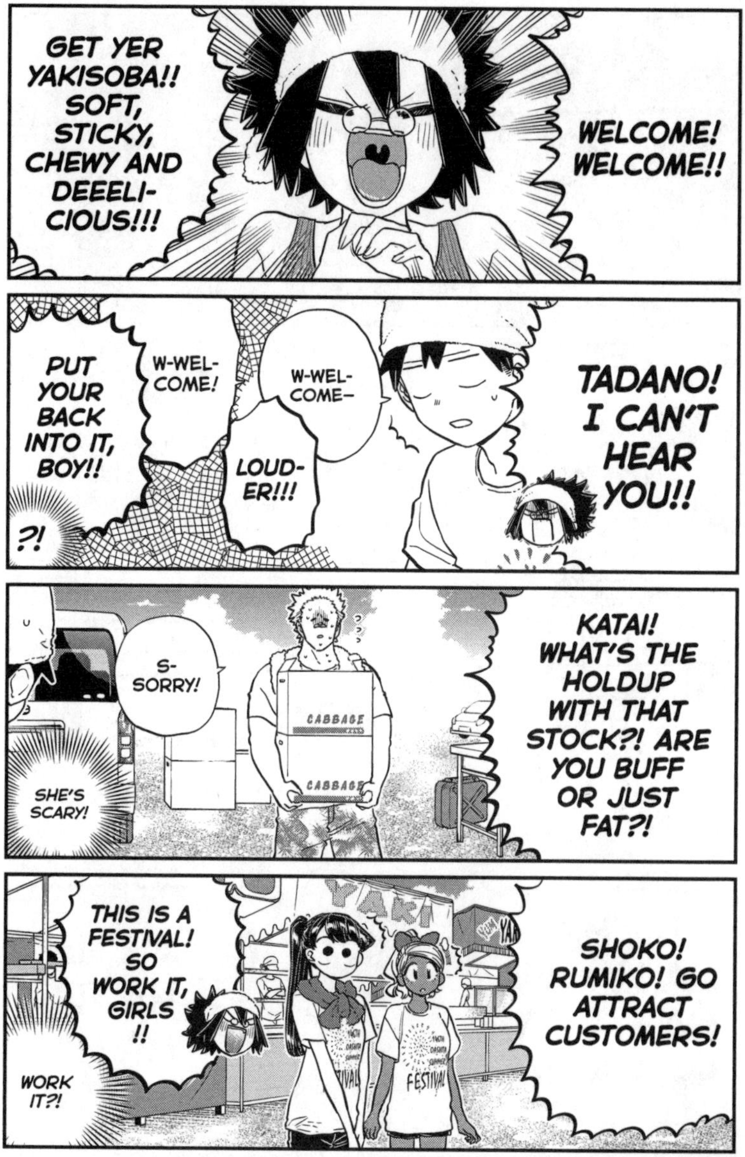
WELCOME! WELCOME!!
GET YER YAKISOBA!! SOFT, STICKY, CHEWY AND DEEELI-CIOUS!!!
TADANO! I CAN'T HEAR YOU!!
W-WEL-COME—
LOUDER!!!
W-WEL-COME!
PUT YOUR BACK INTO IT, BOY!!
?!
KATAI! WHAT'S THE HOLDUP WITH THAT STOCK?! ARE YOU BUFF OR JUST FAT?!
S-SORRY!
CABBAGE
CABBAGE
SHE'S SCARY!
SHOKO! RUMIKO! GO ATTRACT CUSTOMERS!
YAKI
THIS IS A FESTIVAL! SO WORK IT, GIRLS!!
WORK IT?!
FESTIVAL
FESTIVAL

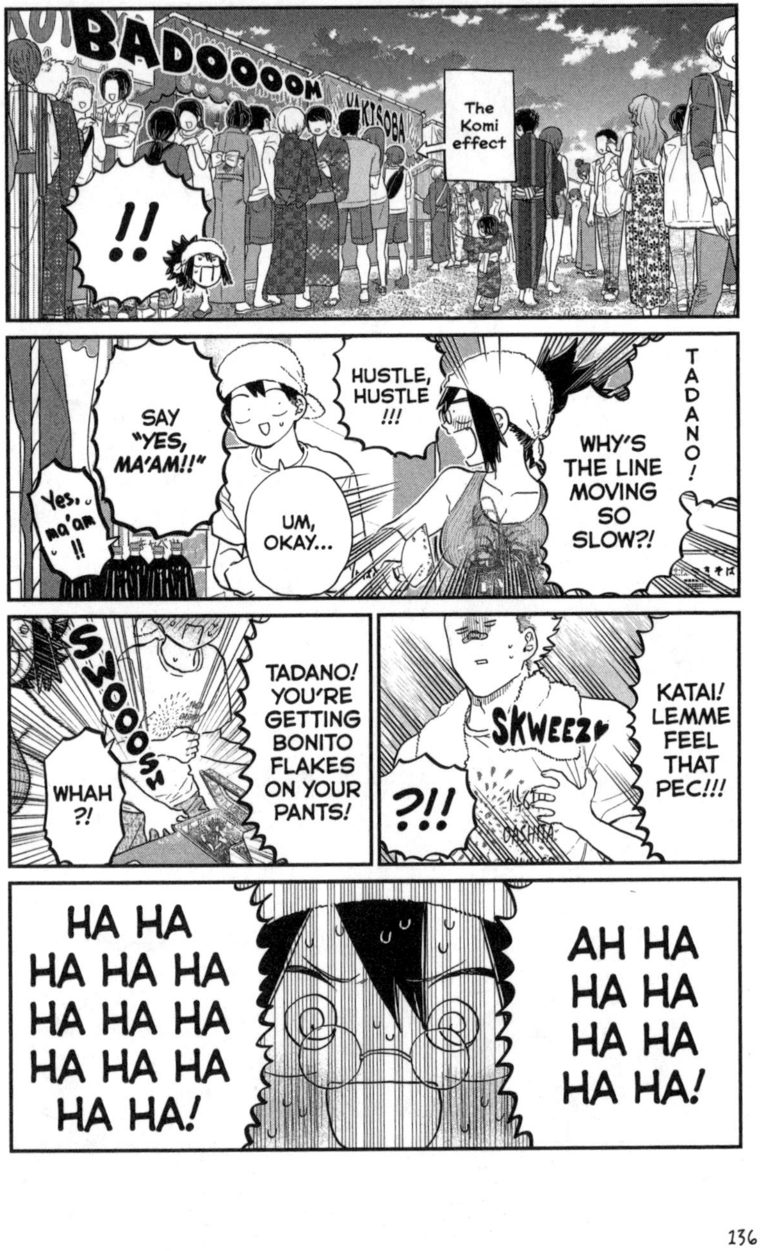

The Komi effect
BADOOOOM
!!
TADANO!
WHY'S THE LINE MOVING SO SLOW?!
HUSTLE, HUSTLE!!!
UM, OKAY...
SAY "YES, MA'AM!!"
Yes, ma'am!!
KATAI! LEMME FEEL THAT PEC!!!
SKWEEZ♥
?!!
TADANO! YOU'RE GETTING BONITO FLAKES ON YOUR PANTS!
SWOOOOSH
WHAH?!
AH HA HA HA HA HA HA HA!
HA HA HA HA HA HA HA HA HA HA HA HA HA!

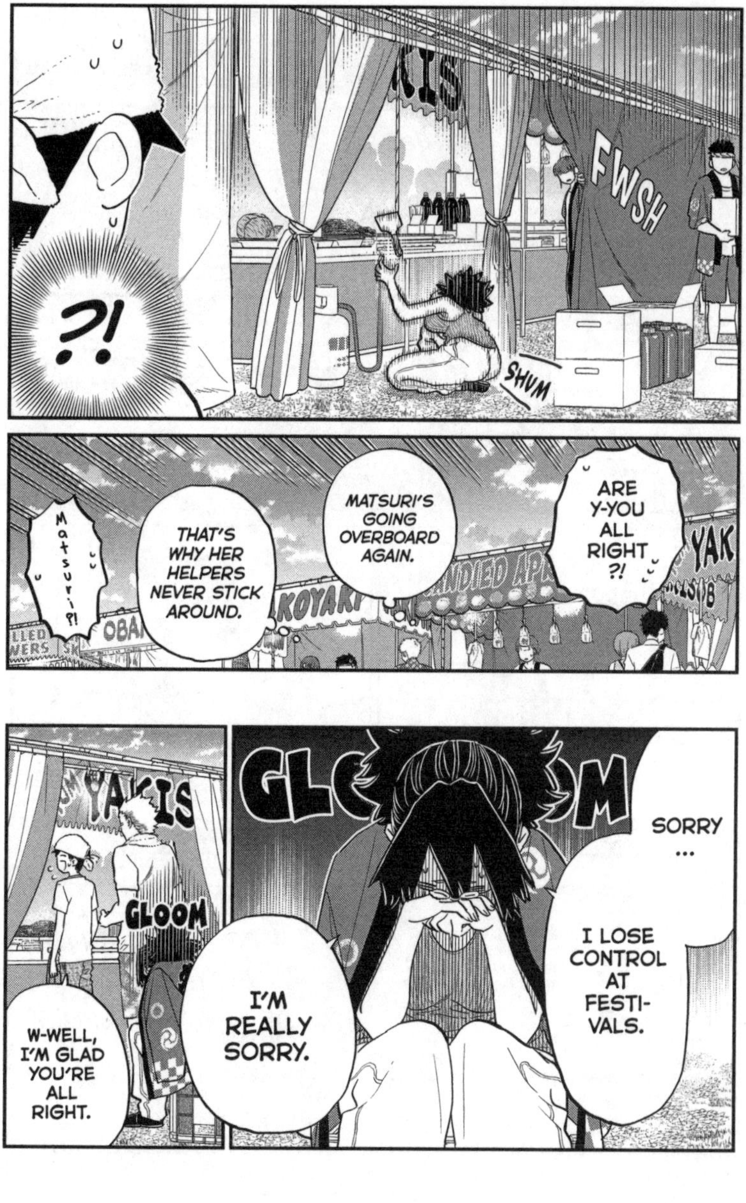
?!
FWSH
SHUM
ARE Y-YOU ALL RIGHT?!
MATSURI'S GOING OVERBOARD AGAIN.
THAT'S WHY HER HELPERS NEVER STICK AROUND.
Matsuri?!
SORRY...
I LOSE CONTROL AT FESTIVALS.
I'M REALLY SORRY.
YAKIS
GLOOM
W-WELL, I'M GLAD YOU'RE ALL RIGHT.

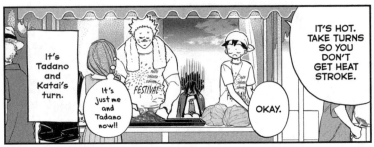

IT'S HOT. TAKE TURNS SO YOU DON'T GET HEAT STROKE.
OKAY.
It's just me and Tadano now!!
It's Tadano and Katai's turn.
I CAME FOR MANGA RESEARCH, BUT...
CHATTER
Saku Fushima
CHATTER
...I GOT STUCK IN A FOOD LINE!
HELLO, FUSHIMA.
CLICK
?!
NO WONDER PEOPLE ARE LINING UP!
YOU FORGOT YOUR FOOD! AND YOUR CHANGE!
Yakisoba ($5)
$9.50

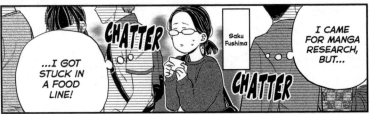

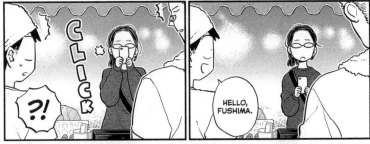

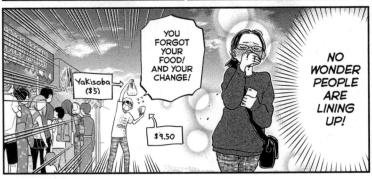

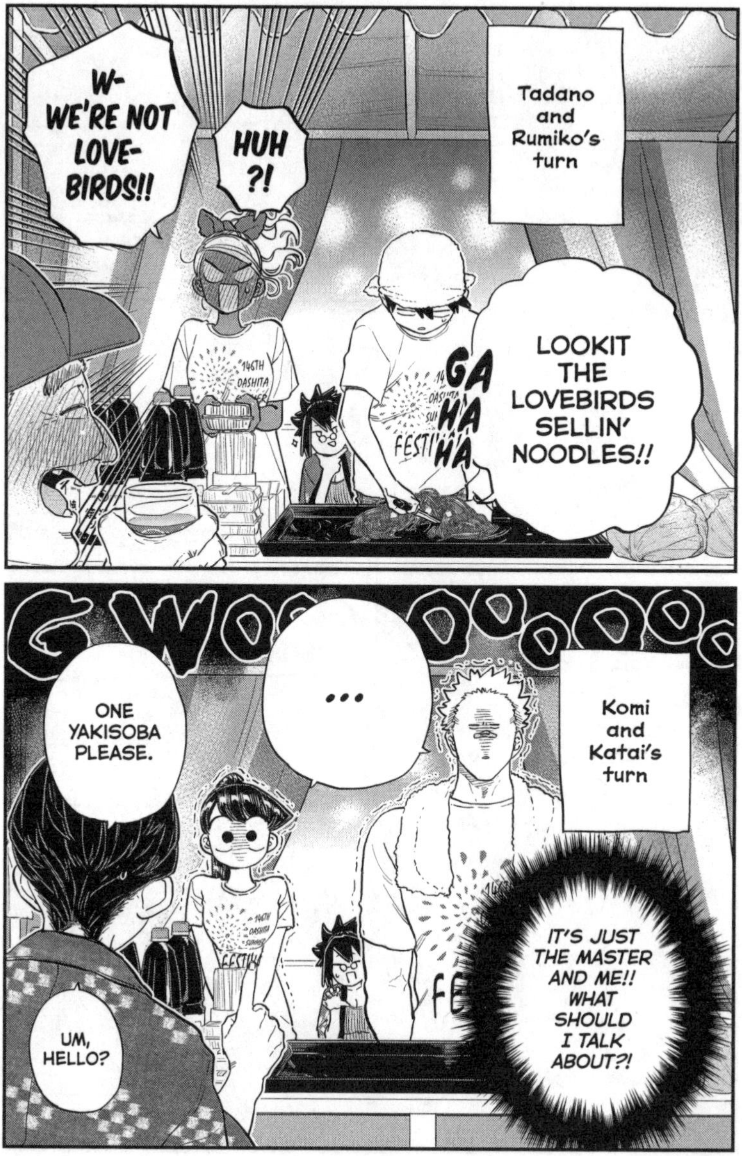

Tadano and Rumiko's turn
LOOKIT THE LOVEBIRDS SELLIN' NOODLES!!
GAHAHA
HUH ?!
W- WE'RE NOT LOVE-BIRDS!!
GWOOOOOOOO
Komi and Katai's turn
...
ONE YAKISOBA PLEASE.
IT'S JUST THE MASTER AND ME!! WHAT SHOULD I TALK ABOUT?!
UM, HELLO?

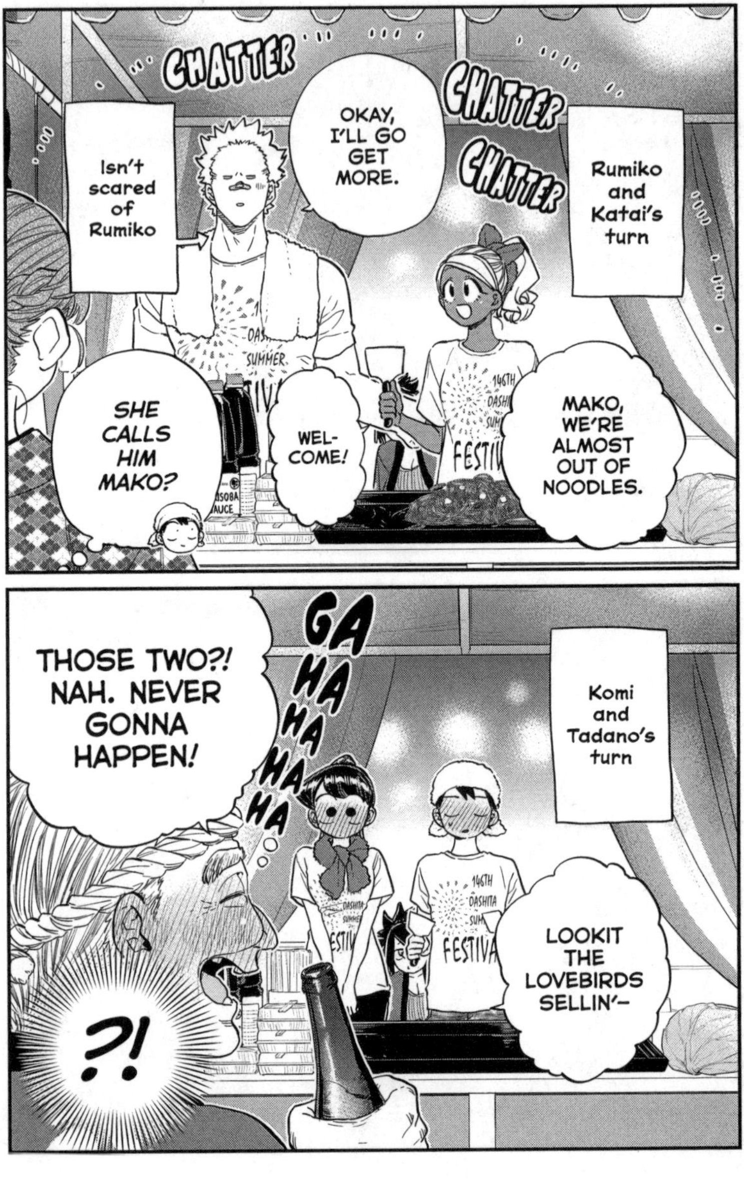
Rumiko and Katai's turn
CHATTER
CHATTER
OKAY, I'LL GO GET MORE.
CHATTER
Isn't scared of Rumiko
MAKO, WE'RE ALMOST OUT OF NOODLES.
WEL-COME!
SHE CALLS HIM MAKO?
Komi and Tadano's turn
GAHAHAHAHAHA
THOSE TWO?! NAH. NEVER GONNA HAPPEN!
LOOKIT THE LOVEBIRDS SELLIN'–
?!

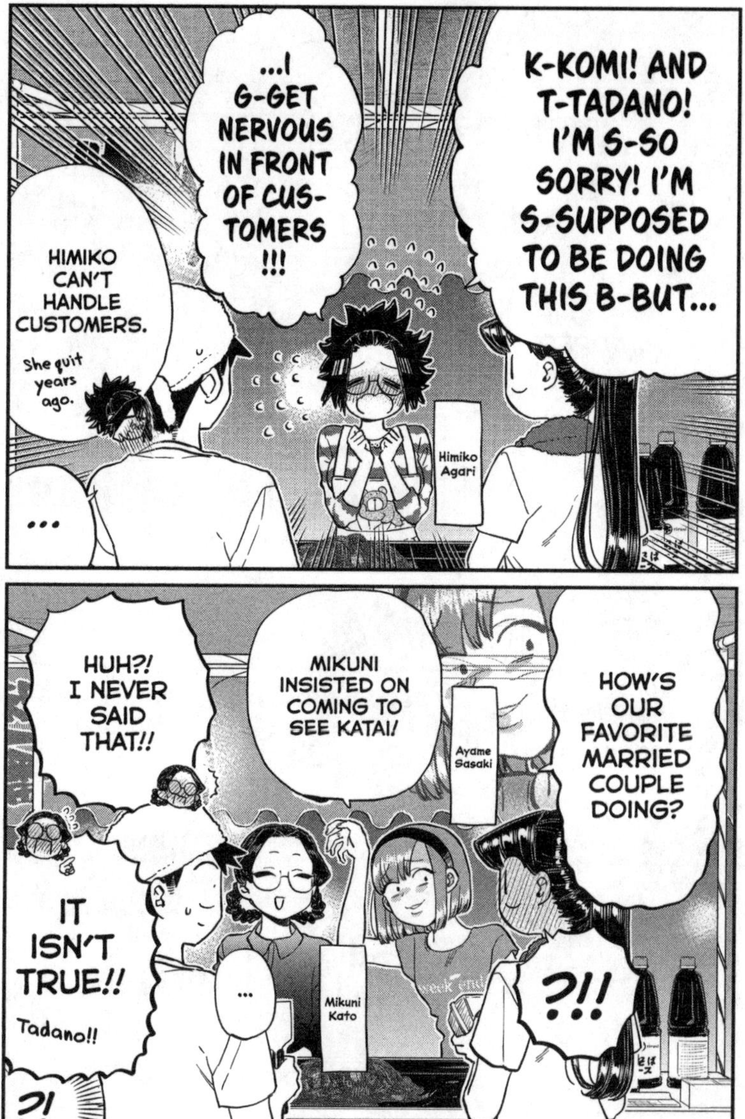
K-KOMI! AND T-TADANO! I'M S-SO SORRY! I'M S-SUPPOSED TO BE DOING THIS B-BUT...
...I G-GET NERVOUS IN FRONT OF CUS-TOMERS !!!
Himiko Agari
HIMIKO CAN'T HANDLE CUSTOMERS.
She quit years ago.
...
HOW'S OUR FAVORITE MARRIED COUPLE DOING?
Ayame Sasaki
MIKUNI INSISTED ON COMING TO SEE KATAI!
HUH?! I NEVER SAID THAT!!
?!!
Mikuni Kato
...
IT ISN'T TRUE!!
Tadano!!
?!

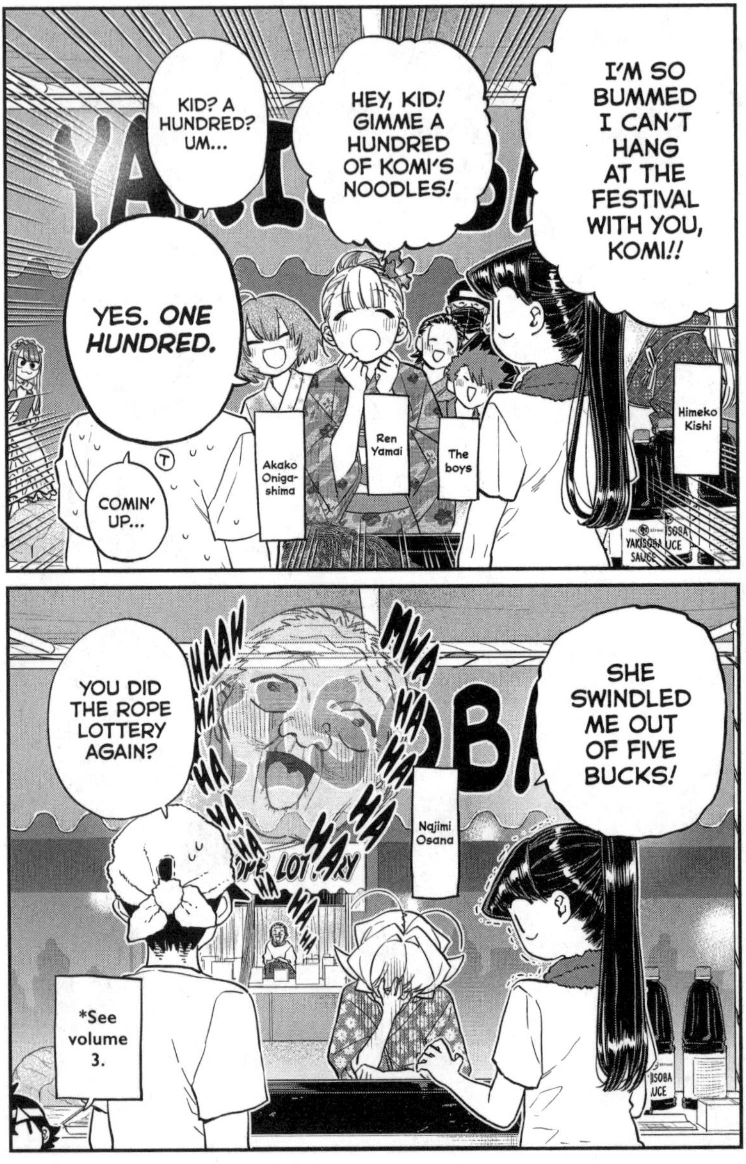
I'M SO BUMMED I CAN'T HANG AT THE FESTIVAL WITH YOU, KOMI!!
HEY, KID! GIMME A HUNDRED OF KOMI'S NOODLES!
KID? A HUNDRED? UM...
YES. ONE HUNDRED.
Himeko Kishi
The boys
Ren Yamai
Akako Oniga-shima
YAKISOBA SAUCE
COMIN' UP...
SHE SWINDLED ME OUT OF FIVE BUCKS!
MWA HA HA HA HA HA HA HA HA HA
Najimi Osana
HAAH HA HA HA HA HA HA HA
YOU DID THE ROPE LOTTERY AGAIN?
ROPE LOTTERY
*See volume 3.

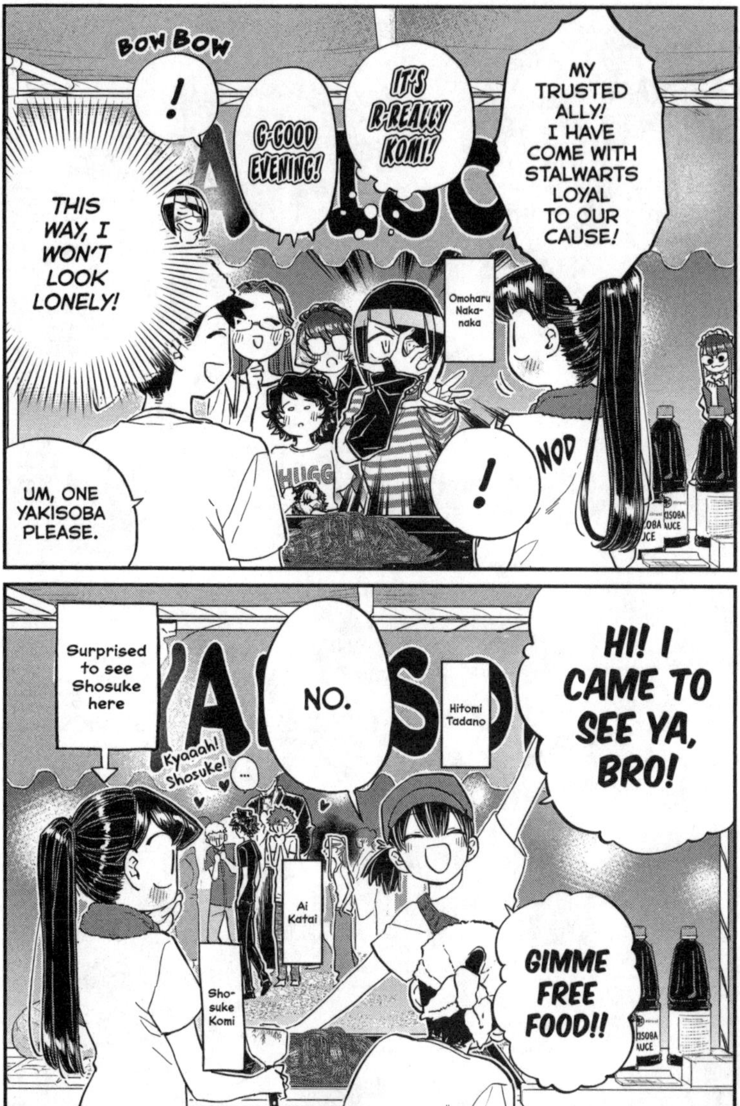
MY TRUSTED ALLY! I HAVE COME WITH STALWARTS LOYAL TO OUR CAUSE!
IT'S R-REALLY KOMI!
G-GOOD EVENING!
BOW BOW
!
Omoharu Naka-naka
THIS WAY, I WON'T LOOK LONELY!
NOD
!
UM, ONE YAKISOBA PLEASE.
HI! I CAME TO SEE YA, BRO!
Hitomi Tadano
NO.
Surprised to see Shosuke here
Kyaaah! Shosuke!
...
GIMME FREE FOOD!!
Ai Katai
Sho-suke Komi

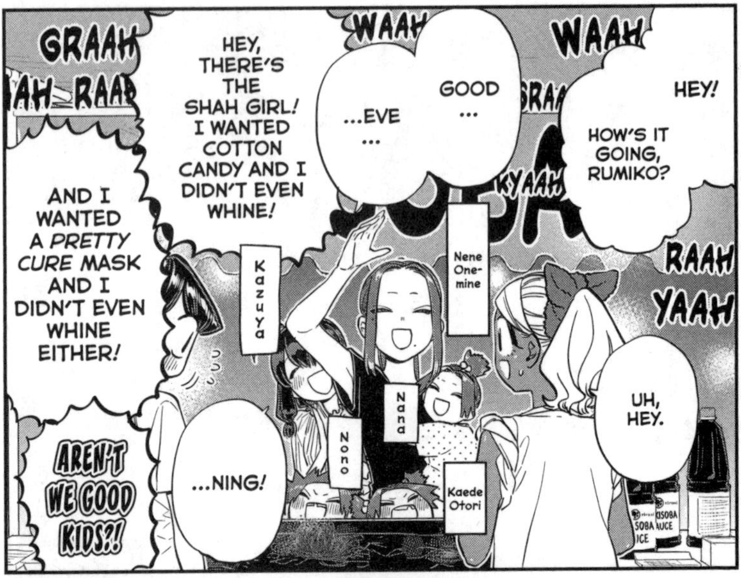
WAAH
HEY!
HOW'S IT GOING, RUMIKO?
GOOD ...
...EVE ...
WAAH
HEY, THERE'S THE SHAH GIRL! I WANTED COTTON CANDY AND I DIDN'T EVEN WHINE!
GRAAH
AH RAAH
AND I WANTED A *PRETTY CURE* MASK AND I DIDN'T EVEN WHINE EITHER!
KYAAH
RAAH
YAAH
Nene One-mine
Kazuya
Nana
Nono
Kaede Otori
UH, HEY.
...NING!
AREN'T WE GOOD KIDS?!

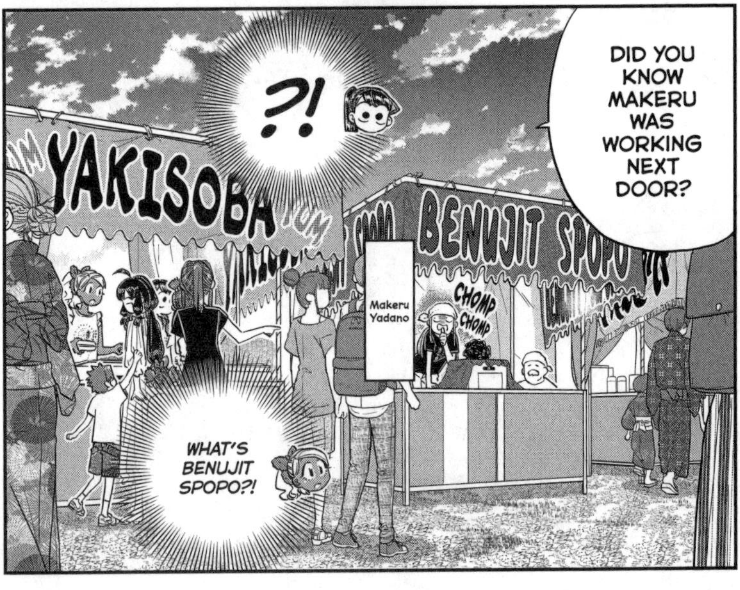
DID YOU KNOW MAKERU WAS WORKING NEXT DOOR?
?!
YAKISOBA
BENUJIT SPOPO
Makeru Yadano
CHOMP CHOMP
WHAT'S BENUJIT SPOPO?!

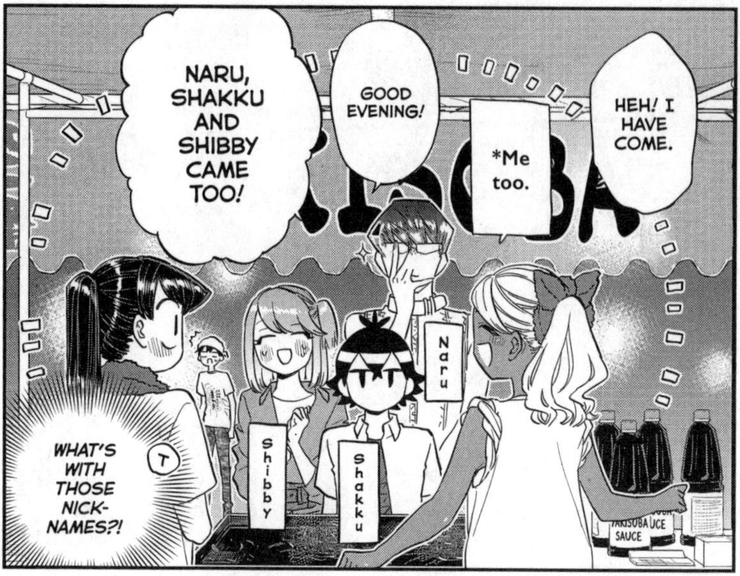
HEH! I HAVE COME.
*Me too.
GOOD EVENING!
NARU, SHAKKU AND SHIBBY CAME TOO!
Naru
Shakku
Shibby
T
WHAT'S WITH THOSE NICK-NAMES?!
YAKISOBA SAUCE

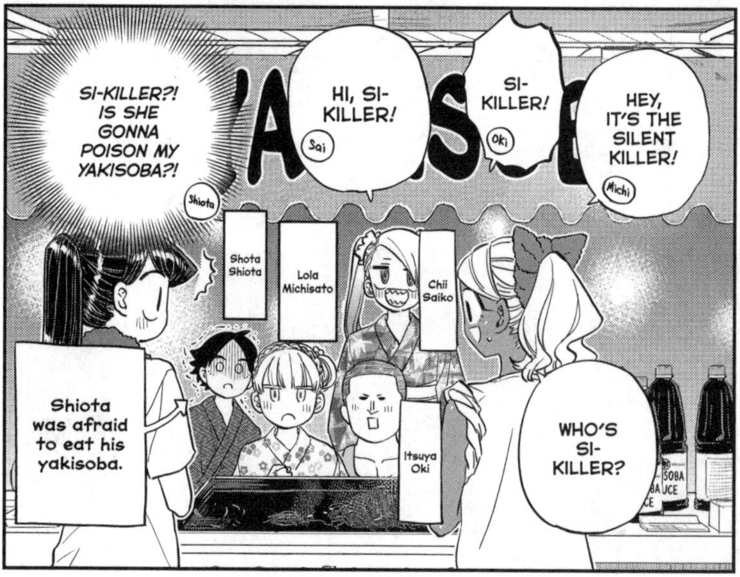
HEY, IT'S THE SILENT KILLER!
Michi
SI-KILLER!
Oki
HI, SI-KILLER!
Sai
SI-KILLER?! IS SHE GONNA POISON MY YAKISOBA?!
Shiota
Chii Saiko
Lola Michisato
Shota Shiota
WHO'S SI-KILLER?
Itsuya Oki
Shiota was afraid to eat his yakisoba.

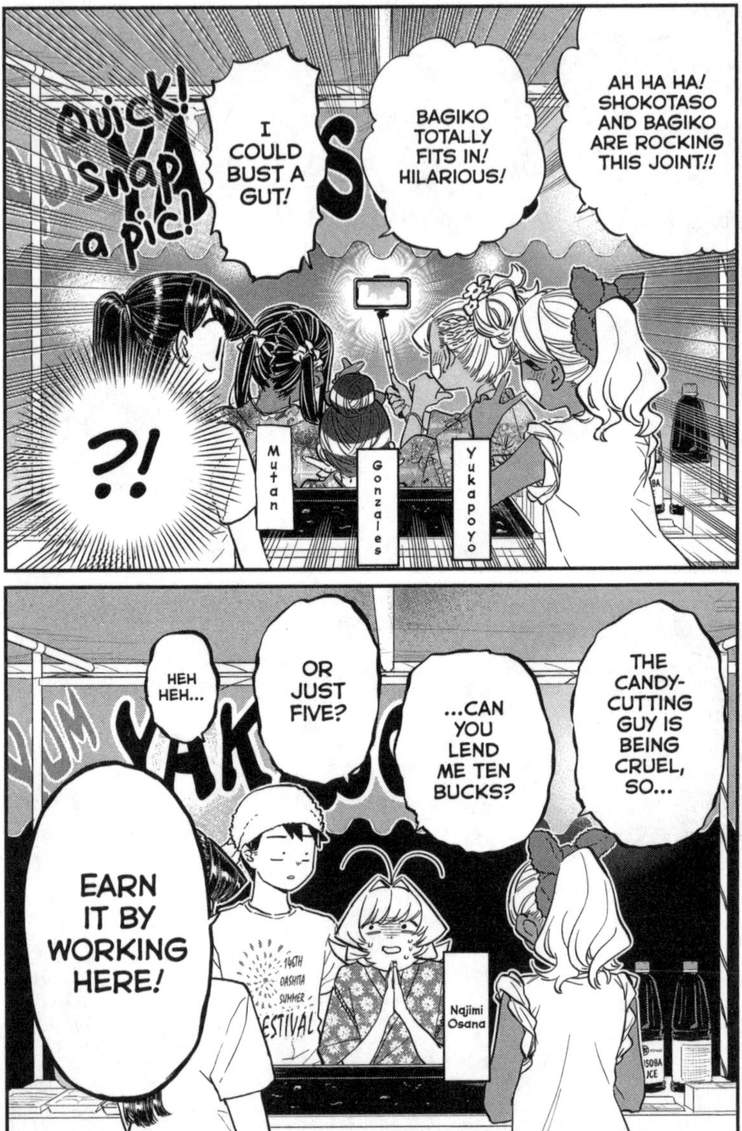
AH HA HA! SHOKOTASO AND BAGIKO ARE ROCKING THIS JOINT!!
BAGIKO TOTALLY FITS IN! HILARIOUS!
I COULD BUST A GUT!
QUICK! Snap a pic!
?!
Yukapoyo
Gonzales
Mutan
THE CANDY-CUTTING GUY IS BEING CRUEL, SO...
...CAN YOU LEND ME TEN BUCKS?
OR JUST FIVE?
HEH HEH...
Najimi Osana
EARN IT BY WORKING HERE!

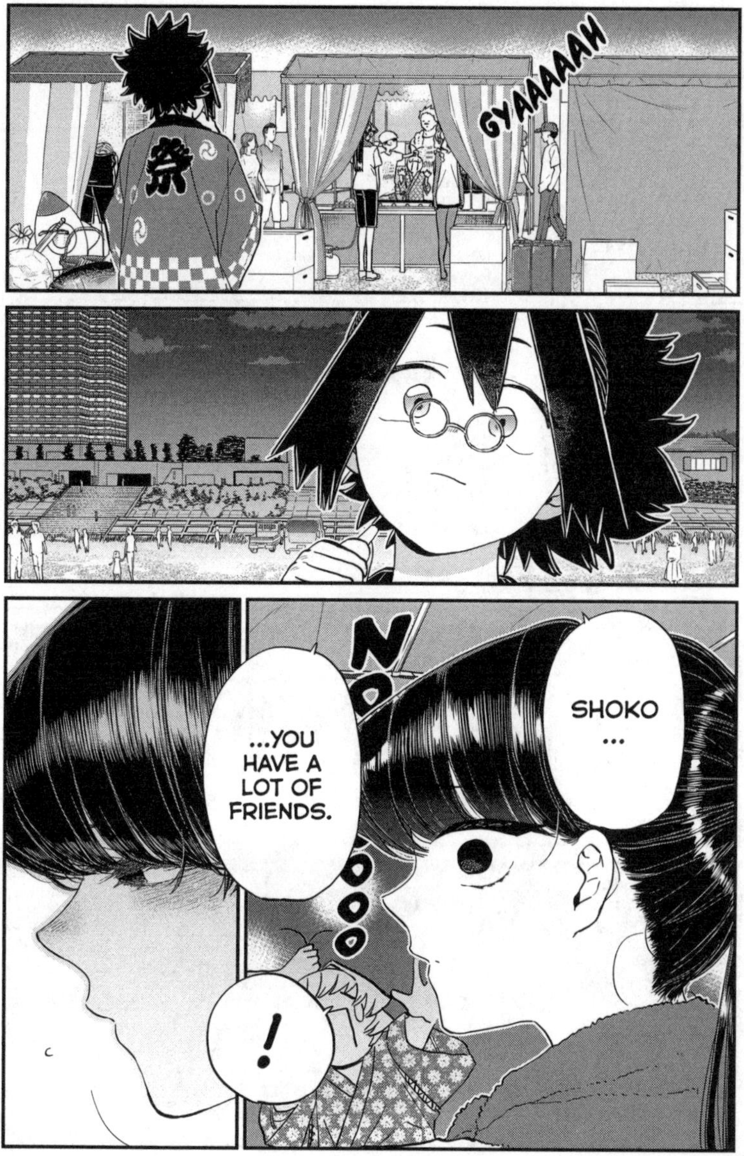
GYAAAAAH
SHOKO ...
NOOOOO
...YOU HAVE A LOT OF FRIENDS.
!

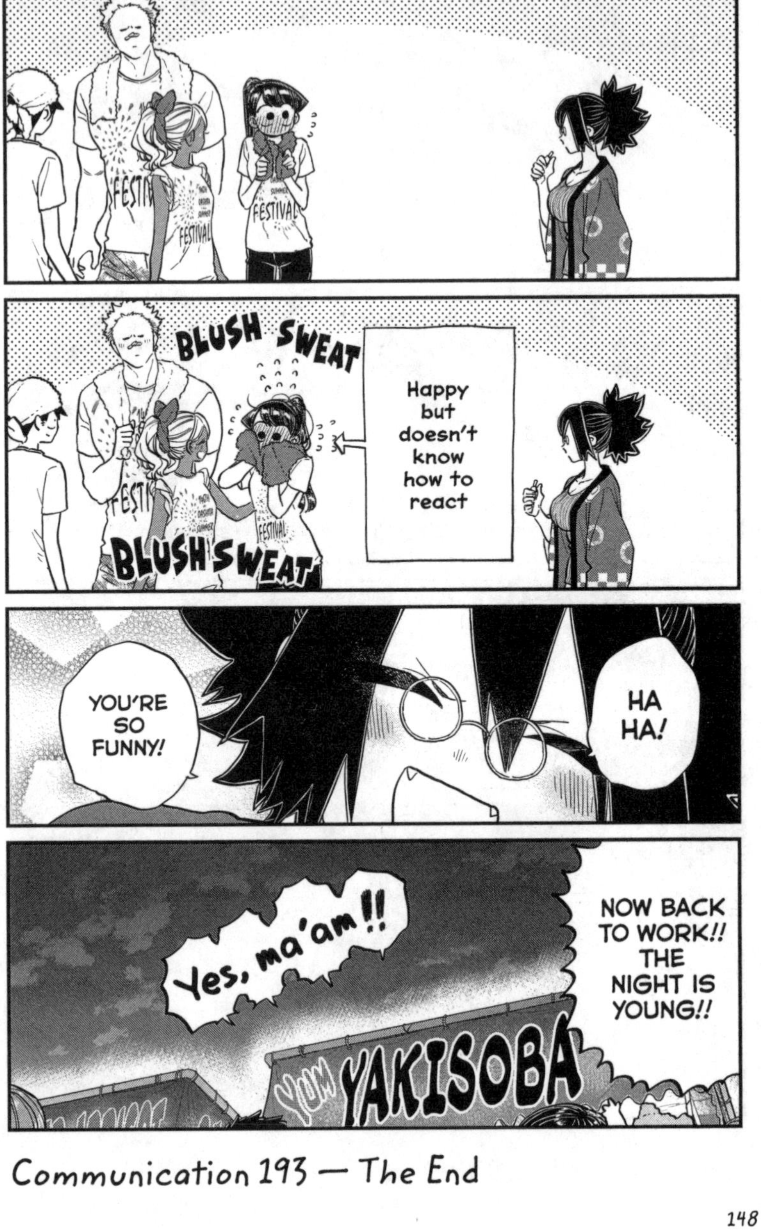
Happy but doesn't know how to react
BLUSH SWEAT
BLUSH SWEAT
HA HA!
YOU'RE SO FUNNY!
NOW BACK TO WORK!! THE NIGHT IS YOUNG!!
Yes, ma'am!!
YUM YAKISOBA

Communication 193 — The End

Komi Can't Communicate

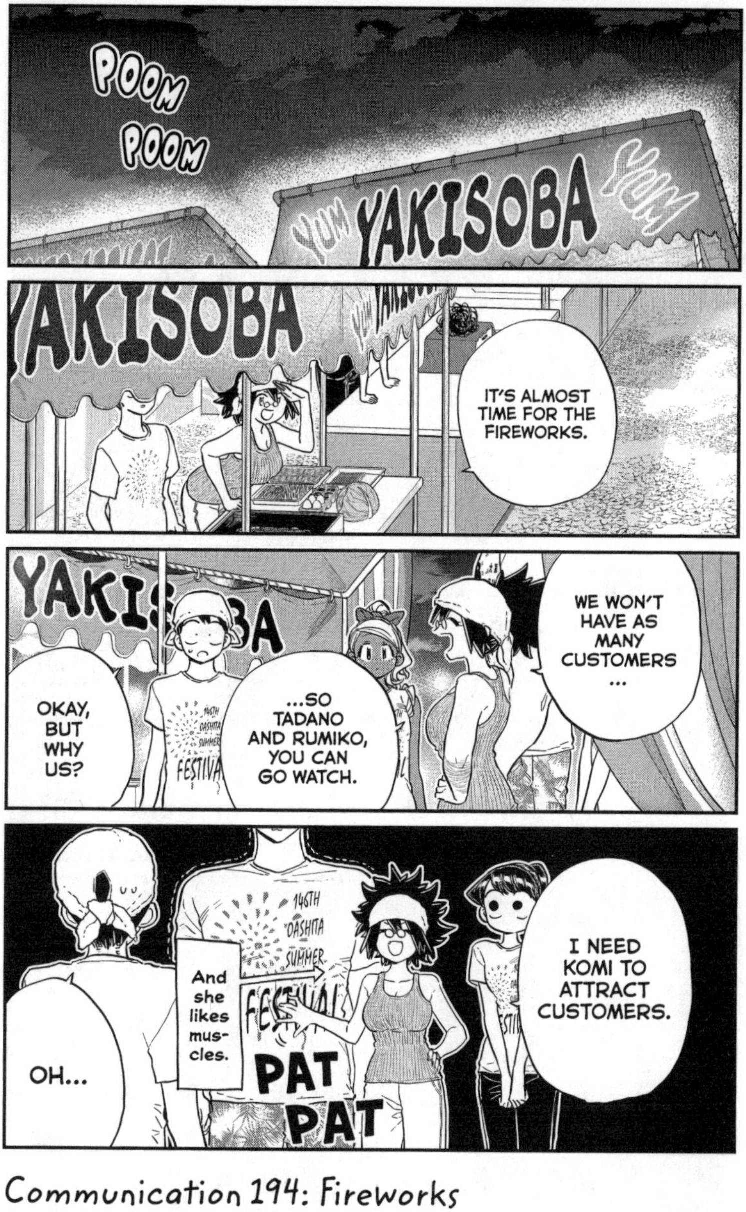
POOM
POOM
YUM
YAKISOBA
YUM
YAKISOBA
IT'S ALMOST TIME FOR THE FIREWORKS.
WE WON'T HAVE AS MANY CUSTOMERS ...
...SO TADANO AND RUMIKO, YOU CAN GO WATCH.
OKAY, BUT WHY US?
I NEED KOMI TO ATTRACT CUSTOMERS.
PAT PAT
And she likes mus-cles.
OH...

Communication 194: Fireworks

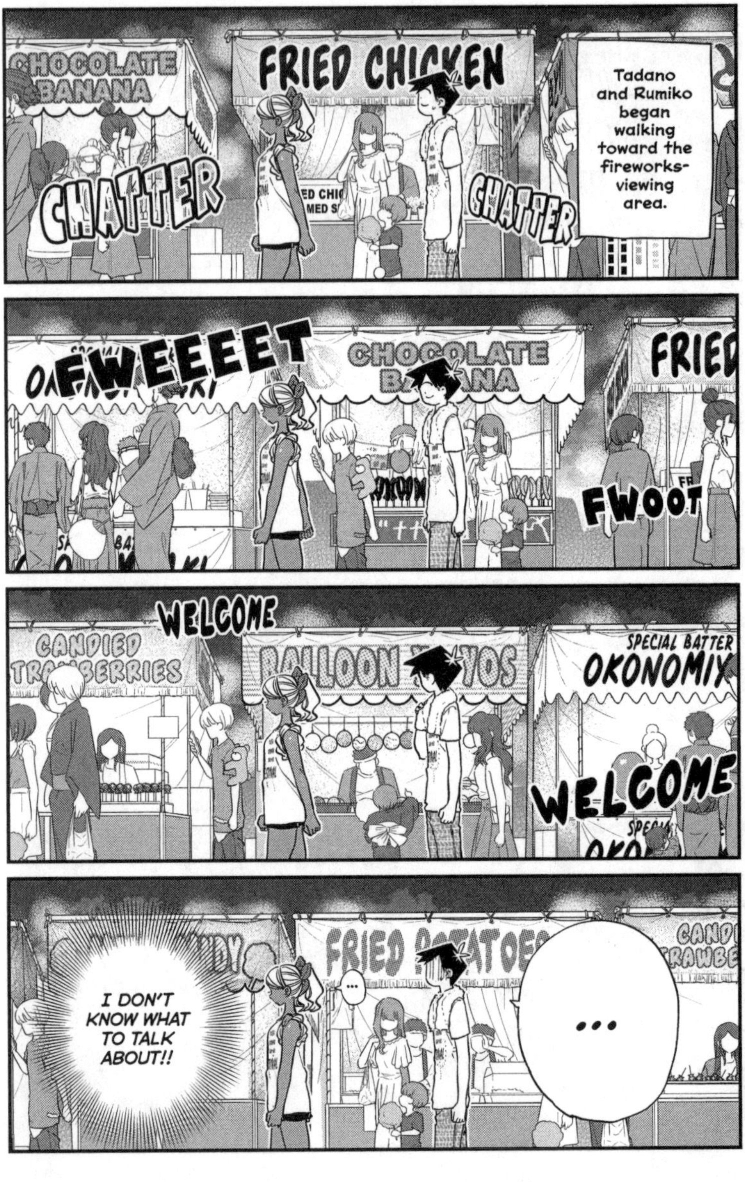
Tadano and Rumiko began walking toward the fireworks-viewing area.
CHATTER
FRIED CHICKEN
CHATTER
CHOCOLATE BANANA
FWOOT
FRIED
CHOCOLATE BANANA
FWEEEET
WELCOME
SPECIAL BATTER
WELCOME
CANDIED
...
...
I DON'T KNOW WHAT TO TALK ABOUT!!

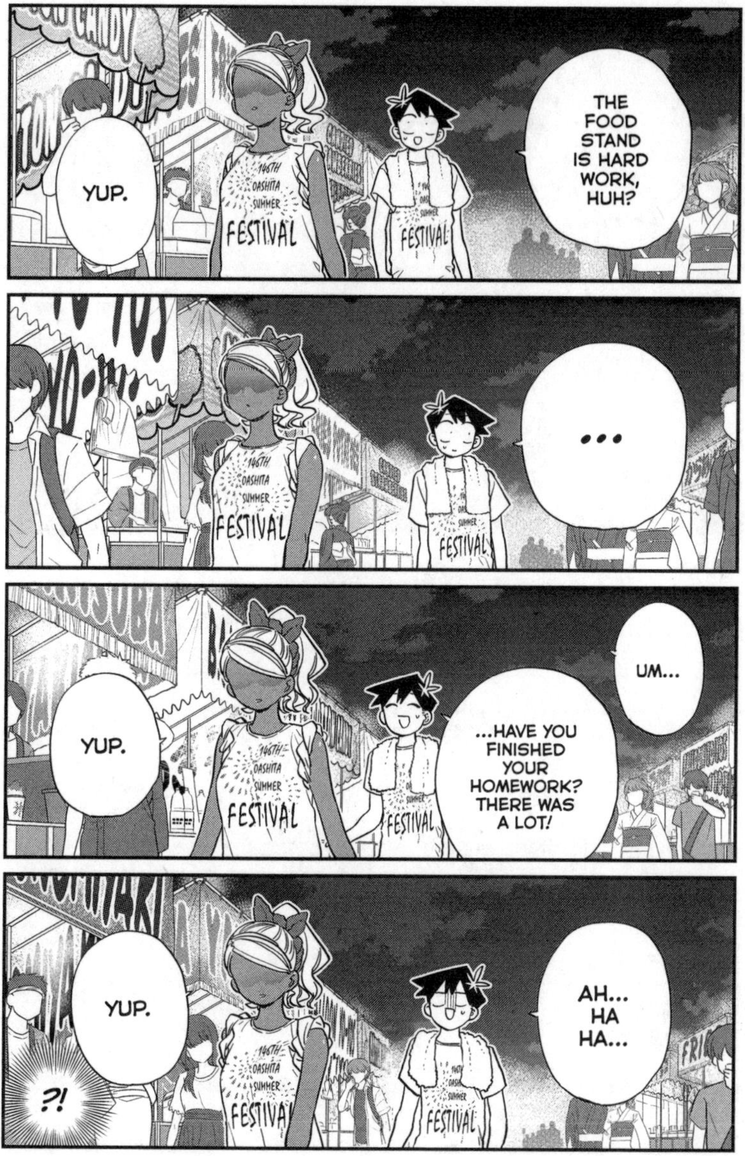
THE FOOD STAND IS HARD WORK, HUH?
146TH OASHITA SUMMER FESTIVAL
YUP.
...
UM...
...HAVE YOU FINISHED YOUR HOMEWORK? THERE WAS A LOT!
YUP.
AH... HA HA...
YUP.
?!

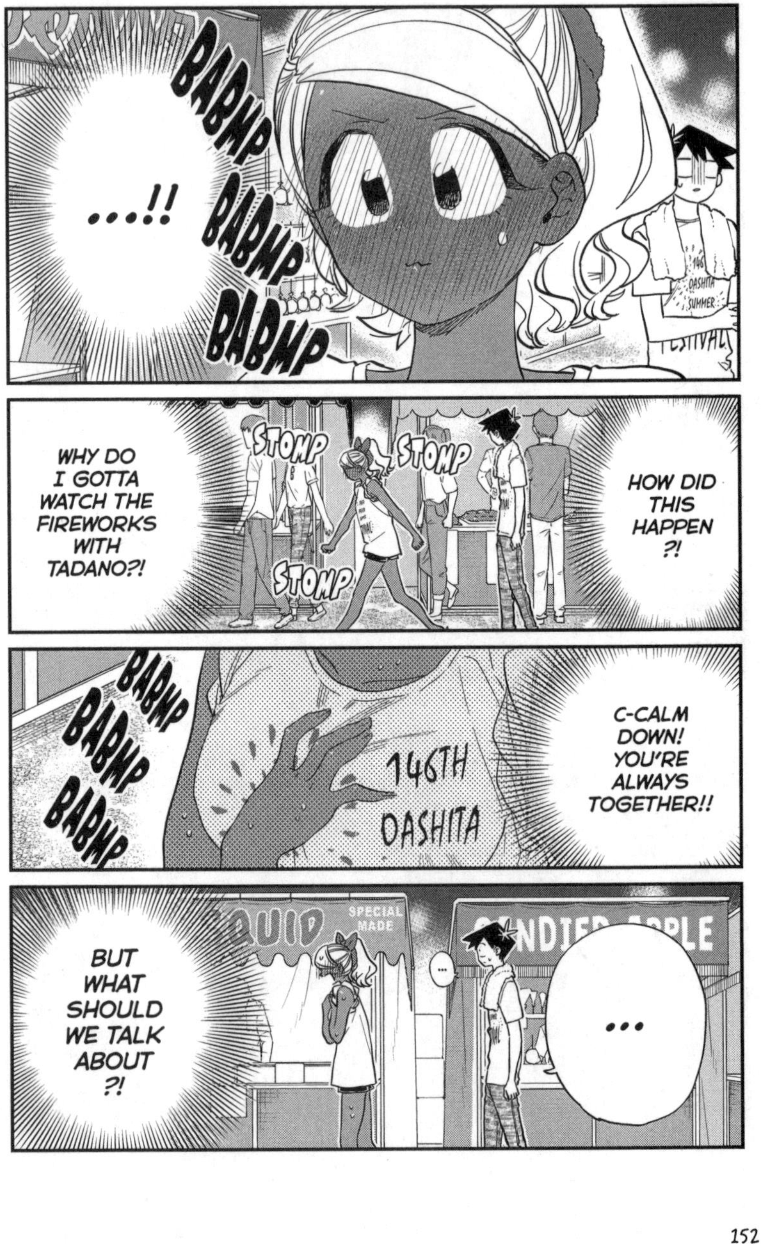
146 OASHITA SUMMER FESTIVAL
BABMP BABMP BABMP BABMP
...!!
HOW DID THIS HAPPEN?!
STOMP
STOMP
STOMP
WHY DO I GOTTA WATCH THE FIREWORKS WITH TADANO?!
C-CALM DOWN! YOU'RE ALWAYS TOGETHER!!
146TH OASHITA
BABMP BABMP BABMP
...
...
SPECIAL MADE
BUT WHAT SHOULD WE TALK ABOUT?!

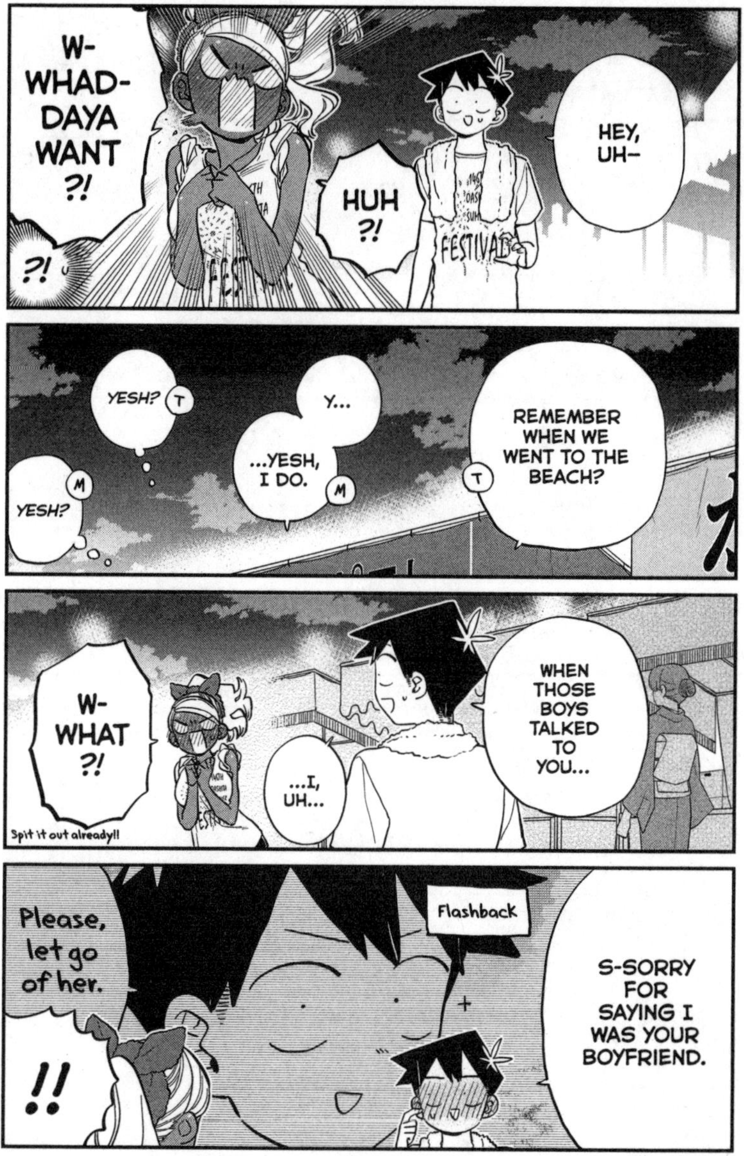
HEY, UH–
HUH ?!
W-WHADDAYA WANT ?!
?!
(T) REMEMBER WHEN WE WENT TO THE BEACH?
Y... ...YESH, I DO. (M)
YESH? (T)
(M) YESH?
WHEN THOSE BOYS TALKED TO YOU...
...I, UH...
W- WHAT ?!
Spit it out already!!
S-SORRY FOR SAYING I WAS YOUR BOYFRIEND.
Flashback
Please, let go of her.
!!

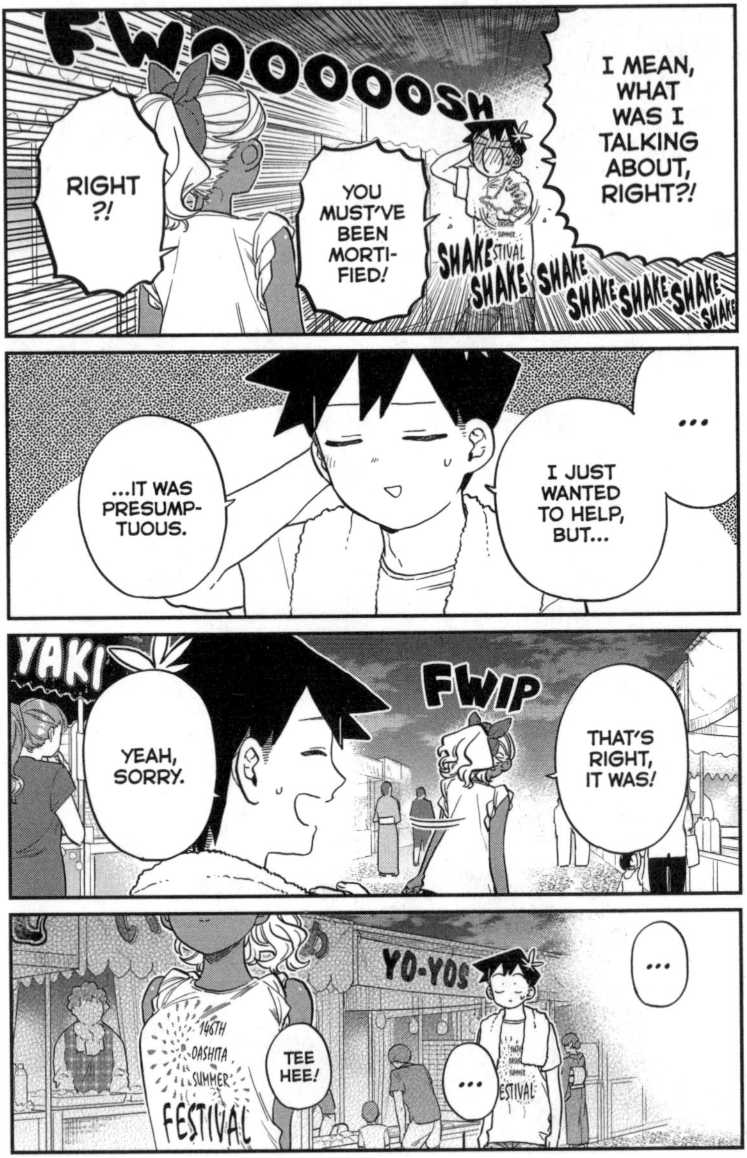
I MEAN, WHAT WAS I TALKING ABOUT, RIGHT?!
FWOOOOOSH
SHAKE SHAKE SHAKE SHAKE SHAKE SHAKE SHAKE
YOU MUST'VE BEEN MORTI-FIED!
RIGHT ?!
...
I JUST WANTED TO HELP, BUT...
...IT WAS PRESUMP-TUOUS.
THAT'S RIGHT, IT WAS!
FWIP
YEAH, SORRY.
YAKI
...
YO-YOS
...
TEE HEE!
146TH OASHITA SUMMER FESTIVAL

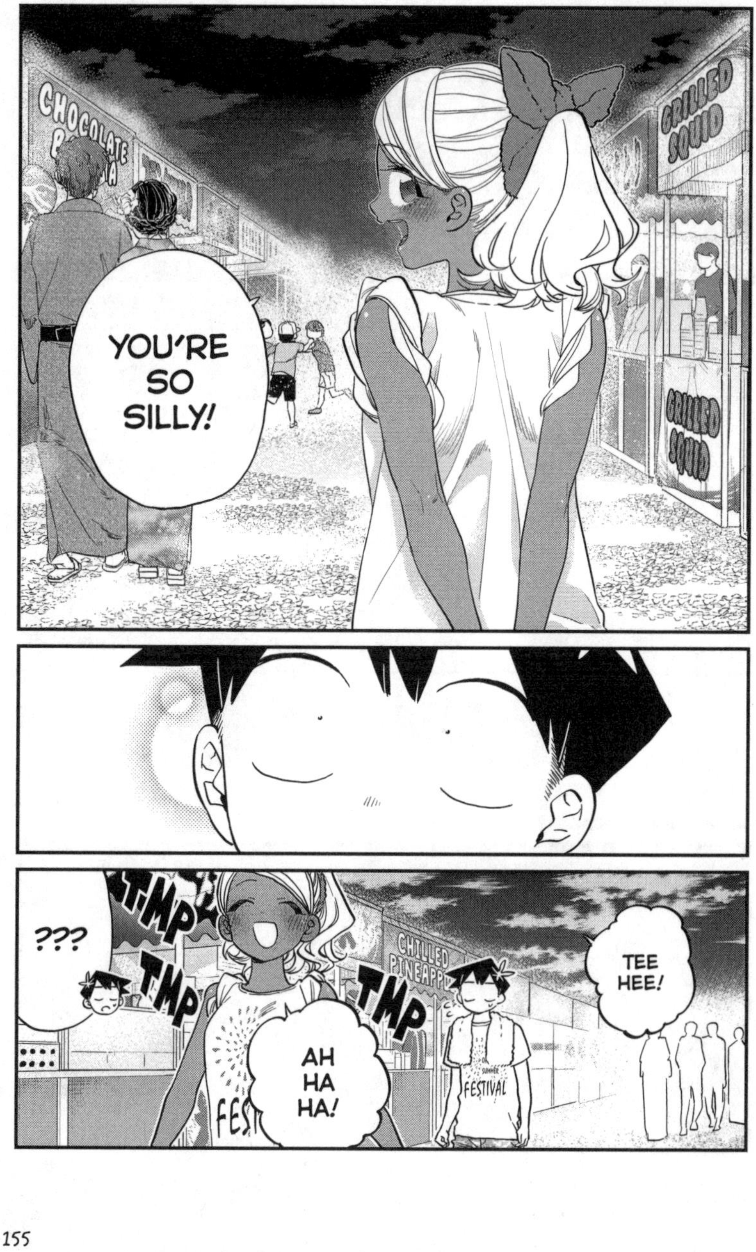
GRILLED SQUID
YOU'RE SO SILLY!
GRILLED SQUID
TEE HEE!
SUMMER FESTIVAL
TMP
AH HA HA!
TMP
TMP
???

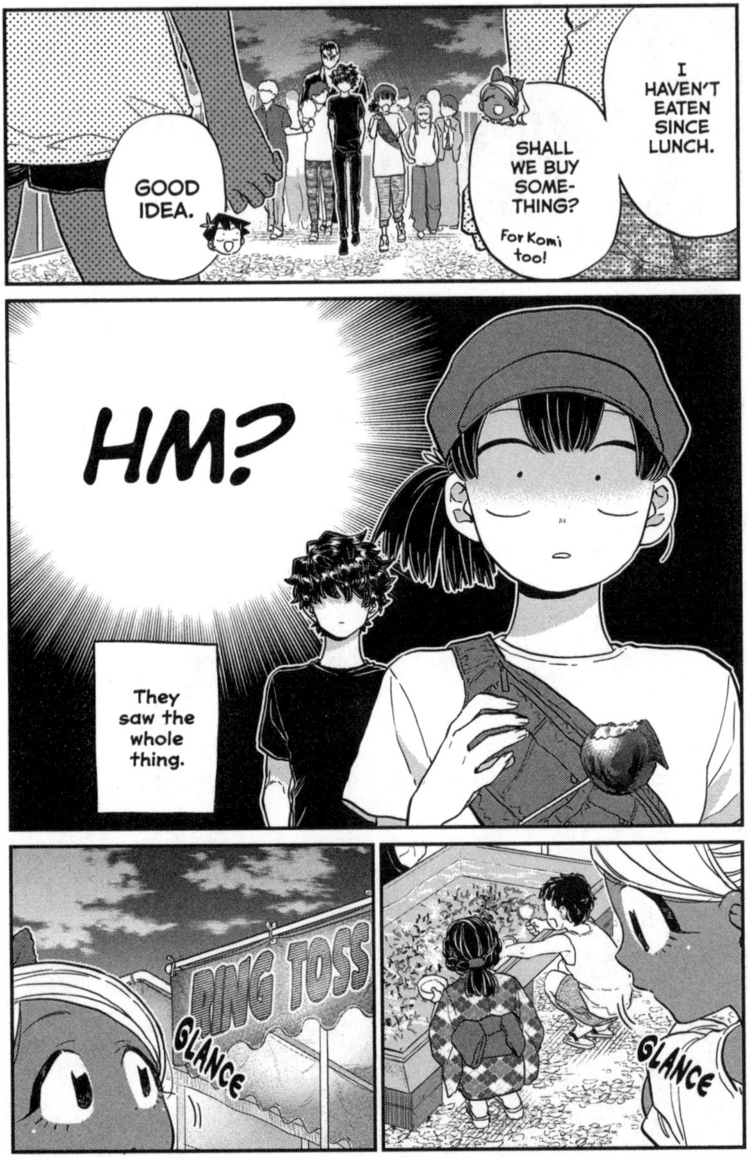
I HAVEN'T EATEN SINCE LUNCH.
SHALL WE BUY SOMETHING?
For Komi too!
GOOD IDEA.
HM?
They saw the whole thing.
GLANCE
RING TOSS
GLANCE

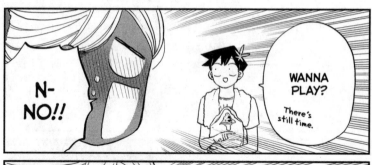

WANNA PLAY?
There's still time.
N- NO!!
...
...
OKAY, JUST A LITTLE!!
I'LL HOLD YOUR THINGS.
ALL RIGHT, THANKS.
BUT YOU SHOULD PLAY TOO!
GRIN
!

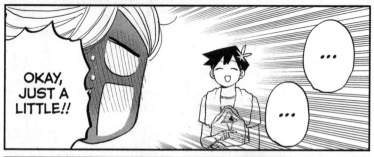

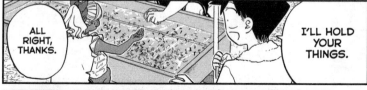

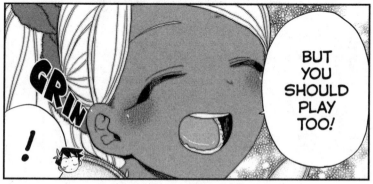

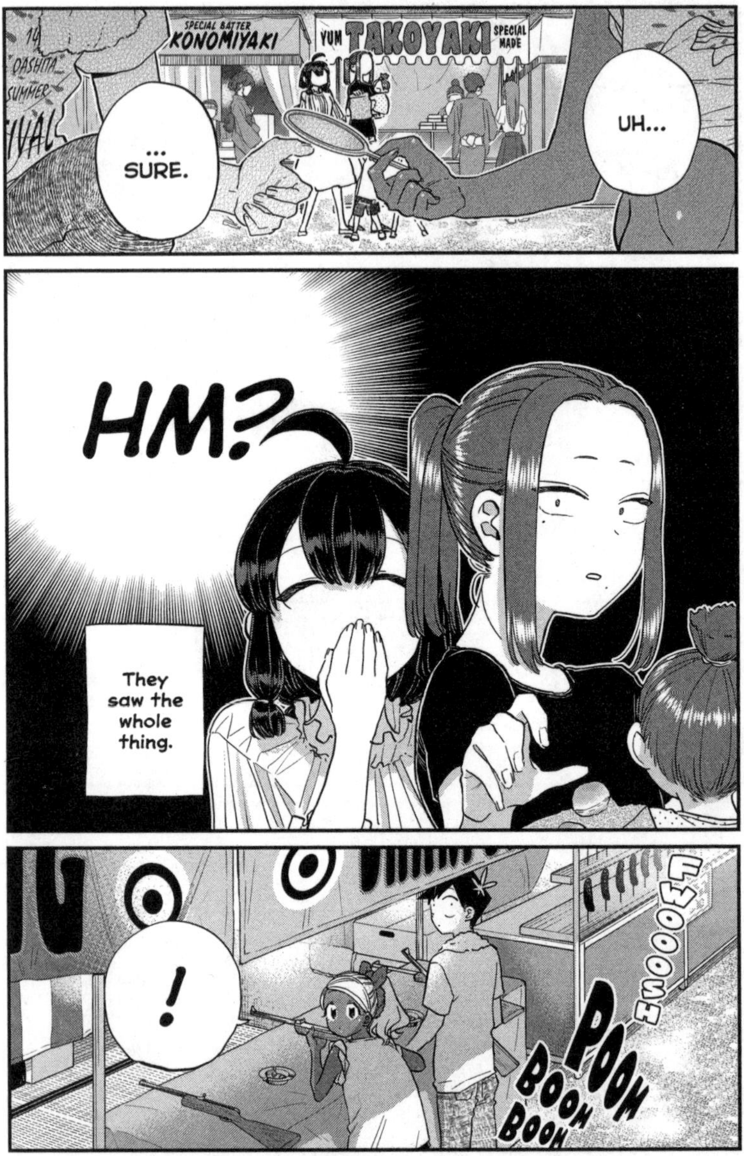
UH...
SPECIAL MADE
YUM TAKOYAKI
SPECIAL BATTER KONOMIYAKI
... SURE.
HM?
They saw the whole thing.
FWOOOSH
POOH
BOOM BOOM
!

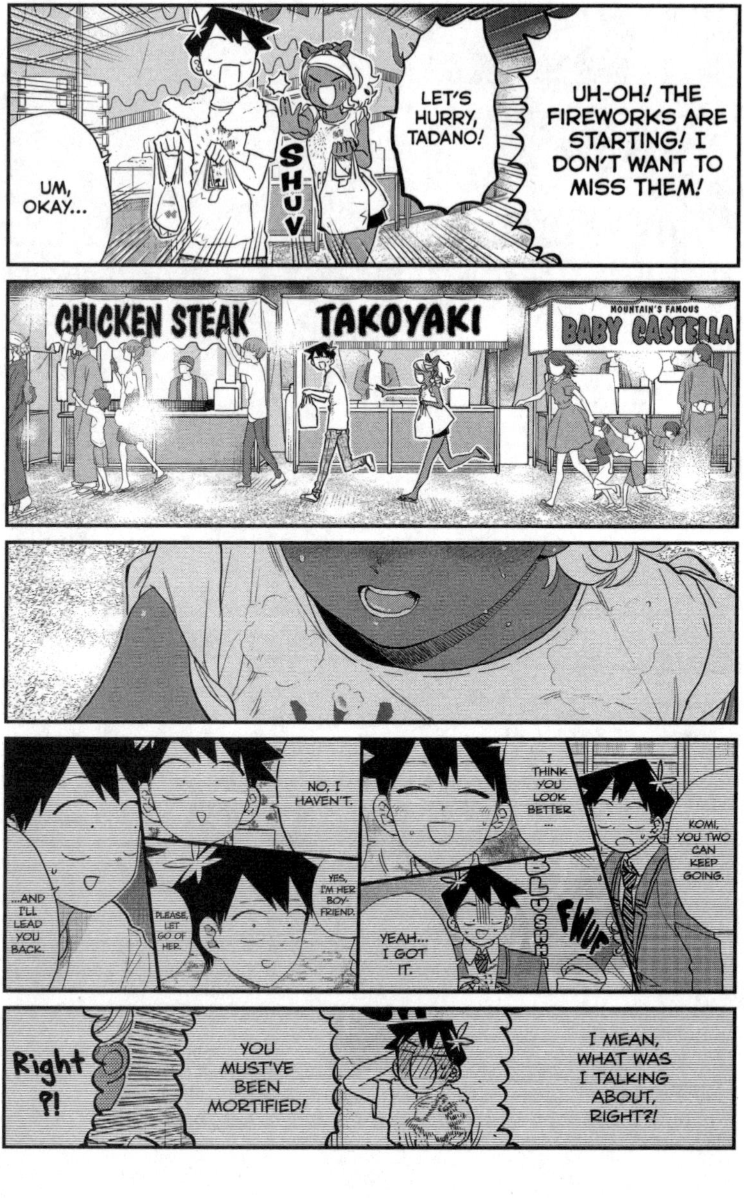
UH-OH! THE FIREWORKS ARE STARTING! I DON'T WANT TO MISS THEM!
LET'S HURRY, TADANO!
SHUV
UM, OKAY...
MOUNTAIN'S FAMOUS
BABY CASTELLA
TAKOYAKI
CHICKEN STEAK
KOMI, YOU TWO CAN KEEP GOING.
I THINK YOU LOOK BETTER ...
BLUSH
FWUF
YEAH... I GOT IT.
NO, I HAVEN'T.
YES, I'M HER BOYFRIEND.
PLEASE, LET GO OF HER.
...AND I'LL LEAD YOU BACK.
I MEAN, WHAT WAS I TALKING ABOUT, RIGHT?!
YOU MUST'VE BEEN MORTIFIED!
Right ?!

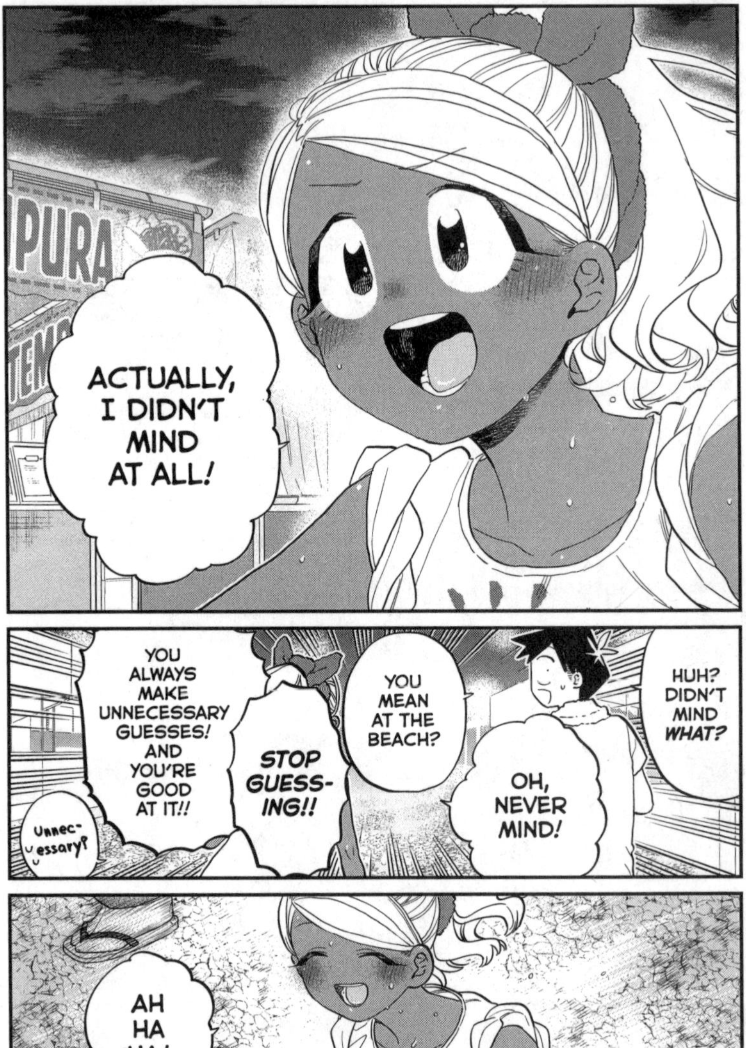
ACTUALLY, I DIDN'T MIND AT ALL!
HUH? DIDN'T MIND *WHAT?*
OH, NEVER MIND!
YOU MEAN AT THE BEACH?
STOP GUESS-ING!!
YOU ALWAYS MAKE UNNECESSARY GUESSES! AND YOU'RE GOOD AT IT!!
Unnec-essary?
AH HA HA!
146TH

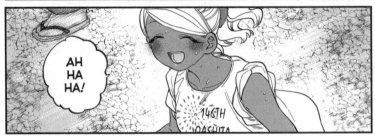

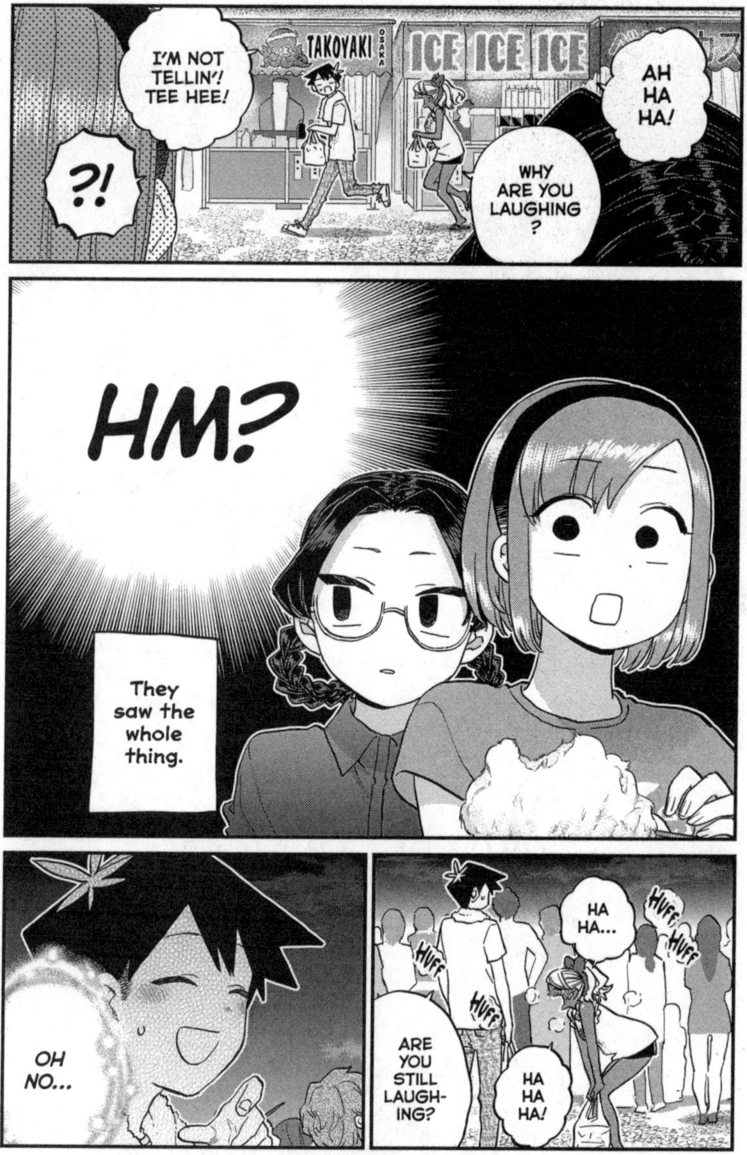
TAKOYAKI
OSAKA
ICE ICE ICE
AH HA HA!
WHY ARE YOU LAUGHING?
I'M NOT TELLIN'! TEE HEE!
?!
HM?
They saw the whole thing.
HA HA...
HUFF
HUFF
HA HA HA!
ARE YOU STILL LAUGH-ING?
HUFF
HUFF
OH NO...

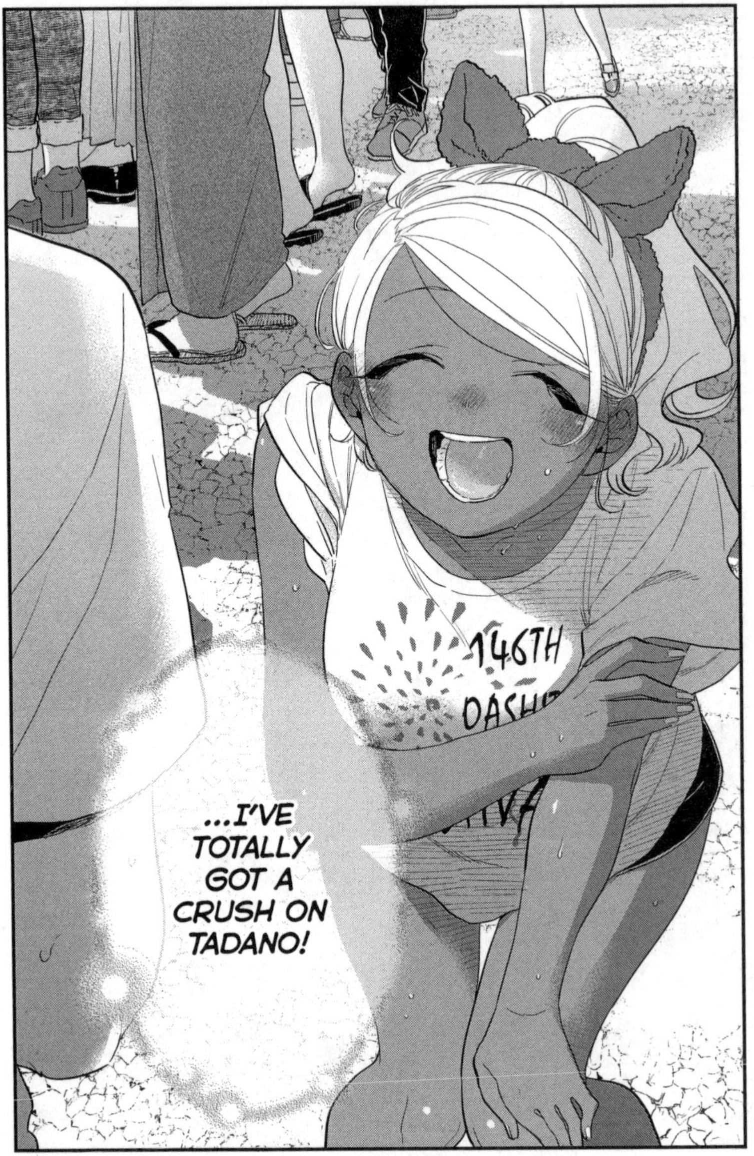
...I'VE TOTALLY GOT A CRUSH ON TADANO!
146TH
OASHI

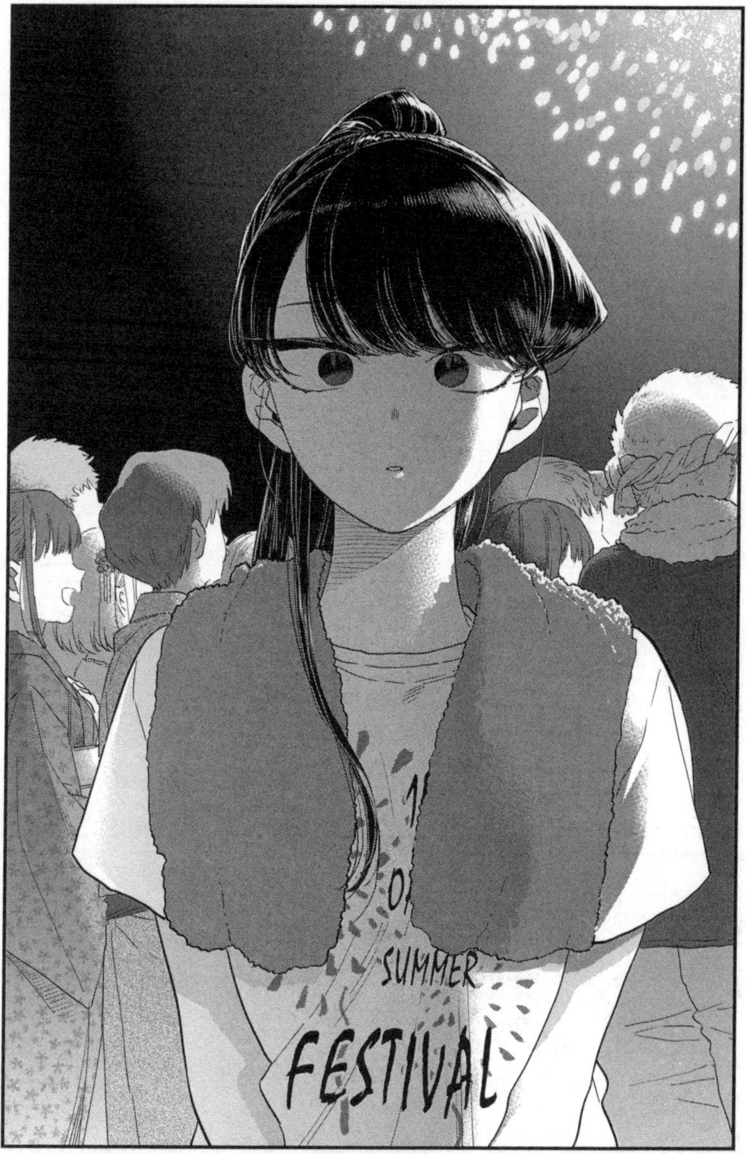
SUMMER
FESTIVAL

OH, THERE'S KOMI!

ALL DONE AT THE STAND?

"I'm supposed to lure in customers."

OH, I SEE.

YOU MUST HAVE PASSED US ALONG THE WAY.

YAY! LET'S WATCH THE FIREWORKS TOGETHER!! WE BOUGHT SNACKS! EAT WITH US!

WHAT'S WRONG, KOMI?

?

...

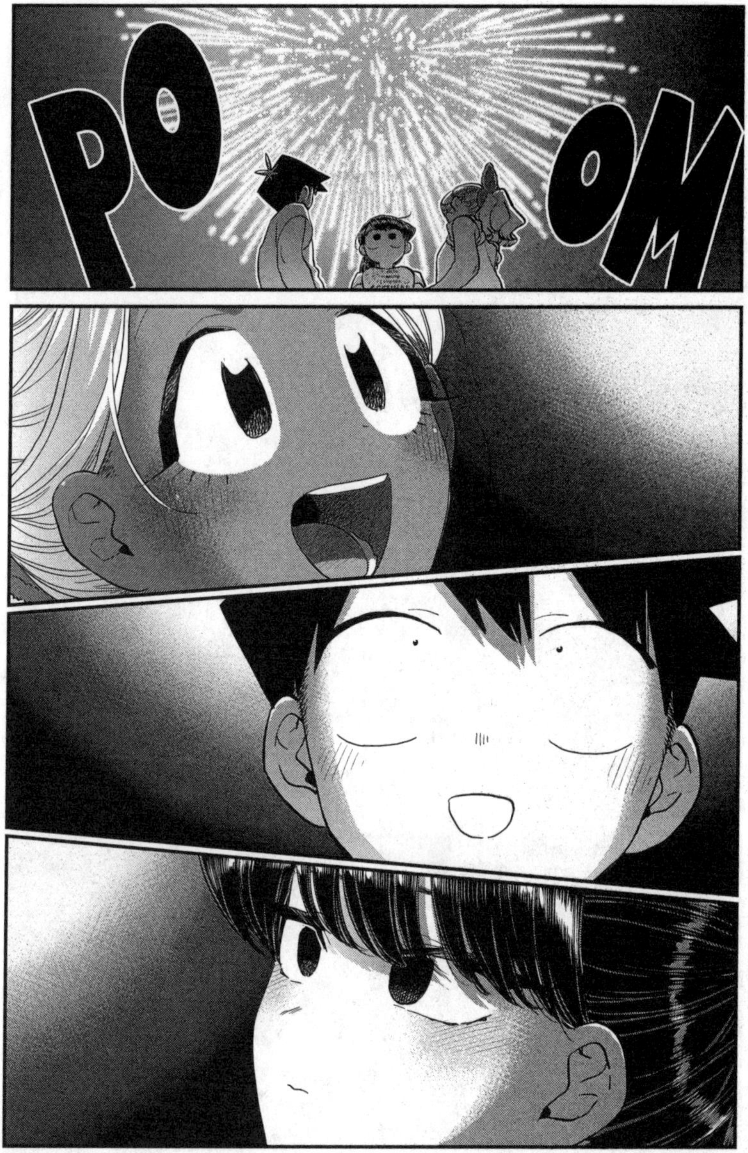
POOM

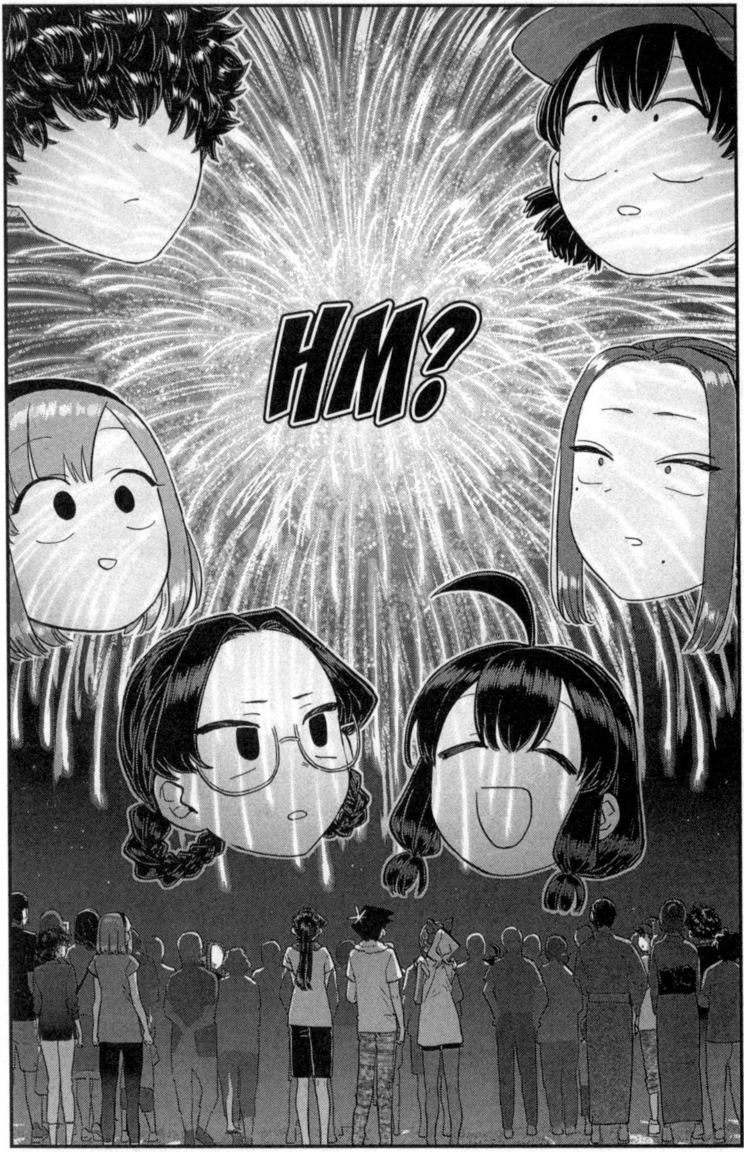
HM?

Communication 194 — The End

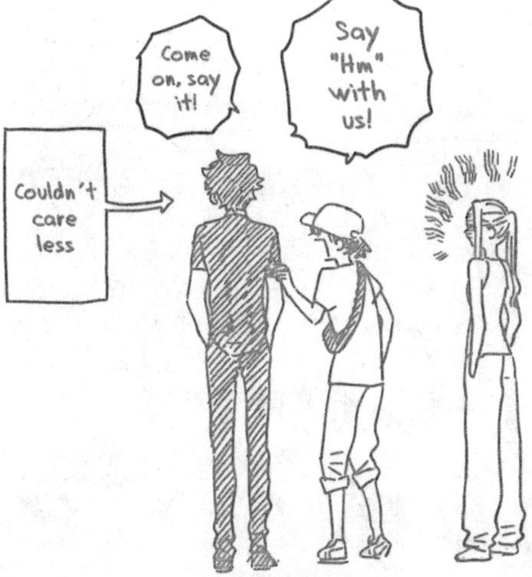
Say "Hm" with us!
Come on, say it!
Couldn't care less

Komi Can't
Communicate

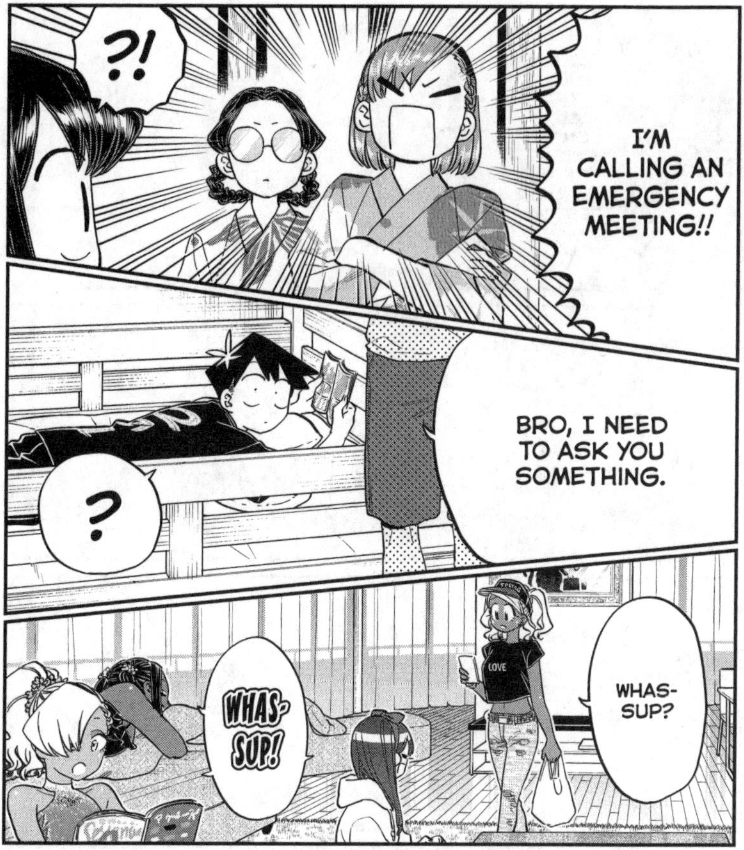
I'M CALLING AN EMERGENCY MEETING!!
?!
BRO, I NEED TO ASK YOU SOMETHING.
?
WHAS-SUP?
LOVE
WHAS-SUP!

Komi Can't Communicate

Communication 195: Three Parties

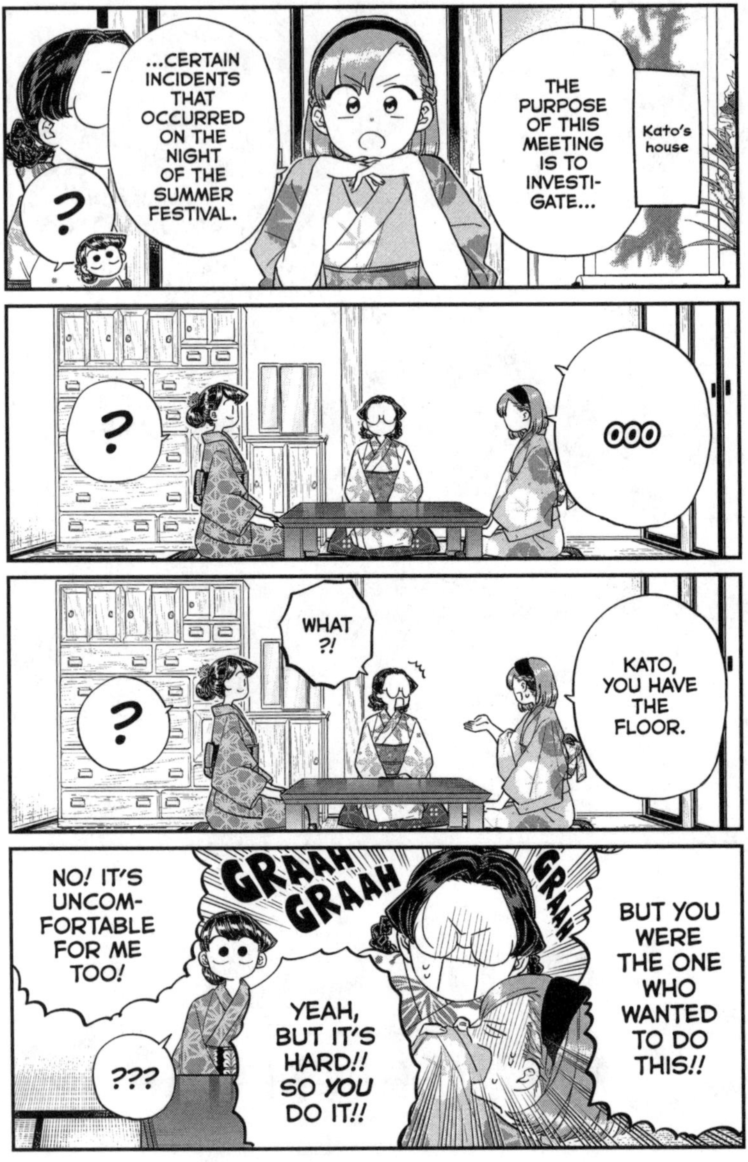
Kato's house
THE PURPOSE OF THIS MEETING IS TO INVESTIGATE...
...CERTAIN INCIDENTS THAT OCCURRED ON THE NIGHT OF THE SUMMER FESTIVAL.
?
OOO
?
KATO, YOU HAVE THE FLOOR.
WHAT?!
?
BUT YOU WERE THE ONE WHO WANTED TO DO THIS!!
GRAAH
GRAAH GRAAH
YEAH, BUT IT'S HARD!! SO YOU DO IT!!
NO! IT'S UNCOMFORTABLE FOR ME TOO!
???

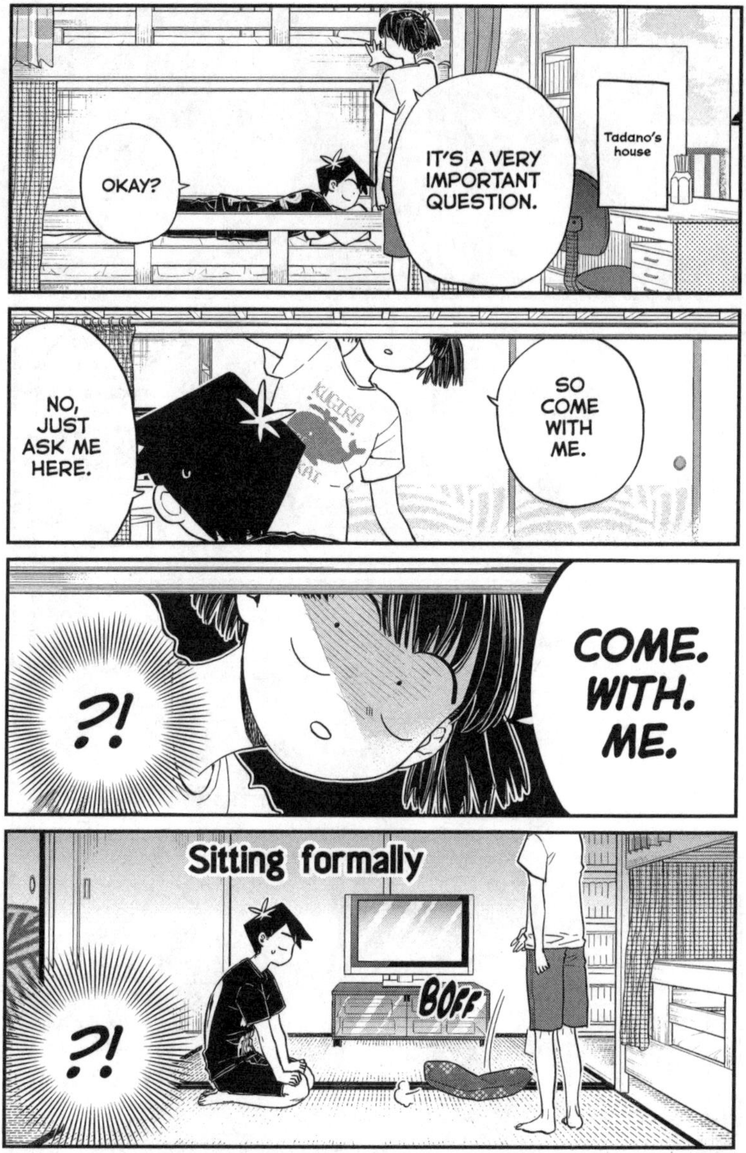
Tadano's house
IT'S A VERY IMPORTANT QUESTION.
OKAY?
SO COME WITH ME.
NO, JUST ASK ME HERE.
COME. WITH. ME.
?!
Sitting formally
BOFF
?!

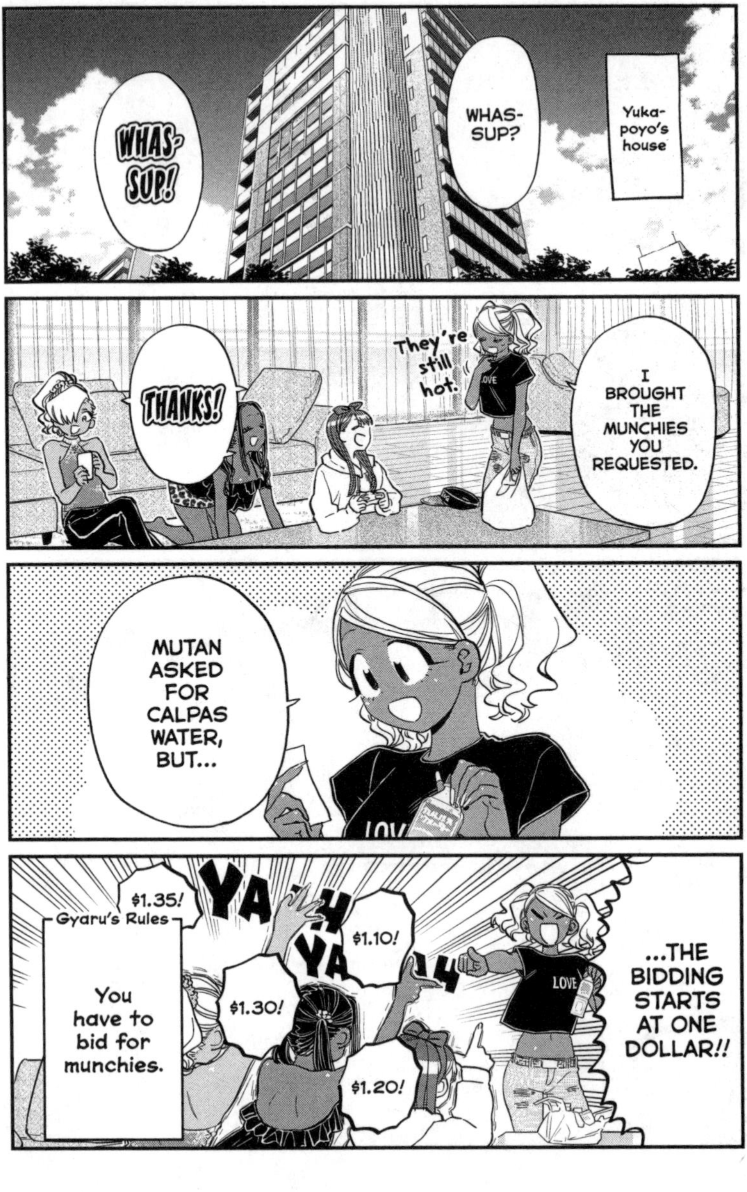

Yuka-poyo's house
WHAS-SUP?
WHAS-SUP!
I BROUGHT THE MUNCHIES YOU REQUESTED.
They're still hot.
THANKS!
MUTAN ASKED FOR CALPAS WATER, BUT...
...THE BIDDING STARTS AT ONE DOLLAR!!
$1.10!
YA
$1.35!
YA
$1.30!
$1.20!
Gyaru's Rules
You have to bid for munchies.

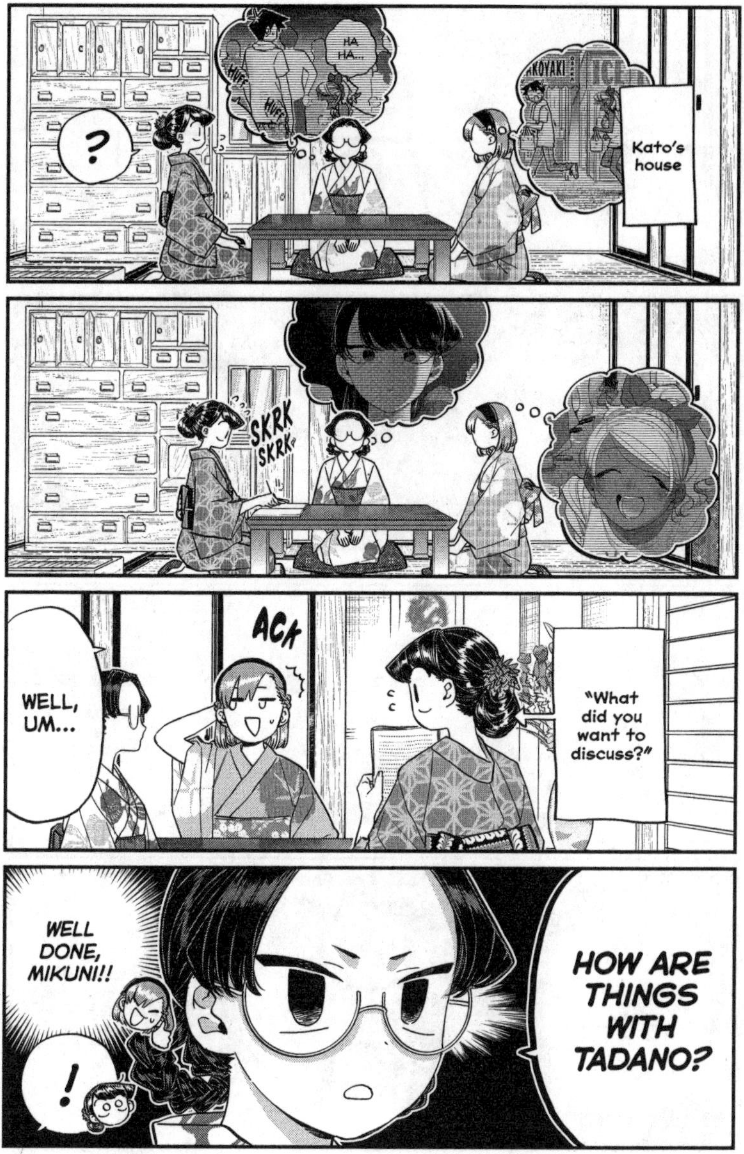
Kato's house
TAKOYAKI
HA HA...
HUFF
HUFF
?
SKRK SKRK
"What did you want to discuss?"
ACK
WELL, UM...
HOW ARE THINGS WITH TADANO?
WELL DONE, MIKUNI!!
!

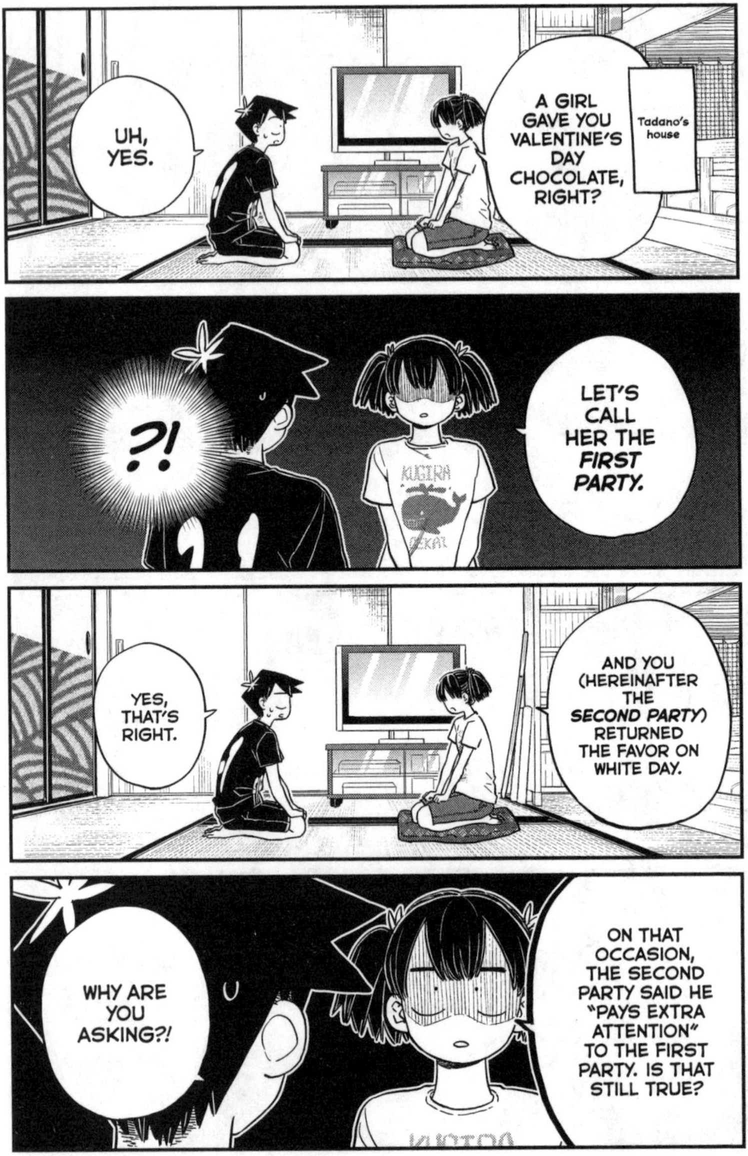
Tadano's house
A GIRL GAVE YOU VALENTINE'S DAY CHOCOLATE, RIGHT?
UH, YES.
LET'S CALL HER THE *FIRST PARTY.*
?!
AND YOU (HEREINAFTER THE *SECOND PARTY*) RETURNED THE FAVOR ON WHITE DAY.
YES, THAT'S RIGHT.
ON THAT OCCASION, THE SECOND PARTY SAID HE "PAYS EXTRA ATTENTION" TO THE FIRST PARTY. IS THAT STILL TRUE?
WHY ARE YOU ASKING?!

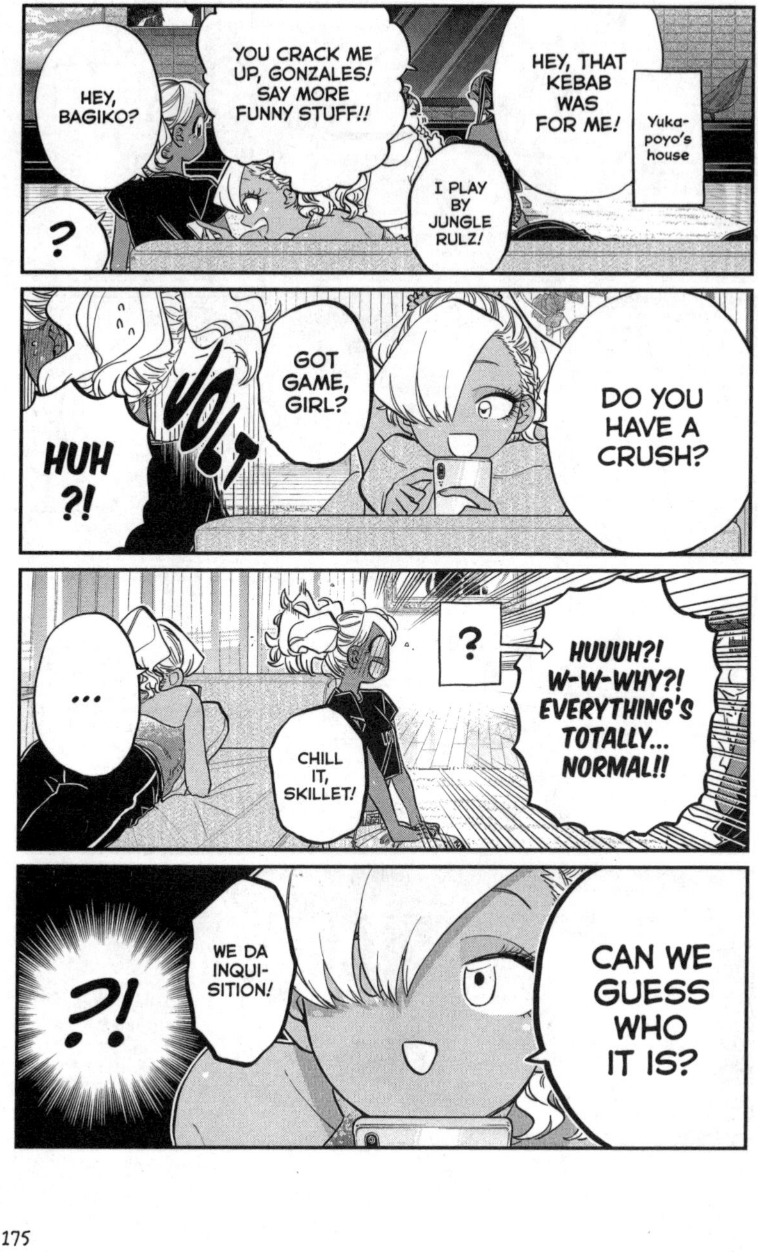
Yuka-poyo's house
HEY, THAT KEBAB WAS FOR ME!
I PLAY BY JUNGLE RULZ!
YOU CRACK ME UP, GONZALES! SAY MORE FUNNY STUFF!!
HEY, BAGIKO?
?
DO YOU HAVE A CRUSH?
GOT GAME, GIRL?
JOLT
HUH ?!
HUUUH?! W-W-WHY?! EVERYTHING'S TOTALLY... NORMAL!!
?
CHILL IT, SKILLET!
...
CAN WE GUESS WHO IT IS?
WE DA INQUISITION!
?!

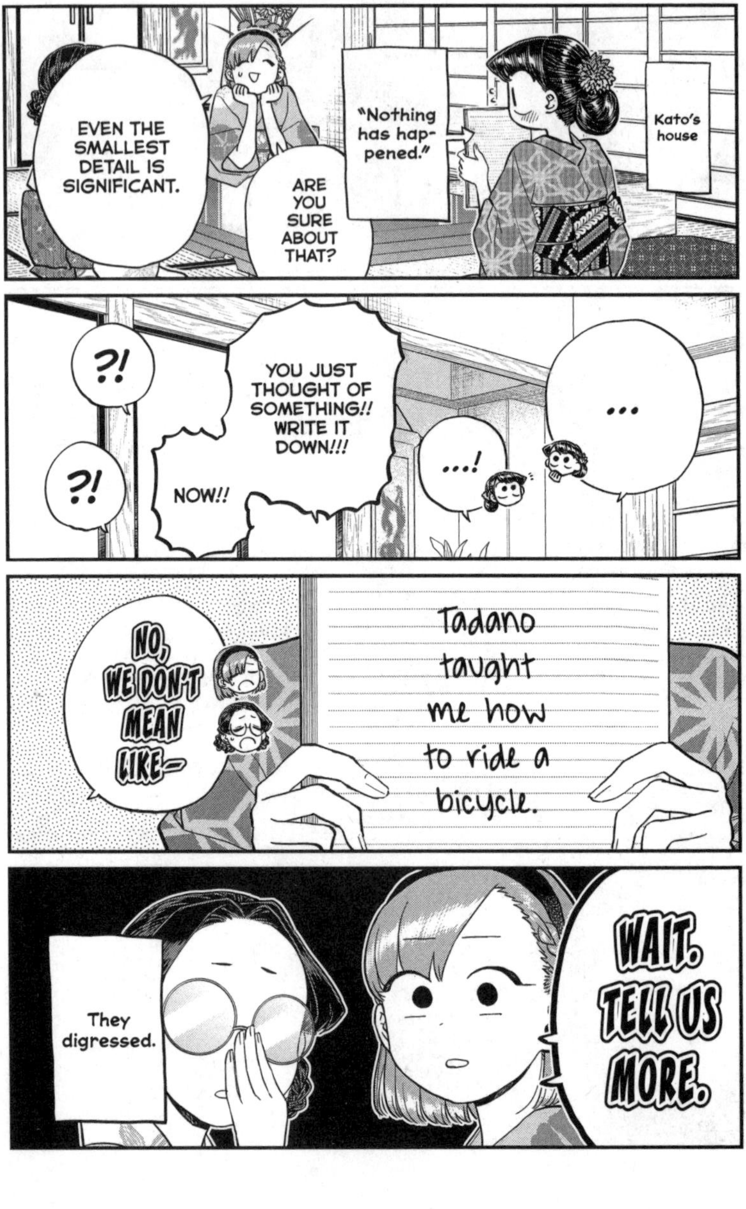
Kato's house
"Nothing has hap-pened."
ARE YOU SURE ABOUT THAT?
EVEN THE SMALLEST DETAIL IS SIGNIFICANT.
...
...!
YOU JUST THOUGHT OF SOMETHING!! WRITE IT DOWN!!!
NOW!!
?!
?!
Tadano taught me how to ride a bicycle.
NO, WE DON'T MEAN LIKE—
WAIT. TELL US MORE.
They digressed.

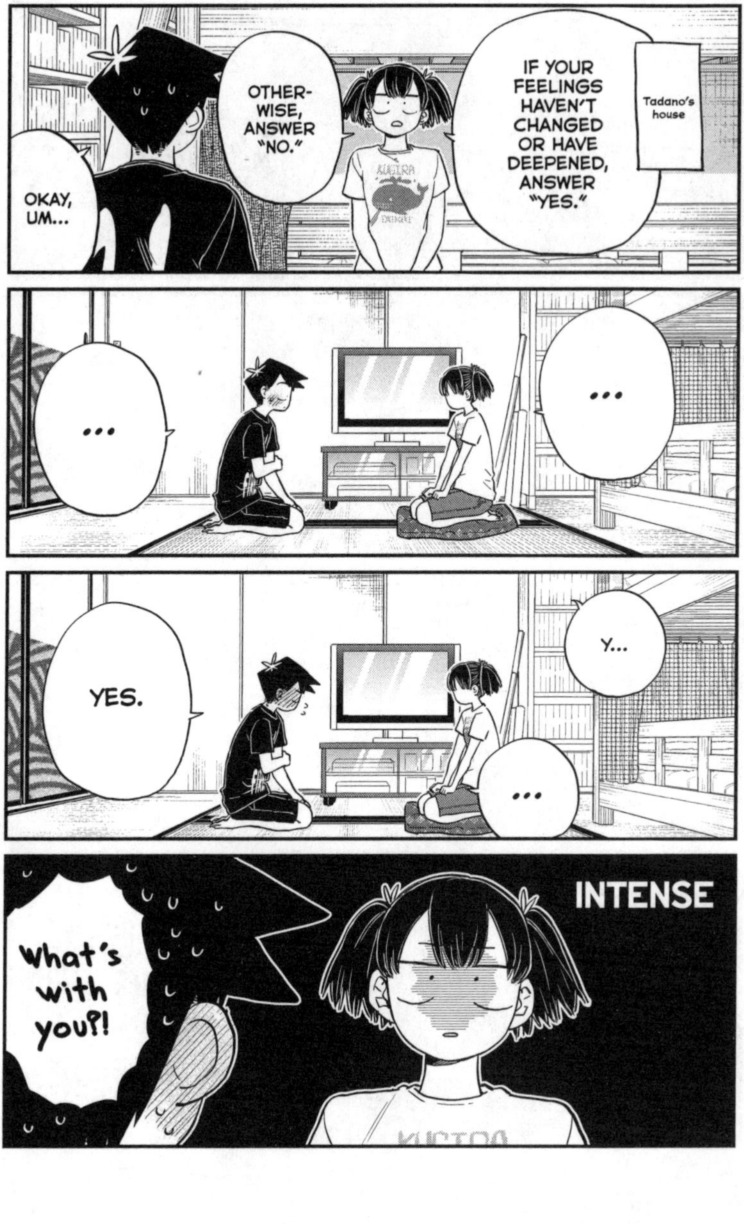

Tadano's house
IF YOUR FEELINGS HAVEN'T CHANGED OR HAVE DEEPENED, ANSWER "YES."
OTHER-WISE, ANSWER "NO."
OKAY, UM...
...
...
Y...
...
YES.
INTENSE
What's with you?!

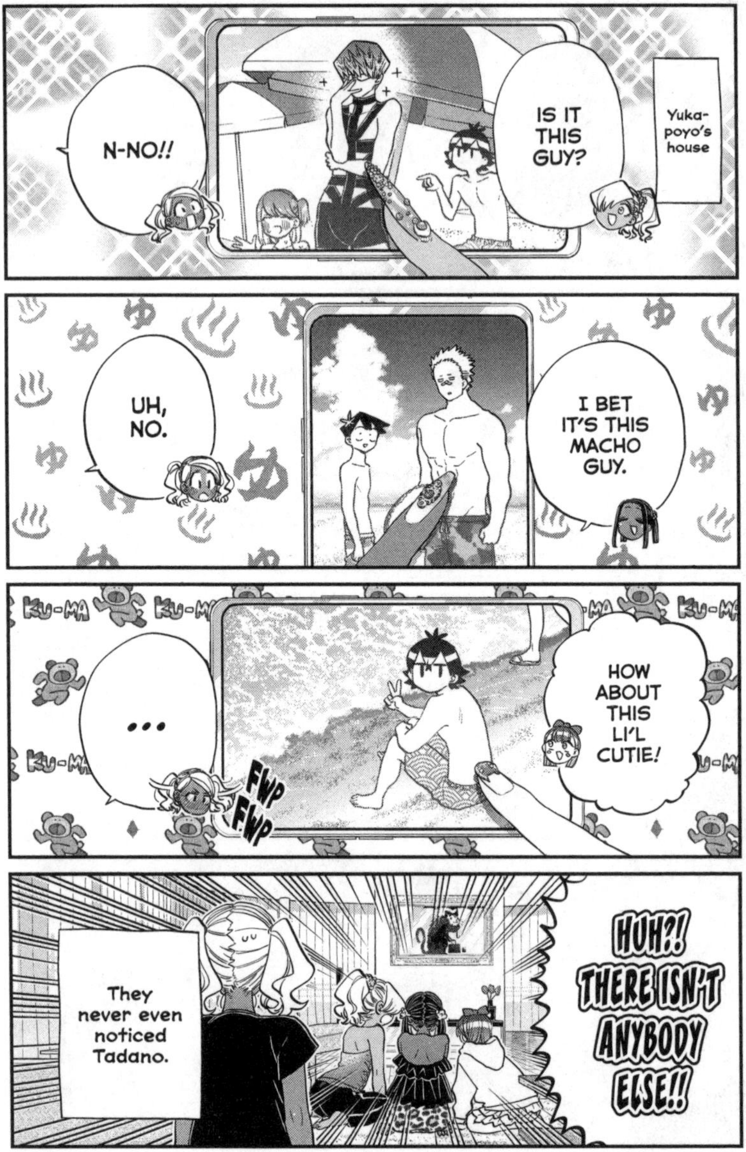
Yuka-poyo's house
IS IT THIS GUY?
N-NO!!
I BET IT'S THIS MACHO GUY.
UH, NO.
HOW ABOUT THIS LI'L CUTIE!
...
FWP FWP
HUH?! THERE ISN'T ANYBODY ELSE!!
They never even noticed Tadano.

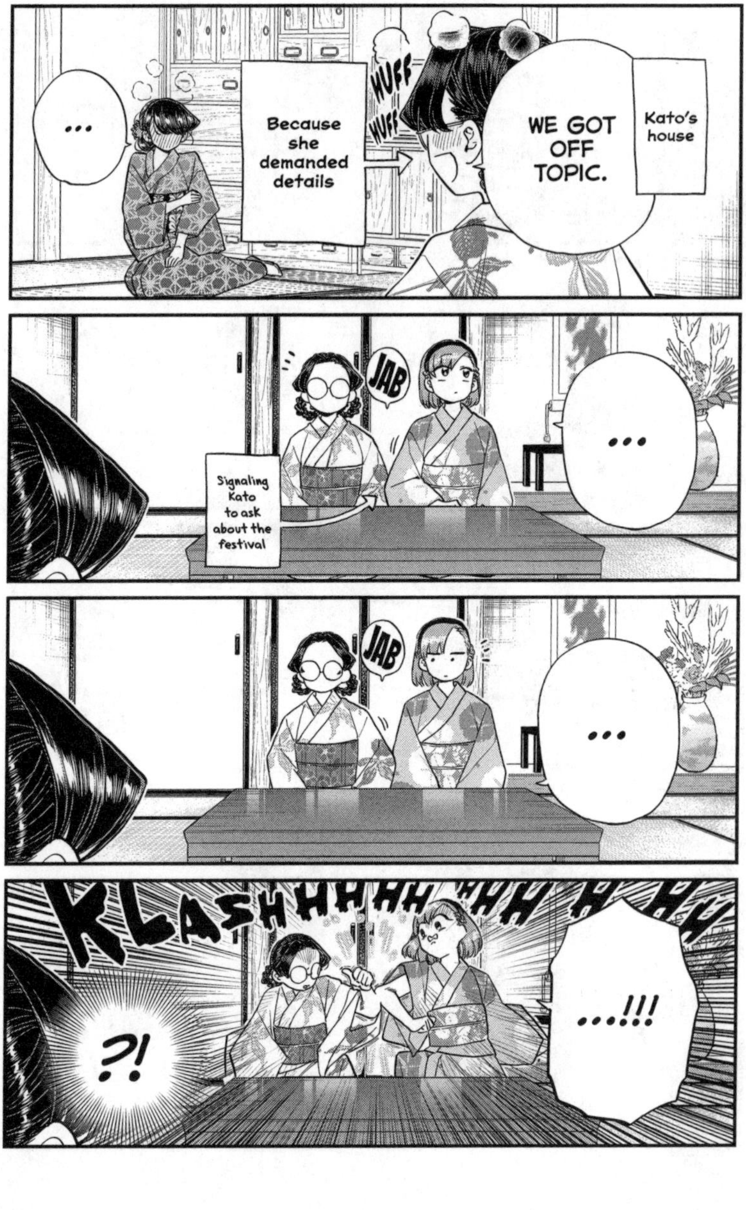
Kato's house
WE GOT OFF TOPIC.
HUFF HUFF
Because she demanded details
...
...
JAB
Signaling Kato to ask about the festival
...
JAB
KLASHHHHHHH
...!!!
?!

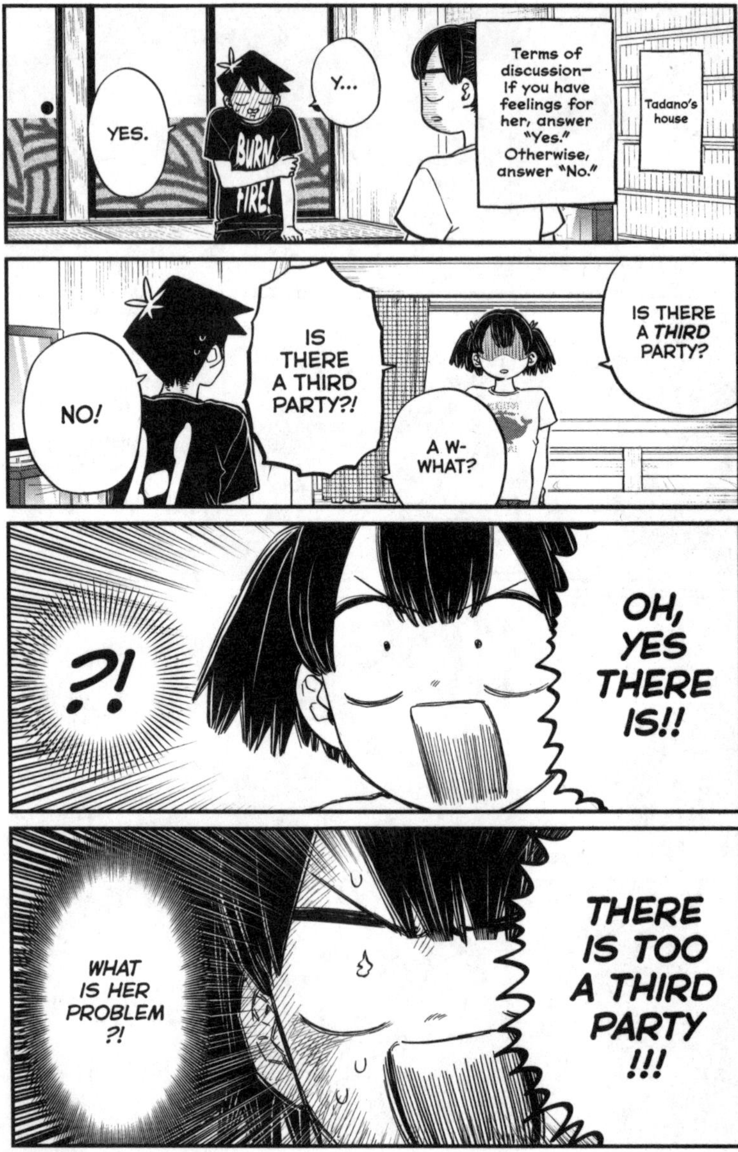
Tadano's house
Terms of discussion— If you have feelings for her, answer "Yes." Otherwise, answer "No."
Y...
YES.
IS THERE A *THIRD* PARTY?
A W-WHAT?
IS THERE A THIRD PARTY?!
NO!
OH, YES THERE IS!!
?!
THERE IS TOO A THIRD PARTY!!!
WHAT IS HER PROBLEM?!

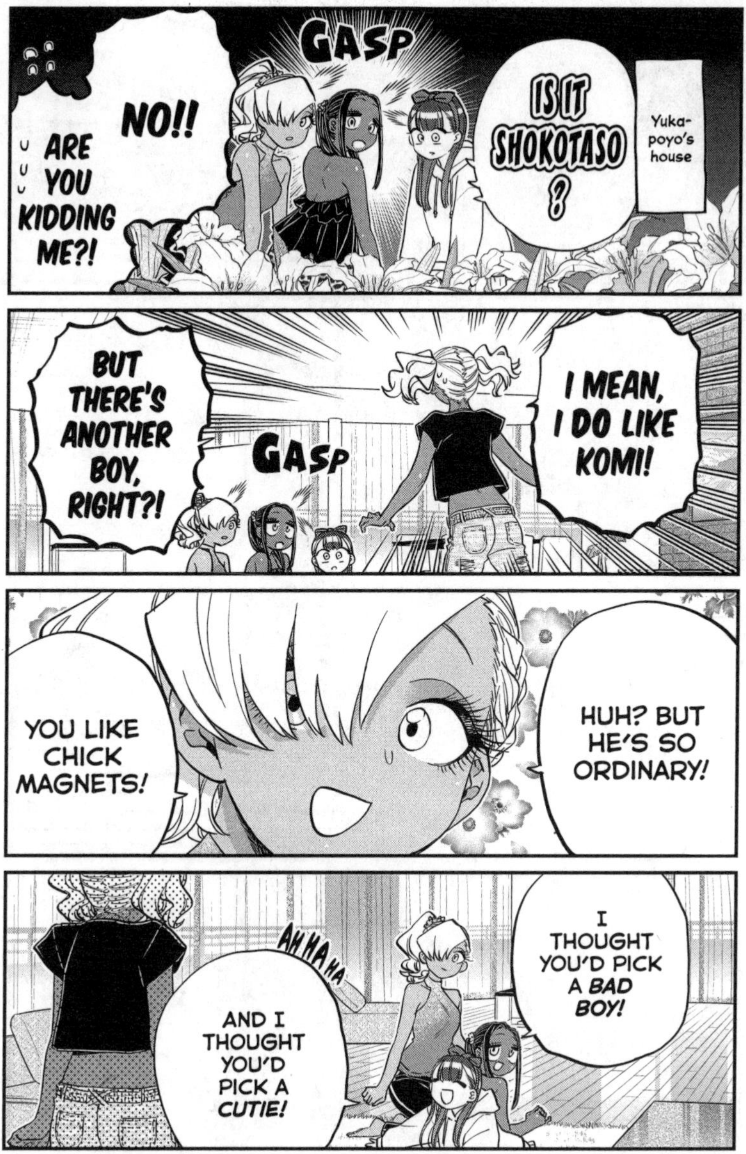
Yuka-poyo's house
IS IT SHOKOTASO?
GASP
NO!!
ARE YOU KIDDING ME?!
I MEAN, I DO LIKE KOMI!
GASP
BUT THERE'S ANOTHER BOY, RIGHT?!
HUH? BUT HE'S SO ORDINARY!
YOU LIKE CHICK MAGNETS!
I THOUGHT YOU'D PICK A *BAD BOY!*
AH HA HA
AND I THOUGHT YOU'D PICK A *CUTIE!*

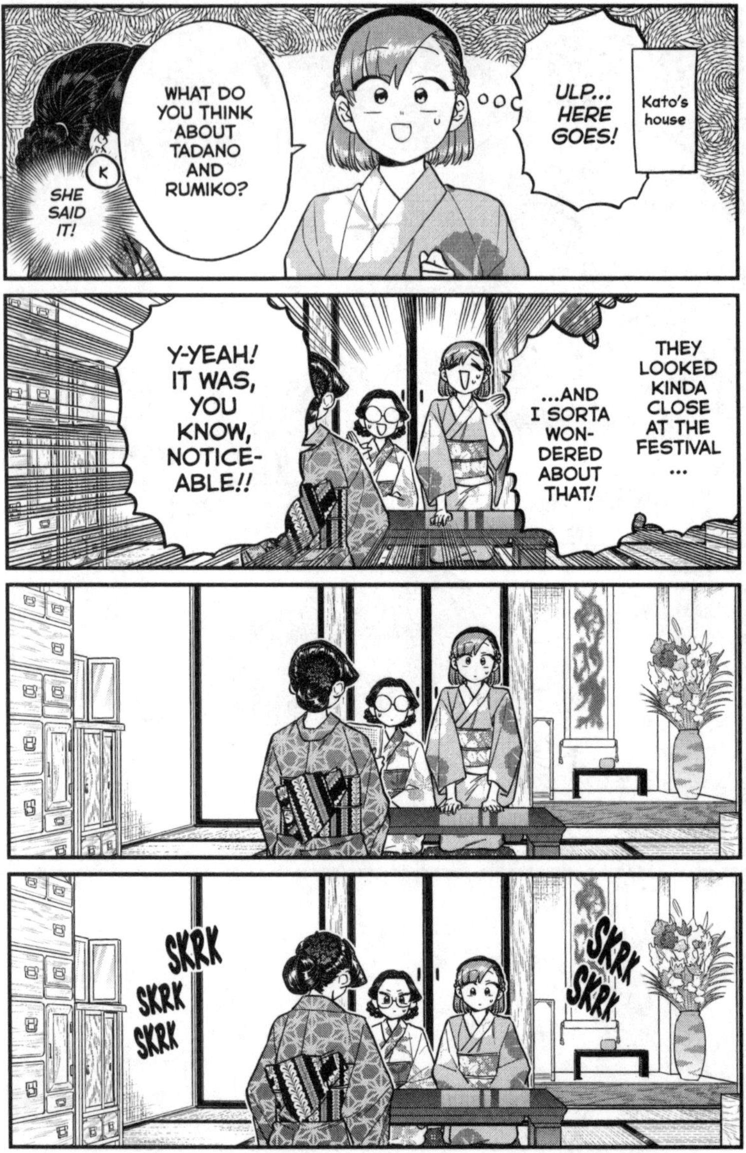
Kato's house
ULP... HERE GOES!
WHAT DO YOU THINK ABOUT TADANO AND RUMIKO?
K
SHE SAID IT!
THEY LOOKED KINDA CLOSE AT THE FESTIVAL ...
...AND I SORTA WONDERED ABOUT THAT!
Y-YEAH! IT WAS, YOU KNOW, NOTICE-ABLE!!
SKRK SKRK
SKRK SKRK SKRK

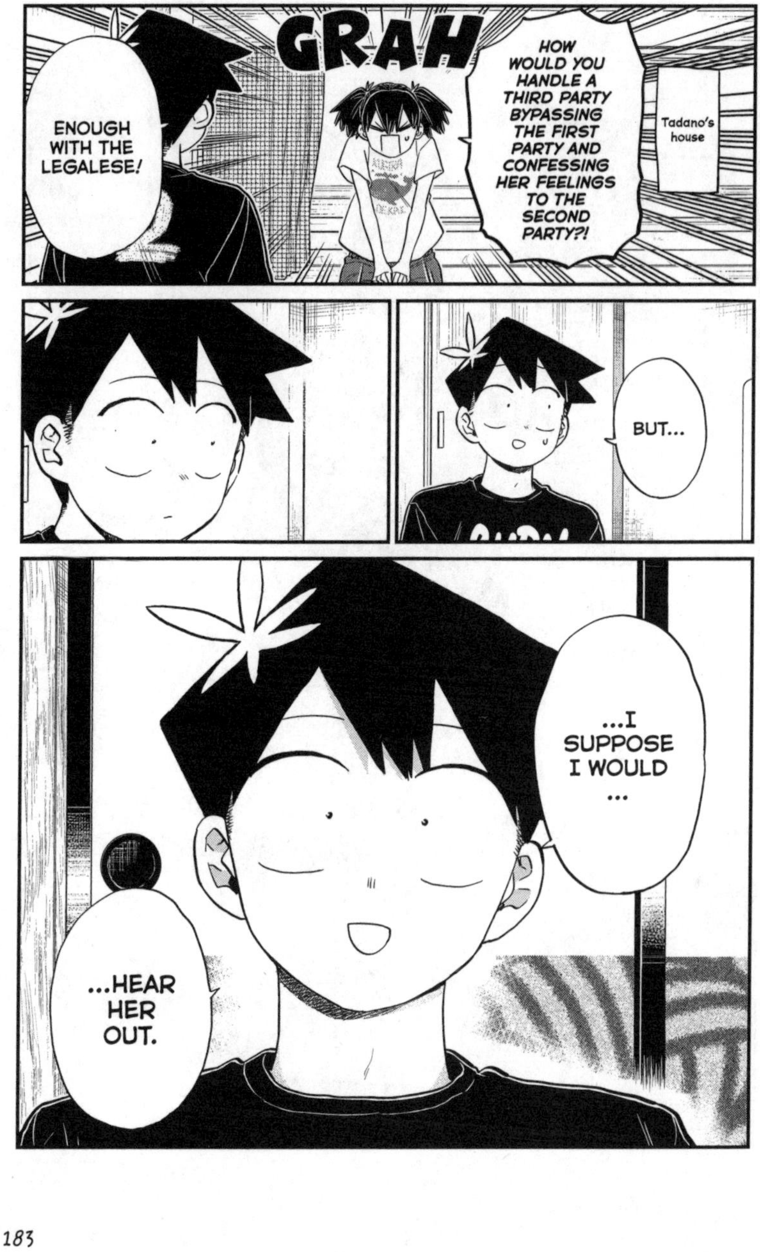
Tadano's house
HOW WOULD YOU HANDLE A THIRD PARTY BYPASSING THE FIRST PARTY AND CONFESSING HER FEELINGS TO THE SECOND PARTY?!
GRAH
ENOUGH WITH THE LEGALESE!
BUT...
...I SUPPOSE I WOULD ...
...HEAR HER OUT.

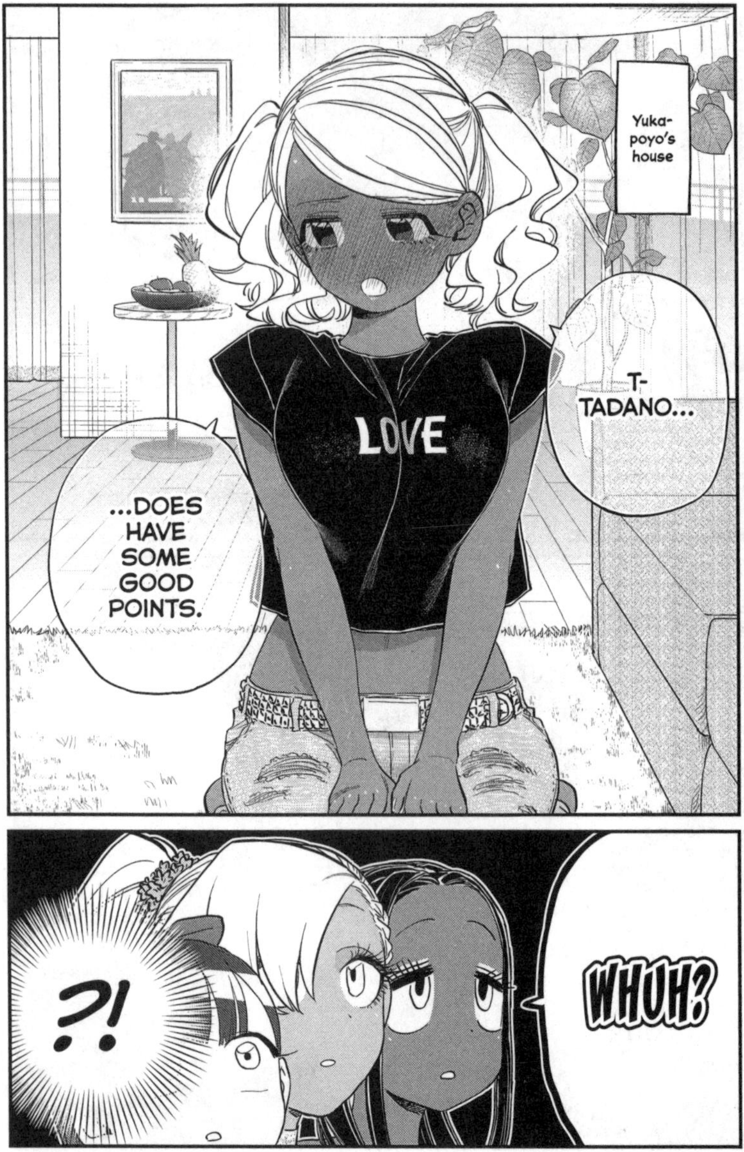
Yuka-poyo's house
T-TADANO...
...DOES HAVE SOME GOOD POINTS.
WHUH?
?!

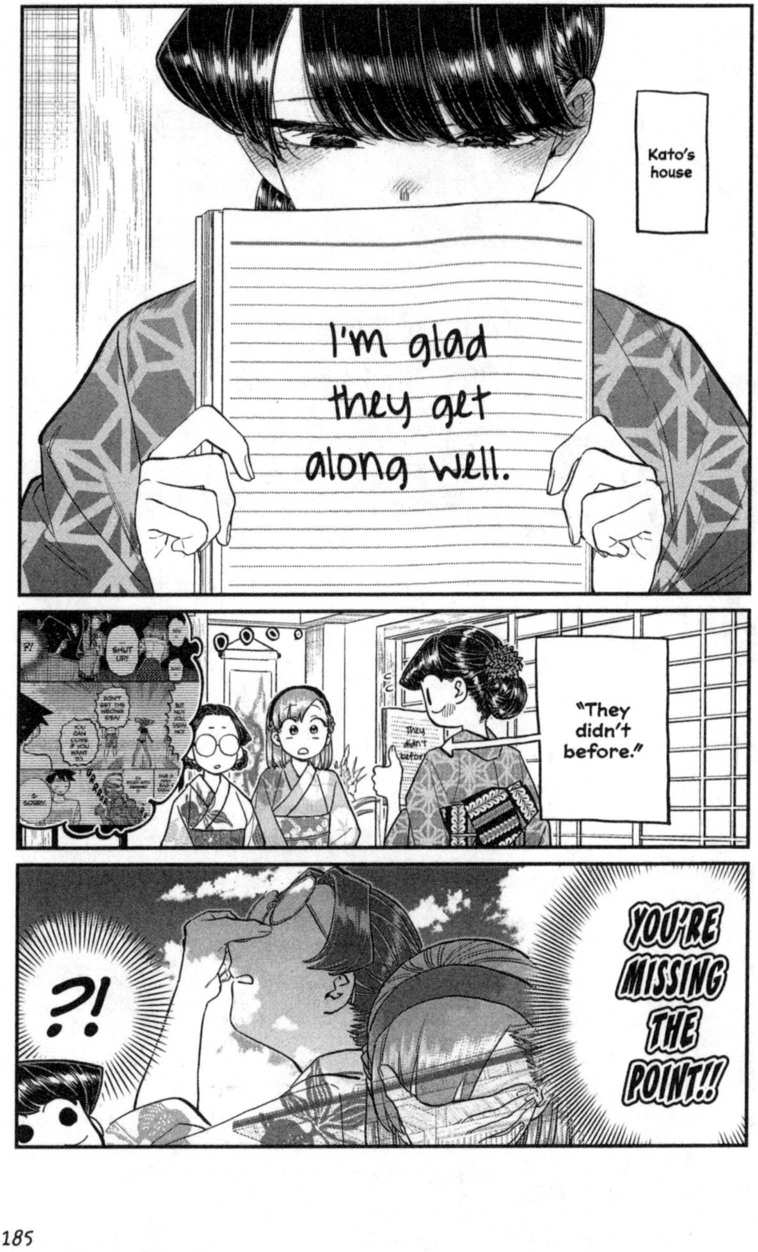
Kato's house
I'm glad they get along well.
"They didn't before."
They didn't before.
SHUT UP!
YOU'RE MISSING THE POINT!!
?!

Tadano's house
AND I'D GIVE A CONSIDERATE REPLY.
BUT THAT WON'T HAPPEN!
WHO WOULD LIKE ME?!
WHAT'S GOTTEN INTO YOU?!
WHAT A BORING ANSWER!
ANYWAY, GOOD LUCK.
WITH *WHAT*?!
One-mine's house
OH, IT'LL WORK OUT SOMEHOW.

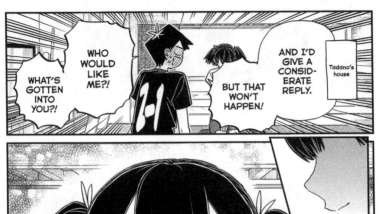

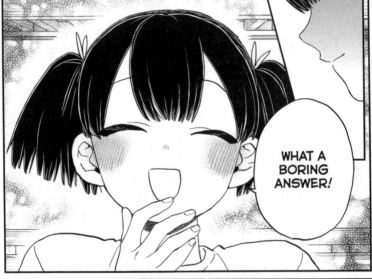

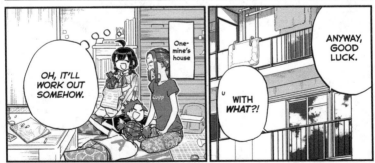

Communication 195 — The End

Komi Can't Communicate

First Party Second Party Third Party

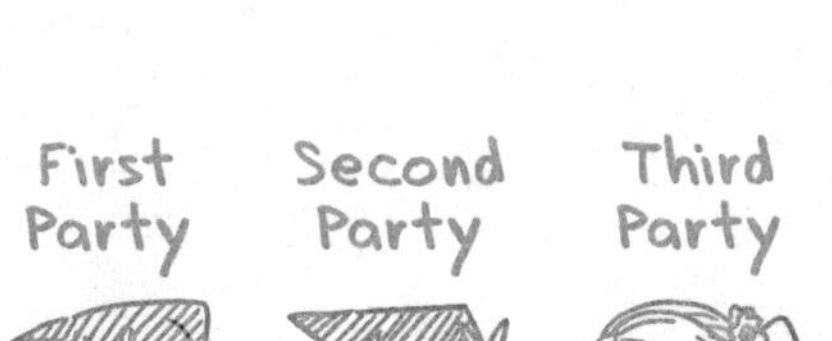

Komi Can't Communicate Bonus

Can Komi Complete Her Summer To-Do List? White Clouds, Red Tomatoes, Blue Summer

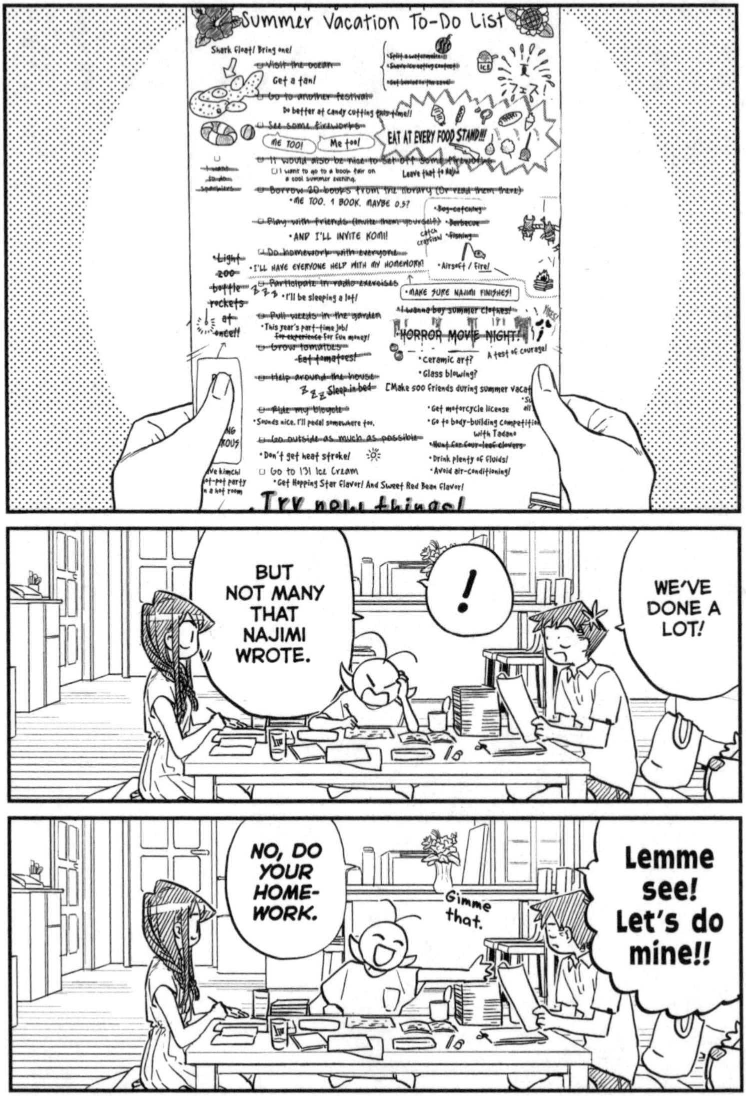
Summer Vacation To-Do List
Shark float! Bring one!
Visit the ocean
Get a tan!
Go to another festival
Do better at candy cutting this time!!
See some fireworks
ME TOO!
Me too!
EAT AT EVERY FOOD STAND!!!
It would also be nice to set off some fireworks
I want to go to a book fair on a cool summer evening.
Leave that to Najimi
Borrow 20 books from the library (Or read them there)
•ME TOO. 1 BOOK. MAYBE 0.5?
Play with friends (invite them yourself)
•AND I'LL INVITE KOMI!
catch crayfish!
•Barbecue
•Fishing
Do homework with everyone
•I'LL HAVE EVERYONE HELP WITH MY HOMEWORK!
•Airsoft / Fire!
•MAKE SURE NAJIMI FINISHES!
•Light 200 bottle rockets at once!!
Participate in radio exercises
•I'll be sleeping a lot!
Pull weeds in the garden
•This year's part-time job! For experience For fun money!
I wanna buy summer clothes!
•HORROR MOVIE NIGHT!
Yikes!
A test of courage!
Grow tomatoes
Eat tomatoes!
•Ceramic art?
•Glass blowing?
Help around the house
Sleep in bed
Ride my bicycle
•Sounds nice. I'll pedal somewhere too.
•Get motorcycle license
•Go to body-building competition with Tadano
Go outside as much as possible
•Hunt for four-leaf clovers
•Don't get heat stroke!
•Drink plenty of fluids!
•Avoid air-conditioning!
Go to 131 Ice Cream
•Get Hopping Star flavor! And Sweet Red Bean flavor!
WE'VE DONE A LOT!
!
BUT NOT MANY THAT NAJIMI WROTE.
Lemme see! Let's do mine!!
Gimme that.
NO, DO YOUR HOMEWORK.

Komi Can't Communicate Bonus

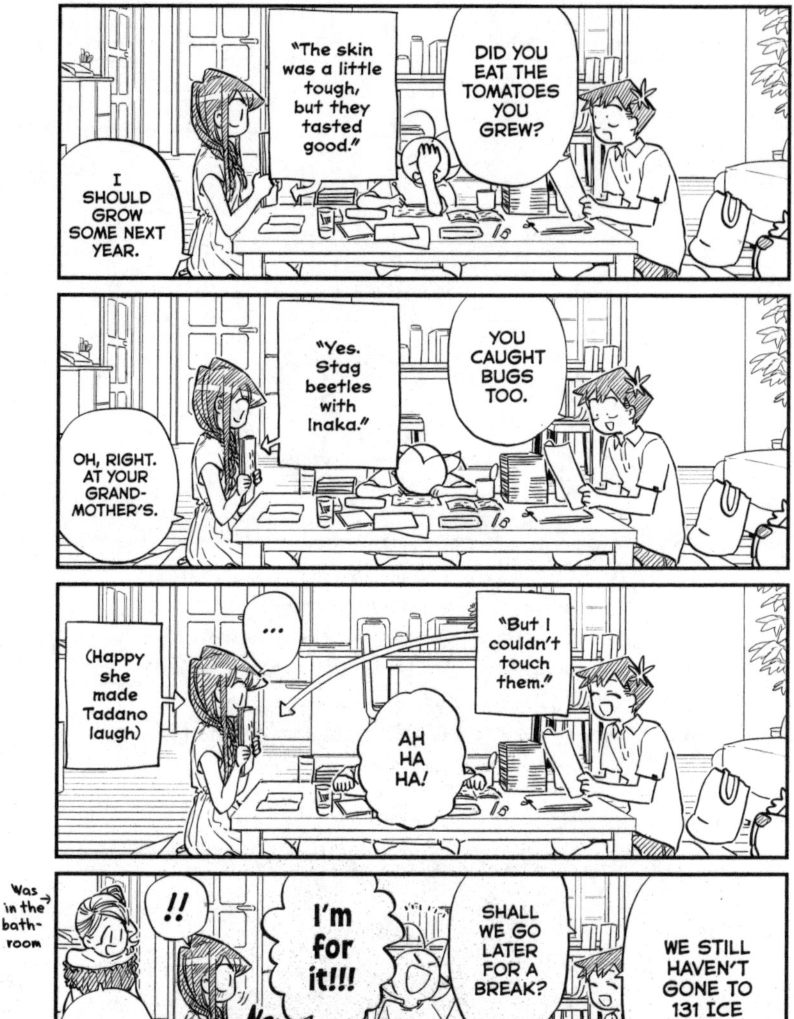
DID YOU EAT THE TOMATOES YOU GREW?
"The skin was a little tough, but they tasted good."
I SHOULD GROW SOME NEXT YEAR.
YOU CAUGHT BUGS TOO.
"Yes. Stag beetles with Inaka."
OH, RIGHT. AT YOUR GRAND-MOTHER'S.
"But I couldn't touch them."
AH HA HA!
...
(Happy she made Tadano laugh)
WE STILL HAVEN'T GONE TO 131 ICE CREAM.
SHALL WE GO LATER FOR A BREAK?
I'm for it!!!
NOD NOD
!!
WE GOING SOME-WHERE?
Was in the bath-room

Tomohito Oda won the grand prize for *World Worst One* in the 70th Shogakukan New Comic Artist Awards in 2012. Oda's series *Digicon*, about a tough high school girl who finds herself in control of an alien with plans for world domination, ran from 2014 to 2015. In 2015, *Komi Can't Communicate* debuted as a one-shot in *Weekly Shonen Sunday* and was picked up as a full series by the same magazine in 2016.

Komi Can't Communicate

VOL. 14
Shonen Sunday Edition

Story and Art by Tomohito Oda

English Translation & Adaptation/John Werry
Touch-Up Art & Lettering/Eve Grandt
Design/Julian [JR] Robinson
Editor/Pancha Diaz

COMI-SAN WA, COMYUSHO DESU. Vol. 14
by Tomohito ODA

Original Japanese edition published by SHOGAKUKAN.
English translation rights in the United States of America, Canada, the United Kingdom, Ireland, Australia and New Zealand arranged with SHOGAKUKAN.

Original Cover Design/Masato ISHIZAWA + Bay Bridge Studio

Printed in the U.S.A.

Published by VIZ Media, LLC
P.O. Box 77010
San Francisco, CA 94107

10 9 8 7 6 5 4 3 2 1
First printing, August 2021

viz.com

shonensunday.com

PARENTAL ADVISORY
KOMI CAN'T COMMUNICATE is rated T for Teen and is recommended for ages 13 and up.

ratings.viz.com

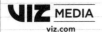

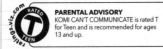

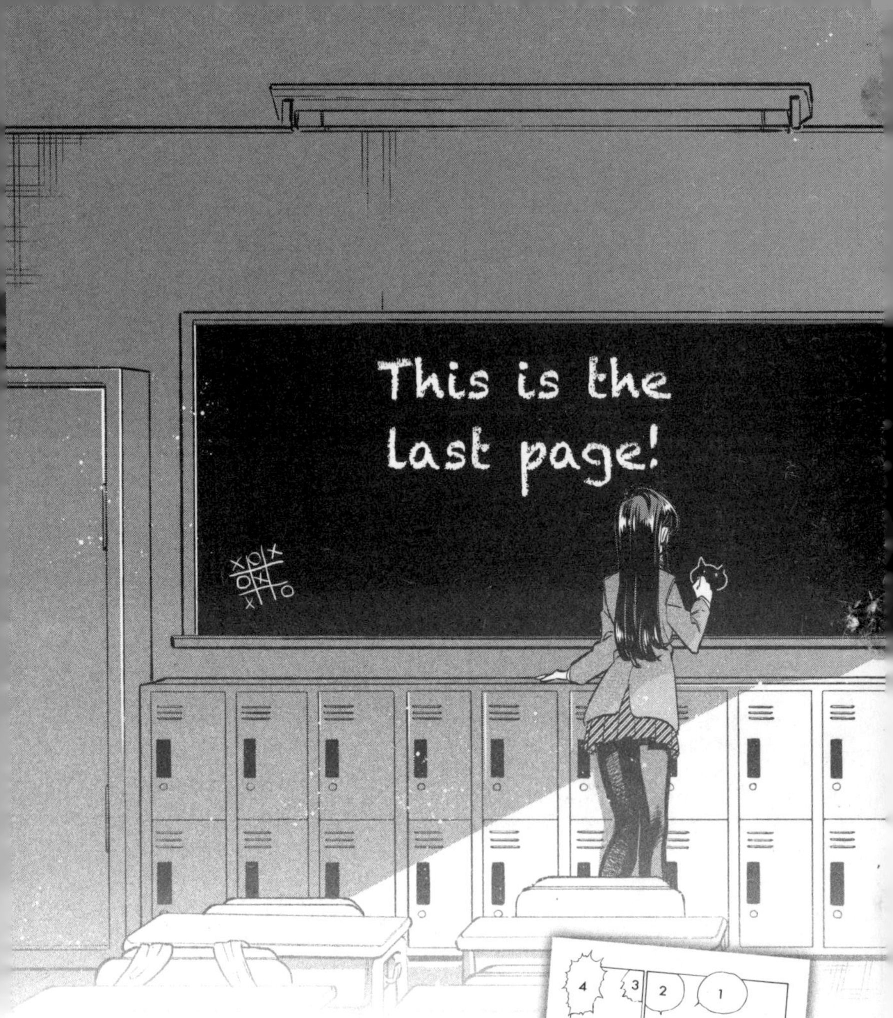
This is the
last page!

Komi Can't Communicate has been printed in the original Japanese format to preserve the orientation of the artwork.

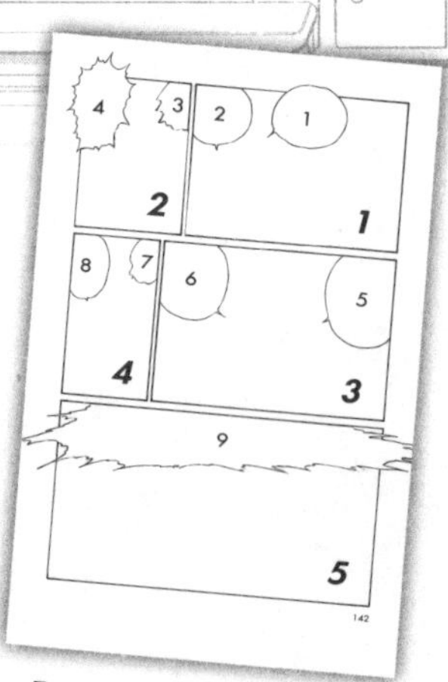
1
2
3
4
5
6
7
8
9
1
2
3
4
5
142

Follow the action this way.